Inside the BBC and CNN
Managing media organisations

Lucy K

D0101467

This book is due for return on or before the last date shown below.

30/06/09

10-4-14

9/3/15

30/4/19

ROUTLEDGE

Don Gresswell Ltd., London, N21   Cat. No. 1207   DG 02242/71

London and New York

First published 2000
by Routledge
11 New Fetter Lane, London EC4P 4EE

Simultaneously published in the USA and Canada
by Routledge
29 West 35th Street, New York, NY 10001

Routledge is an imprint of the Taylor & Francis Group

© 2000 Lucy Küng-Shankleman

Typeset in Garamond by Taylor & Francis Books Ltd
Printed and bound in Great Britain by TJ International Ltd,
Padstow, Cornwall

British Library Cataloguing in Publication Data
A catalogue record for this book is available from the British Library

Library of Congress Cataloging in Publication Data
A catalog record for this title has been requested

ISBN 0–415–21321–5 (hb)
ISBN 0–415–21322–3 (pb)

Contents

Illustrations

Tables

Figures

Acknowledgements

The book and the study that underlies it would not have been possible without the support and encouragement of a great many individuals and institutions. First of all, I am indebted to the two organisations that provided the focus for this study, the BBC and CNN, for their open-minded support for the project and their readiness to open themselves to academic scrutiny. Within this context, I am particularly grateful to Bob Nelson at the BBC and to Tom Johnson, Lynn Gutstadt and Ken Tiven at CNN, all of whom not only made so much of their own time available, but also helped to open many other doors, both inside and outside their own organisations. As a result of their backing, a great many individuals declared themselves willing to share some of their innermost perspectives on their professional lives. I am deeply appreciative of the ready accessibility and openness shown by all of those I interviewed.

This book began its life as a PhD thesis at the University of St Gallen and my thanks also go to my two academic mentors, Professor Louis Bosshart and Professor Peter Gomez, whose interest and guidance enhanced my work enormously.

Writing a PhD is at times a tortuous process but the effort is amply rewarded if, as in this case, the author has the opportunity to broadcast her findings to a wider audience. I am therefore extremely grateful to Rebecca Barden and her colleagues at Routledge for their enthusiastic response to this project.

Particular thanks are also due to those who provided friendship and hospitality during the many international research trips this project entailed. Many, many individuals helped turn potentially arduous experiences into pleasurable ones and I am grateful to all of them, particularly Fran Clark, Gill Hudson, Brian and Anke Ma Siy, Sue Mack, Olive and Allen Synge, Jill Shankleman and Martin Shankleman in the UK, and Robert Kronley, Wendy Puriefoy and Jane Starr in the US.

Finally, my deepest appreciation is to my husband Gebi for his unfailing good humour, intellectual engagement and unflinching support during what must have appeared a tedious and unending process of writing and rewriting. I dedicate this book to him, and to the memory of my parents.

Lucy Küng-Shankleman
Zürich, November 1999

Abbreviations

ABC	American Broadcasting Corporation
BBC	British Broadcasting Corporation
CBC	Canadian Broadcasting Corporation
C4	Channel 4 (UK)
CD-Rom	Compact disc read-only memory
CNN	Cable News Network
DBS	Direct broadcast satellite
DTH	Direct to home (broadcast satellite)
ISDN	Integrated systems digital network
IT	Information technology
LAN	Local area network
NVOD	Near video on demand
PBS	Public broadcasting service
PC	Personal computer
PSB	Public service broadcaster
TBS	Turner Broadcasting Systems Inc.
TV	Television
VCR	Video cassette recorder
VOD	Video on demand

Introduction

> By (say) 2020 a large number of suppliers may be offering broadcasting products to millions of viewers in several different ways ... Broadcasting will no longer be the pre-eminent example of a public good, but instead a host of broadcasting services and products will seek customers like other private goods.
>
> (Congdon, 1991: xv)

At the turn of the millennium the world's broadcasting industries are undergoing a period of tumultuous and unparalleled change. A cocktail of closely interwoven changes ranging from the digitisation of information to the development of global electronic networks, from dramatic increases in computing power and bandwidth capacity to the emergence of the internet, are combining to change the world's media industries for ever.

Whenever environmental change is discussed in management literature, it is inevitably coupled with a set of adjectives so over-used as to have become clichés. It is almost always 'rapid', 'radical' and 'discontinuous'. These default descriptions have become so familiar that they have virtually lost their meaning. However, when applied to the world of broadcasting, such extreme terms are for once absolutely correct. The developments under way in the global media arena are so far-reaching that none of the industries involved will ever be the same again.

Since its inception, television broadcasting has been a classic example of a 'public good', with a distinctive financing sector and special regulatory arrangements. The industry was traditionally characterised by stable, nationally bounded spheres of activity that were clearly circumscribed by regulation, markets that tended towards the oligopolistic, processes that were rooted in well-established technologies, strong organisational cultures derived from the confluence of a variety of professional, national and individual influences, and audiences who clearly understood their role in the broadcasting process.

However, from the late 1980s onwards a series of tremors, including market liberalisation, the introduction of new transmission technologies, and changing social attitudes, triggered the beginnings of an industry restructuring. This was followed by a series of even stronger technologically driven shocks which have provoked the so-called 'digital revolution'. Developments such as the internet and World Wide Web, digitisation, rapid advances in computing power and bandwidth availability and the development of open global networked electronic platforms are gradually eroding the structural barriers between the media, telecommunications and information technology industries. This phenomenon, known as convergence, is leading to profound change. For broadcasters, channel capacity is fast becoming unlimited. The potential to design specialist channels for niche audiences, even for an audience of one, now exists. Viewers are increasingly able to dictate which broadcasting products they want to consume and when, and to pay for these directly. Undreamed of categories of interactive products and services are now possible. Every single element of the broadcasting business model – whether funding, programming, production, delivery or audience – is subject to forces of disaggregation and fragmentation.

As a result, the characteristics of television supply have been altered. Broadcasting is evolving into a wholly market-orientated system. It is no longer the pre-eminent example of a public good, but a private good which must compete for customers like any other. Public service broadcasters can no longer assume automatic access to every home in the country, nor automatic funding from the public; they must now fight to maintain access to viewers and, even if publicly financed, expect to find a significant proportion of their income from commercial sources. As a consequence, the way in which they fulfil their basic function (or, in some cases, whether they are able to fulfil their basic function at all) is open to re-examination. For all players, competition is rising steeply, with new competitors coming from outside national boundaries and from within, as well as from other industry sectors. Partnering the rise in competition is a rise in uncertainty. How will media audiences react to these new products and services? Are they willing to become 'senders' as well as 'receivers', consumers as well as viewers?

The broadcasting world to come will be very different than that in which the current players grew up. Environmental change means that new strategic directions are inevitable. The question explored in this book is how the cultures of these organisations are responding to the change in strategic direction. What is the nature and extent of their impact on strategic process in broadcasting organisations?

The BBC and CNN

Against such a backdrop, this study focuses on two organisations.[1] The BBC, the world's oldest public service broadcaster (PSB), operates according to a clear public mandate, is financed by a universal licence fee, and broadcasts the traditional 'PSB' wide range of programming. It has always been accustomed to some level of protection against commercial forces and holds the dominant position in UK broadcasting. CNN is a relatively young US cable broadcaster that specialises in news and, because it broadcasts on cable and satellite, is considered to be outside the mainstream of US television. In 1996 it was catapulted into the big league of US broadcasting when it was bought by Time Warner Inc. and became part of the largest media organisation in the world.

These organisations were selected on grounds of their dissimilarity, because they offer the maximum possible range of circumstances to be found among English-speaking broadcasting organisations, and thus the widest possible range of cultural influences. The study does not attempt to compare 'like with like'. Rather, through examining two organisations which exhibit strong differences in terms of fundamental mission, national context, product range and financial basis, it seeks to expose the wide range of value orientations possible within the same industry, and the way in which different organisational value orientations create different strategic responses to fundamentally similar environmental contexts: different organisations, different business models, same business, same dilemmas.

By the same token this book does not seek to provide any type of judgement, qualitative or quantitative, on the organisations' respective performance or output. Its goal is to understand how culture affects strategy in these organisations, not to assess the respective merits of their actual strategies. It is important for readers to understand that of the two organisations the BBC is by far the longer established and the more complex entity. This provides a wonderfully fertile ground for research, but inevitably creates a much greater scope for analysis and comment. As a result, this book devotes more space to the unique challenges and dilemmas faced by the BBC than it does to those of CNN, but this should not be construed as implying that of the two organisations one is better or worse managed than the other. To repeat, this book does not attempt to compare and judge the two organisations' corporate strategies or performance.

Theoretical foundations

This book is concerned with the challenges of managing media organisations. It explores these issues through close analysis of two leading players in the Anglo-Saxon media world, the BBC and CNN. Of course, any type of empirical research into organisations needs to be conducted from a specific perspective; a theoretical 'lens' must be adopted through which the objects under scrutiny can be observed. In this work, the 'lens' through which the BBC and CNN are scrutinised is culture, a frustratingly elusive organisational element which nevertheless has a powerful impact on an organisation's strategic options. The model of culture that provides the theoretical underpinnings of this research was developed by Schein (1992). He contends that at the heart of every organisation there is a paradigm of interrelated and unconscious shared assumptions which directs how members of that organisation think, feel and act.

However, this book is not just about organisation culture and its role in the management of media organisations. A particular feature of the research described here is its broad scope both in terms of the range of academic disciplines encompassed and the span of organisational activities – functional and geographic – analysed. Although about management of media organisations, its theoretical 'roots' include the social sciences, media and mass communication studies, national media systems in Europe and North America, as well as the technology of communications. Pluralism is reflected also in the variety of ways in which the term 'culture' is used: this book focuses on the 'culture' of organisations concerned with 'cultural' products, viewing 'culture' from national, industry and organisation perspectives.

About the research

The in-company research underpinning this analysis of the BBC and CNN was conducted between 1994 and 1995. During that period twenty-one senior members of staff were interviewed at the BBC and thirteen at CNN. The majority of these individuals were interviewed twice, once for the initial data-gathering and once for feedback. In addition, nineteen expert interviews were carried out with senior industry figures and academics in the UK and US. Full details of the research methodology used can be found in the Appendix.

Guide to this book

This book falls broadly into four parts. The first part, comprising Chapters 1 to 3, provides the theoretical background and context to the study. Readers whose primary interest is the organisations and not their industrial, organisational or competitive context, are recommended to skip this portion of the work and move straight to Chapter 4 onwards. Chapter 1, 'What is organisation culture', discusses current theoretical understanding of the concept of organisation culture and its links to strategic processes and organisational performance. The study's central model, the Schein model of culture, is introduced and explained, as are related theories concerning how culture is founded and transmitted and the nature of subcultures, professional cultures and national cultures. The strategic terms and concepts which are highlighted by the Schein model are briefly discussed.

Chapter 2 is entitled 'The status quo is not an option' and has as its subject broadcasting's changing environmental context. It analyses the global trends shaping today's and tomorrow's television industry and considers their implications for broadcasting organisations. Developments such as market liberalisation and deregulation, changes in social structures and attitudes to the digital revolution, convergence and media mergers and alliances are discussed.

The changing nature of broadcasting itself is the subject of Chapter 3, entitled 'The mass paradigm fragments'. This provides an explanatory back-drop to the analysis of the BBC and CNN by defining and explaining the broadcasting industry and some of the terms and concepts particular to the sector. It discusses the various options for funding, delivery, programming and regulation, major organisational types, the role and function of broad-casters in general and of public service broadcasters in particular, and surveys academic research on the culture of broadcasting, the culture of journalism, and of national differences in journalists' role perception. The chapter closes by exploring the phenomenon of fragmentation which is currently affecting many dimensions of the broadcasting industry.

The second part of the book concentrates on the two organisations which are the focus of this research, the BBC and CNN. Chapter 4, 'Serving the nation' and Chapter 5, 'The "Mouth of the South" and his "Chicken Noodle Network"' provide introductions to these organisations by analysing their origins, span of activities and performance, and discussing each organisa-tion's national context – including national and industry culture, regulation and national media policy and levels of industry competition.

Chapter 6, 'Continuous revolution' and Chapter 7, 'Reinventing the news', provide assessments of the BBC and CNN as businesses. They consider the organisations' respective strategic goals and missions, organisa-tional competencies, strengths and weaknesses, key stakeholder demands and environmental challenges.[2]

The unique cultures of these organisations and their implications for managing media companies are explored in the third part of this book, which in some respects is its heart. Chapter 8, 'Part of the British way of life' and Chapter 9, 'Underdogs and outsiders', present the cultures of the BBC and CNN in terms of an interlinked paradigm of basic assumptions. Chapter 10, 'Reithianism versus Birtism' and Chapter 11, 'Adrenaline', explore the implications of the BBC's and CNN's unique cultures for how these organisations are managed. They explore how culture underpins strategic processes, look at how culture governs general attitudes towards strategy, assess the level of 'fit' between culture and strategic processes and priorities, and analyse dilemmas arising from the confluence of culture and strategy.

Chapter 12, 'A special case?' concludes the book by exploring the impli-cations of this analysis for the management of media firms in particular and for organisations in general.

A brief outline of the research methodology, describing the research design, methodology, interview sample and themes and methods of data-collection and analysis can be found in the Appendix.

Chapter 1

What is organisation culture?

> Corporate culture – a chameleon-like lizard of such variegated hues that, while everyone acknowledges its splendour, few can agree on a description.
>
> (Hampden-Turner, 1990: 134)

In recent years the term 'corporate culture' has become part of the standard vocabulary of management.[1] An organisation's culture is widely accepted as one of its 'vital organs' just like strategy, structure or processes, a key element of its basic functioning and an important contributory factor to success or failure.

Culture's prominence derives from its widely credited power over critical but intangible aspects of organisational life, 'the non-rational qualities of an organisation' (Morgan, 1986). Culture is variously credited with the ability to decipher phenomena such as myths, ceremonies and rituals (Bolman and Deal, 1991), define behaviour and resolve ambiguity (Hampden-Turner, 1994), stimulate organisational learning (Argyris, 1993; Gomez and Probst, 1995; Senge, 1990), legitimise organisational actions, ideas and demands (Pettigrew, 1985), determine an organisation's ability to master environmental change (Schein, 1992), and even directly influence economic performance (Peters and Waterman, 1982).

Constructs of culture

Although, however, the existence and power of culture is widely acknowledged in both academic and managerial discourse, it remains a frustratingly abstract concept ('the most nebulous area of corporate management, and by far the most challenging', Tichy and Sherman, 1993: 68). Culture resists operational definition. All too often it is defined evocatively but imprecisely, for example, the 'expressive social tissue around us … a system of terms, forms, categories and images [which] interprets a people's own situation to themselves' (Pettigrew, 1985: 44); 'distinctive beliefs and patterns over time … unconscious or taken for granted … reflected in myths, fairy stories, rituals, ceremonies, and other symbolic forms' (Bolman and Deal, 1991: 268); the 'most important stuff around' (Peters, 1984, cited in Sackmann, 1991: 7).

In short, corporate culture appears to have become a ubiquitous shorthand term for the 'soft', irrational, symbolic aspects of an organisation which are hard to grasp but nonetheless exert a powerful effect on what happens both inside and outside it.

Links between culture and performance

Although now firmly ensconced in management vocabulary, culture is an awkward import from the world of social sciences into that of organisations.[2] Early attempts to apply the term 'culture' in an anthropological[3] sense to the world of organisations were made by Barnard (1938), who called attention to the unconscious shared beliefs at work in organisations. This approach was carried further by Selznick (1957) and others. However, it was not until a positive relationship between culture and performance was mooted that the concept of organisation culture was taken seriously. The suggestion that culture had a strong influence on the economic performance of organisations brought it to the attention of general management theorists, and from there into the mainstream of management thinking.

This began in earnest in the 1980s. Culture became a metatheory for the explanation and prediction of corporate effectiveness (Linstead and Grafton-Small, 1992). This was the era of the 'best fit' approach (Sackmann, 1991), which proposed that an 'appropriate' culture – a particular configuration of values, norms, and behaviours – that supports the strategy of the organisation will promote organisational effectiveness (Peters and Waterman, 1982; Pascale and Athos, 1981; Ouchi, 1980; and Gordon in Frost et al., 1991). Understanding of the relationship between the elements was both prescriptive and functional. If high (or 'excellent' as the buzzword ran) performance results from the internal coherence and consistency of culture and strategy, then it was the task of senior management to ensure that the culture was brought into line with strategic initiatives. Henceforth, strategy needed to be supported not only by structures and systems, but also by culture.

Such approaches were somewhat simplistic. Little acknowledgement was given to the intricacies and challenges posed by reconciling the elements involved, nor to the complex human systems that organisations represent. At best culture was simply another organisational variable that managers could manipulate, at worst an obstacle to be circumvented or neutralised in order to achieve strategic goals. Unsurprisingly, reconciling culture and strategy proved far from straightforward in practice. Culture was far more deeply rooted and intractable than anticipated. In the words of Schein (1992: xi), 'perceiving the potential power of culture proved easier than manipulating it'.[4]

As the 1990s progressed, so too did the understanding of the complexity and power of the phenomenon known as culture, reflecting in part a growing academic interest in the symbolic aspects of organisations, and a growing emphasis on seeing organisations as constructs resulting from human thought and action, host to social cognitive processes which over the course of time develop their own dynamics (Gomez, 1993). By the close of the decade culture had developed from 'potential nuisance' to 'latent power'. It was increasingly seen as a symbolic frame ('the pattern of beliefs, values, practices, and artefacts that define for its members who they are and how they do things'), a root metaphor which 'encodes an enormous variety of meanings and messages into economical and emotionally powerful forms' (Bolman and Deal, 1991: 250). It ceased to be viewed as a troublesome element that simply needed to be factored into the strategy process but became instead a mysterious organisational force whose strength needed to be 'harnessed' if strategy was to be successfully implemented, and which was less easily engineered than best-fit proponents had suggested.

As its 'latent power' grew, so too did its perceived influence on strategic processes. Research by Kotter and Heskett (1992) concluded that it could have a significant impact on long-term economic performance. Firms with cultures that emphasised key constituency groups – customers, shareholders, employees – and leadership from all levels, outperformed by a large margin companies that did not display these characteristics. Indeed, culture became the starting place for strategy:

> strategy must be a natural expression of the potential latent in a culture. Because corporate cultures are unique, the products inspired by a culture can be original and incomparable to the offerings of competitors. Hence, a competitive strategy should begin with the culture of the organisation.
>
> (Hampden-Turner, 1990: 253)

Schein's concept of culture

> Culture is to the organisation what character is to the individual.
>
> (Schein, 1992: 196)

Culture is normally imprecisely defined – typically as an emergent pattern of shared beliefs, norms and values, unique to the organisation concerned. In contrast, Schein[5] offers a definition that is both comprehensive and precise, and therefore suitable as a basis for empirical research. For Schein, culture is:

> a pattern of shared basic assumptions that a group learned as it solved its problems of external adaptation and internal integration, that has worked well enough to be considered valid, and therefore is taught to

new members of the group as the correct way to perceive, think and feel in relation to those problems.

(Schein, ibid.: 12)

Culture is essentially, therefore, nothing more than the accumulated learning shared by a set of members of an organisation. This learning has been acquired as the group deals with the challenges posed by the environment and by the organisation as it develops and matures. In the course of this problem-solving process a number of precepts emerge which repeatedly prove themselves effective. These represent a set of basic tacit assumptions about how the world is and ought to be, assumptions which determine perceptions, thoughts, feelings and, to some degree, overt behaviour. They come to function as heuristics, shortcuts to future problem-solving. New members learn these assumptions as part of their socialisation, and thus the culture is perpetuated (Schein, ibid.).

Levels of culture

Culture is often approached from the surface level, whereby researchers attempt to 'read' the superficial aspects of an organisation – its rituals, its dress style, even its logo or the design of its corporate communications – and use these as clues to decipher the underlying beliefs. Schein approaches culture 'in reverse', working from the covert to the overt, starting by accessing the hidden assumptions and using these to interpret more tangible organisational phenomena. Culture, according to Schein, manifests itself at three levels: artefacts, espoused values and basic underlying assumptions.

Artefacts are the 'top' layer of a culture, the superficial phenomena including everything that can be seen, heard and felt, including day-to-day behaviour, physical environment, communication style, dress style, rituals and ceremonies, publications, myths, stories and so on. Artefacts are easy to access, but hard to interpret, representing 'a complex compromise between espoused values, deeper assumptions, and situational contingencies' and should be interpreted in the light of underlying assumptions. From this point springs Schein's criticism of climate[6] surveys as a means of analysing culture. Surveys are by their nature highly reductionist tools, inadequate as a means of accessing subtle and complex phenomena. Culture surveys therefore offer access only to culture's most superficial layers: 'in that regard the data are perfectly valid cultural artifacts[7], but they are artifacts that have to be interpreted and deciphered in the same way as other artifacts' (Schein, ibid.: 185).

The second level of culture comprises the *espoused values*, the group's officially expressed strategies, goals and philosophies. This level of culture also needs to be interpreted with care. Mission statements and corporate philosophies may appear to reveal a culture's underlying beliefs, but in reality

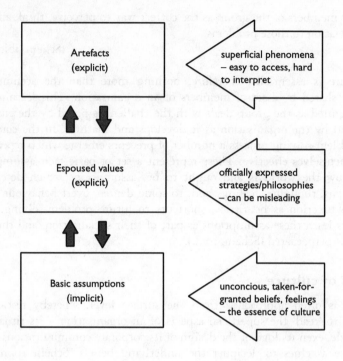

Figure 1.1 Levels of culture

represent little more than how a group feels it should present itself publicly to important audiences, or how it would like to be ideally (see below). Espoused values can be used therefore to check hypotheses about underlying assumptions, but are neither an accurate representation of them, nor a guide to deciphering them.

Basic assumptions represent the third and 'deepest' level of a culture and also its essence. These are the unconscious, taken-for-granted beliefs, perceptions and feelings about the organisation and its environment which act as the ultimate source of values and drivers of actions. By accessing underlying assumptions a researcher not only acquires the 'key' to the culture under review, but also the necessary clues to decipher the other two levels. Only when assumptions have been uncovered can artefacts be correctly interpreted and the credibility of espoused values assessed.

> When we see the essence of a culture, the paradigm by which people operate, we are struck by how powerful our insight into that organisation now is, and we can see instantly why certain things work the way they do, why certain proposals are never bought, why change is so difficult, why people leave and so on.
>
> (Schein, ibid.: 207)

Assumptions do not stand alone, but form an interrelated belief system, or paradigm.[8] This is central to Schein's conception of culture: it is because cultures contain belief systems, rather than an assortment of stand-alone assumptions and beliefs, that they are so powerful. In order to decipher a culture, a researcher must understand not only the assumptions, but the complex interrelationships between them:

> Unless we have ... attempted to identify the paradigm by which the members of a group perceive, think about, feel about, and judge situations and relationships, we cannot claim that we have described or understood the group's culture. Unless we achieve this level of analysis, however, we should not make any statement at all about culture, however superficial.
>
> (Schein, ibid.: 142–3)

Assumptions serve many functions at once. They enable a group or organisations to create and preserve integrity and autonomy and differentiate itself from the environment; they also create a sense of group identity and promote group stability by reducing complexity, confusion, uncertainty and anxiety, and by increasing predictability, even functioning as a cognitive defence mechanism.

Schein is not alone in positing that a powerful set of tacit assumptions drives organisational behaviour. His ideas echoed those of Argyris ('theories-in-use', 1977), Senge ('mental models', 1990) and even McGregor ('assumption

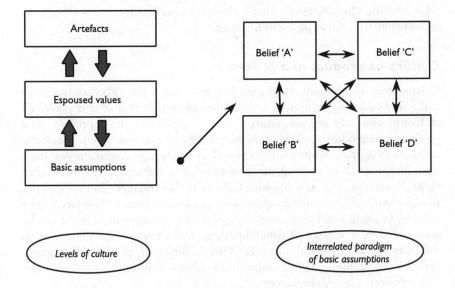

Figure 1.2 Assumptions as a paradigm

sets', 1960). Bolman and Deal (1991: 30–1) provide an accessible explanation of how and why assumptions function as they do:

> People rarely enjoy … feeling out of control. They want their world to be understandable, predictable, and manageable. Even in the face of inconsistent evidence, people will try to make the world fit their current theories about it … What they want above all is a theory that works for them and helps them figure out what is going on in a particular situation. The theories that we learn and carry with us determine whether a given situation is confusing or clear, meaningful or cryptic, a disaster or a learning experience. Theories are essential because of a simple – but very basic – fact about human perception in organisations: there is simply too much happening in any given situation for an individual to attend to everything. To understand what is going on and to take action, the individual needs theories that will tell the individual both what is important and what can be safely ignored and group a great deal of different pieces of information into patterns or concepts.

Assumption sets bring benefits, creating security, building identity, speeding decision-making and so on. But they are also inhibiting, restricting group members to familiar ways of thinking and acting (Senge, 1990; Schein, 1992; Bolman and Deal, 1991). Because they are hidden and therefore seldom confronted, and because much effort has been invested in developing and learning them, they are also difficult to change. Altering basic assumptions requires 'double loop learning' (Argyris, 1977), or 'generative learning' (Senge, 1990), that is, learning that involves reassessing basic assumptions and releasing basic anxieties.

Culture as product and process

Culture may be difficult to change but it is not static. The last point to make in relation to theoretical conceptions of culture is that it is perceived as living, vital and organic. Culture is both a product and a process. As a product it embodies the accumulated wisdom of previous group members. As a process it is continually renewed as changing circumstances force assumptions to be re-assessed, and re-created as new members are introduced to, and question, 'old' assumptions. Culture is also emergent in that it is not uni-dimensional. Postmodern approaches to culture stress the subjectivity of culture (Linstead and Grafton-Small, 1992). Any organisational event can be interpreted in a variety of different ways, and therefore 'contains' several different meanings simultaneously. This 'differential process of meaning construction' (Young, 1989) undermines cultural uniformity and reinforces culture's evolutionary characteristics.

Cultural pluralities

Underlying the 'superficial' approaches to culture discussed earlier is an assumption that organisation cultures are monolithic. Certainly, a basic cultural homogeneity was implicit in many 'best fit' prescriptions for matching culture to strategy. However, as understanding of culture has advanced, it has also become clear that while every organisation culture exhibits certain homogeneous, organisation-wide characteristics, it is also affected by a wide range of other cultural influences, inter- and extra-organisational, which both exist alongside the common organisation culture and cut across it, and which need to be understood and integrated if the organisation is to work effectively (Schein, 1993b).

Occupational communities and other subcultures

The cultural processes at work in society at large are also at work within organisations. Members of an organisation are simultaneously members of many other social and cultural institutions, all of which share common frames of reference, common languages and common unconscious assumptions, and which therefore exert influence on an organisation's culture. These include:

- *professional cultures or occupational communities* (Van Maanen and Barley, 1984, in Schein, 1993b) – groups of practitioners who share a common base of knowledge, a common jargon and similar background and training[9]
- *industry cultures* – the value orientation common to those working in a certain industry (Fombrun *et al.*, 1984)
- inter-organisational *subcultures* based around cultural groupings such as hierarchical level, function departments, gender and ethnic subgroups (Pettigrew, 1985; Sackmann, 1991).

National cultures

National groups also display shared cultural traits – value orientations, beliefs and attitudes – and these permeate every aspect of organisational behaviour. A national population, like the members of an organisation, shares a common heritage, language, approaches to dealing with each other and with the world outside. 'National assumption sets' have a pervasive influence on organisations.

Such influence has been widely researched, and empirical results show consistent differences and general patterns (although they have also been criticised for treating culture as a residual factor to which 'national variations that have neither been postulated before the research nor explained after its completion' are attributed (Child, 1981, in Tayeb, 1994)). National groups display differences in value structures, need orientations and the attribution of meaning (Hofstede, 1991; Trompenaars, 1993; Laurent, 1983), and corporate cultures act out themes and patterns in the wider culture (Hampden-Turner 1990; Hampden-Turner and Trompenaars, 1993).

National cultures have a pervasive impact on strategic processes (Schneider, 1989). They affect how organisations scan the environment, their preferences for types and sources of information, methods of interpretation and validation, and their criteria for establishing priorities. Environmental assessments therefore are heavily affected by the values, beliefs, attitudes and perceptions common to that national culture.[10]

Culture's beginnings and the role of the founder

Schein, like other theorists (Bolman and Deal, 1991; Kotter and Heskett, 1992; Kay, 1993), ascribes to the founder of a culture a disproportionate and decisive role in shaping its subsequent development (1983). Even in mature companies, cultural assumptions can be traced back to the beliefs and values of founders and early leaders. Once a culture has been established, the founder plays an important role in correcting cultural dysfunction, which includes recognising and taking action should the organisation be threatened because elements of its culture have become maladapted, particularly

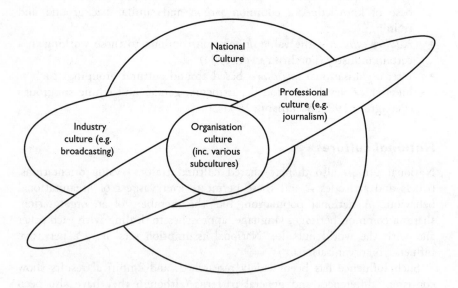

Figure 1.3 Interaction between organisation, professional, industry and national cultures

to environmental developments. The cultural researcher must ensure that an organisation's founder and founding circumstances are included in cultural investigations.

> Cultures basically spring from three sources: the beliefs, values and assumptions of founders of organisations; the learning experiences of group members as their organisation evolves; and new beliefs, values and assumptions brought in by new members and leaders. Though each of these mechanisms plays a crucial role, by far the most important for cultural beginnings is the impact of founders. Founders not only choose the basic mission and the environmental context in which the new group will operate, but they choose the group members and bias the original responses that the group makes in its efforts to succeed in its environment and to integrate itself.
>
> (Schein, 1992: 211–12)

The process by which a leader's values, solutions and ways of looking at the world become part of shared assumption sets is as follows:

- the founder of a new group starts with some beliefs, values and assumptions about how to proceed and teaches these to new members
- the founder's basic reality becomes a set of interim values and beliefs for the group
- the group behaves in a certain way based on the founder's beliefs and values, and either succeeds or fails
- if it fails, the group eventually dissolves and no culture is formed
- if it succeeds, and this process repeats itself, the founder's beliefs, values and assumptions come to be validated in the shared experiences of the group.

Culture's link to strategy

An assumption that some type of relationship exists between performance and culture, that the alignment of strategy and culture is a prerequisite of organisational success, has become almost a *sine qua non* of current management thinking. However, in keeping with the general vagueness surrounding the concept of culture, theoretical attention to the relationship between these elements has tended to concentrate on the output of the relationship, on its impact on performance, rather than on the nature of the relationship itself or on the link between the elements.

The Schein model, however, addresses with some clarity the issue of how exactly the culture of an organisation affects its strategic processes, and translates such concepts into empirically applicable detail. Schein proposes that at the heart of an organisation's culture lie an interrelated set of assumptions.

These assumptions have arisen out of group learning processes. This learning relates to two categories of problem-solving: 'external' problems concerned with responding to the environment, and 'internal' problems arising from managing the internal development of the organisation. Learning that arises from the response to environmental challenges leads to the creation of a number of different assumptions, all contained within the organisation's overall culture, and a number of these relate to issues of mission and strategy (Schein, 1992: 53).

Culture, therefore, plays an important role in determining firstly how environmental developments are perceived by members of an organisation, and secondly how members of the organisation react to the strategies designed to respond to those environmental developments. This perception of culture's impact on strategy is broadly echoed elsewhere in management literature, for example:

> for every manager, the strategy-making process starts with a funda-mental strategic choice: which 'theoretical picture of human activity and environment fits most closely with his or her own view of the world, his or her personal "theory of action"'.
>
> (Argyris, 1977: 119–34)

Where Schein differs from his peers is in offering an empirically tested method to access the assumptions which relate to matters of strategy. This

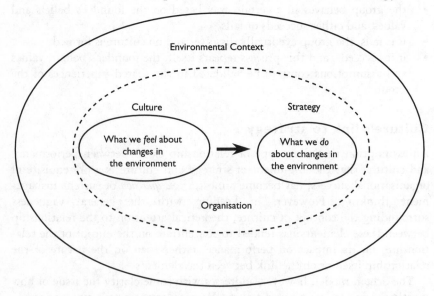

Figure 1.4 Theoretical understanding of culture, strategy and environmental context

can be done by holding broad discussions about the following issues with group members involved in the strategic process:[11]

*   the organisation's *core mission*, basic function in society, manifest and latent functions[12]
*   *stakeholders*: which groups are the most important and how good relationships with them can best be maintained
*   the nature of the organisation's external *environment*
*   the organisation's *core competencies*.

To summarise, Schein asserts that the essence of an organisation's culture is contained in an underlying paradigm of commonly held unconscious assumptions. An important set of these assumptions relates to the organisation's strategic processes and priorities, and functions as a quintessential and often unacknowledged driver of strategic decisions and activities. This assumption set can, however, be accessed by holding broad-based discussions with members of the organisation about key strategic issues such as mission and strategy, environment, core competencies and stakeholders. This approach serves as the basis for the empirical research in this study, and the purpose of the following pages is to discuss these themes more fully.

Culture, success and environmental myopia

Culture, then, governs how an organisation perceives its environment and the strategies judged as appropriate to respond to it. If 'aligned', cultural assumptions, strategic processes and environmental developments create a virtuous circle. Cultural assumptions determine how the environmental context is perceived; on the basis of such perspectives an organisation develops coherent strategic processes for dealing with the environment. Provided that the underlying cultural assumptions are in line with the environment (and, of course, that organisations have the necessary resources), the organisation experiences success; that success leads to the reinforcement of dominant assumptions about the environment.

Thus culture is both forged and reinforced by organisational success, and the greater the success, the stronger the culture is likely to become. But, ironically, the greater the success, the greater the extent also to which the organisation becomes divorced from forces in its environment. Success causes an ever increasing decoupling of the organisation from its surroundings. If the environmental context shifts significantly, this can transform a virtuous circle into a vicious one:

> Cultural assumptions are the product of past successes. As a result they are increasingly taken for granted and operate as silent filters on what is perceived and thought. If the organisation's environment changes and

new responses are required, the danger is that the changes will not be noticed or, even if noticed, that the organisation will not be able to adapt because of embedded routines based on past success. Culture constrains strategy by limiting what the CEO and other senior managers can think about and what they perceive in the first place.

(Schein, 1992: 382)

Strong 'successful' cultures can therefore be a liability as well as an asset. The stronger the culture, the greater the risk of organisational inflexibility and the greater the extent to which the culture is divorced from its environment, unless assumptions specifically address the need to learn, develop and flex to changing environmental circumstances. An organisation is unlikely spontaneously to examine or challenge the assumptions which have contributed to its success and have become a source of pride and self-esteem. But in a changed environment, the same assumptions can become blinkers, limiting understanding of contextual developments and filtering out appropriate strategic options because they are out of line with shared assumptions about the mission of the organisation and its way of working (Lorsch, 1985).

Strategic concepts highlighted in the Schein model

Mission

Mission is a ubiquitous management term with a somewhat vague meaning. In some senses it can be seen as occupying the soft middle ground between strategy and culture. In everyday usage the term 'mission' is often used interchangeably with 'vision',[13] to mean an integration of individual and organisational goals comprehensible at a personal, individual level. Mission is perhaps the human expression of corporate strategy: individuals cannot form deep emotional attachments to corporate strategy, but they can identify personally with the fundamental purposes an organisation seeks to serve.

In the 1980s published declarations of an organisation's explicit mission, known as mission statements, were much in vogue (Campbell *et al.*, 1990). These synthesised the strategy, purpose, values and expected standards of behaviour of an organisation into a few pithy sentences which fulfilled a symbolic role in clarifying and defining a firm's overall strategic goals. However, the importance and sensitivity of these statements, and the number of hands they usually went through in the course of development, meant that the majority ended up as somewhat banal documents, all too often dismissed as public relations puffery. This led to their fall from management grace:

If we took the mission statements of a hundred large industrial companies, mixed them up tonight while everyone was asleep, and reassigned them at random, would anyone wake up tomorrow and cry, 'My gosh, where has our mission statement gone?'

(Hamel and Prahalad, 1994: 133)

The fashion for mission statements, which are usually little more than a prosaic enumeration of an organisation's goals in terms of core functions and key constituencies, has helped to obscure the true value of the concept. An individual's conception of an organisation's mission represents a complex internal synthesis, a prioritisation of the organisation's many functions – latent and overt – and the demands of its stakeholder groups (Johnson and Scholes, 1993; Schein, 1992).

Schein defines mission as 'an organisation's primary task, or reason to be, a set of beliefs about its core competencies and basic functions in society' while 'strategy concerns the evolution of an organisation's basic mission' (1992: 53). He is clear about how researchers can access assumptions relating to these areas:

> One of the most central elements of any culture will be the assumptions the members of the organisation share about their identity and ultimate mission or functions. These assumptions are not necessarily conscious but one can bring them to the surface by probing the organisation's strategic decisions.
>
> (Schein, 1992: 56)

> A more useful way to think about ultimate or core mission is to change the question to 'What is our function in the larger scheme of things?' Posing the question in this way reveals that most organisations have multiple functions reflecting the multiple stakeholders.
>
> (Schein, 1992: 53–4)

Stakeholders

> Every new group or organisation must develop a shared consensus of its ultimate survival problem, from which it usually derives its most basic sense of core mission, primary task, or reason to be. In most organisa- tions this shared definition revolves around the issue of economic survival and growth, which in turn involves the maintenance of good relations with major stakeholders.
>
> (Schein, 1992: 53)

Stakeholder groups are various constituencies of an organisation which have a legitimate interest in its activities and the ability directly to affect its performance (the term derives from the fact that they have a stake in the performance of the organisation). They can be internal (such as employees, unions), or external (competitors, suppliers, customers, shareholders, the local community, etc.).

According to Schein, cultural assumptions steer an organisation's stakeholder relations, directing where emphasis is to be placed and how priorities are to be assigned. Contextual approaches to organisations stress the need to expand the frame of analysis to include the wider social, political and economic environmental trends. One way in which such trends are operationalised is via the demands of an organisation's stakeholder groups. Understanding the perspectives and expectations of an organisation's various stakeholder communities is an essential stage in reconciling the complex demands of the environment with those of the organisation, thus allowing an organisation to achieve a level of autonomy from its environment (Gomez, 1993; Gomez and Probst, 1991, 1995; Morgan, 1986).

For these reasons the analysis of stakeholder demands has long been viewed as a necessary precursor to formulating strategy. During the 1960s and 1970s some large multinationals elevated this task to complex analytic exercises in which the needs of various interest groups were systematically assessed and factored into the planning process, an approach which has long since fallen out of favour:

> so mechanistic one has to wonder if logic became the problem instead of the solution. Even if planners really did exhibit the assumed objectivity to stand aside (or above) and calculate everybody else's needs, even if such calculations were possible in the first place ... the result would be so sterile that any stakeholder with a shred of sensitivity would reject the whole exercise out of hand.
>
> (Mintzberg, 1994: 143)

'Managing' stakeholder demands is a complex and challenging task. Even separating out the various constituencies and identifying their interests can be problematic since stakeholders do not fall into neat, self-contained groups – distinctions blur and an individual can belong to many stakeholder groups at once. Further, the relative influence of stakeholder groups shifts in step with the changing environment. An organisation must inevitably prioritise the needs of its various stakeholders, since all cannot be pursued with equal emphasis, but the interests of any one stakeholder group cannot be neglected, since a group whose needs are consistently ignored may remove its support (Goold et al., 1994).

Competencies

> Corporate success derives from a competitive advantage which is based on distinctive capabilities ... successful strategies result when organisa-

tions understand and exploit what they are distinctively good at in an adaptive and opportunistic way to meet the challenges of the business environment they face.

(Kay, 1993: 11)

Competencies have been a dominant concept in contemporary strategy literature. They are traditionally understood as distinctive organisational attributes that create sustainable competitive advantage and, critically, a platform for future growth ('gateways to tomorrow's opportunities' (Hamel and Prahalad, 1994); the key to a 'strong corporate future' (Quinn, 1992)).

The concept has a long history. The term 'distinctive competence' was coined in 1957 by Selznick. During the 1960s Ansoff took the concept further, and in 1965 developed the 'Competency Grid'. From the 1980s onwards the concept surfaced again in connection with the 'resource-based school' which focused on the resources and capabilities that lead to a sustained competitive advantage (Wernerfelt, 1984, 1989; Barney, 1991). However, it was Hamel and Prahalad's 1990 article in the *Harvard Business Review*, 'The core competencies of the corporation', that brought the concept to mainstream strategic prominence.

Recently the term 'competence' has acquired a new specificity (if not semantic clarity, for where one author will speak of 'competencies' another will refer to 'capabilities'; however, for the purposes of this study, the two terms can be used interchangeably). A core competence is distinguished by a number of commonly agreed characteristics (Hamel and Prahalad, 1990 (see above), 1994; Quinn, 1992; Kay, 1993). A competence therefore:

- represents a 'bundle' of individual skills and technologies that are integrated and company-wide
- integrates multiple streams of technologies
- involves many levels of individuals in an organisation and all functions
- creates a real and meaningful distinctiveness in customers' minds
- is unique to the organisation concerned
- cannot be easily reproduced by competitors (a competence ubiquitous to an industry is not core, unless an organisation's level of competence is substantially superior or the competence is under-exploited by its competitors)
- delivers real and meaningful customer benefit
- provides an engine for new business development.

The roots of distinctive capabilities often extend back to the foundation of an organisation, emerging originally as a means by which an organisation could fulfil its primary mission. They are thus deeply embedded in culture, and contribute not only to competitiveness but also to the psycho-social 'glue' that creates identity, differentiation and cohesion (Schein, 1992: 303).

This relationship between an organisation's culture and its competencies is stressed by Drucker:

> Ever since ... Prahalad and Hamel's pathbreaking article ... we have known that leadership rests on being able to do something others cannot do at all or find difficult to do even poorly. It rests on core competencies that meld market or customer value with that special ability of the producer or supplier. Core competencies are different for every organization, they are, so to speak, part of an organization's personality.
>
> (Drucker, 1998: 92)

However, a strong link between culture and competence can make organisations vulnerable. A culture that values a particular competence, and is proud of the organisation's mastery of that competence, can put that organisation at a disadvantage should technological or other changes render the competence irrelevant.

From theory to practice

This book explores the strategic implications of corporate culture, and seeks to uncover the impact of organisation culture on strategic developments in two broadcasting organisations. Within this context, this chapter serves a double function, first to describe the theoretical underpinnings of the study and second to provide a context for the discussions of culture and strategy presented here.

Chapter 2

'The status quo is not an option'[1]

Broadcasting's changing environmental context

The often-heated discussions of the strategic changes undertaken by long-established broadcasters such as the BBC, or analysis of the activities of newer international players such as CNN, frequently omit to mention the environmental and market developments which can play a decisive role in determining those organisations' activities. This chapter examines why issues of strategy are becoming critical for media organisations, and why, in the words of the BBC, 'the status quo is not an option'.

The broadcasting industry is finding itself embroiled in a period of unforeseen turbulence and far-reaching change. The form in which it will finally emerge from this turmoil, and whether indeed it will emerge from this turmoil as a stand-alone sector, is far from clear.

The tumult in the broadcasting sector is the result of the interplay between an intertwined and broad-ranging set of forces at work in the industry's larger environment. Some can be classified as destabilising, others as enabling, but the net result has been identical: to create unprecedented levels of contextual turbulence and cumulatively to dismantle the paradigm which had been governing the activities of television broadcasters for decades.

These environmental developments are closely intertwined; it is neither feasible nor appropriate to attempt to disentangle them in order to establish cause and effect relationships. Instead, the goal of this chapter is to distinguish and discuss any clear strands that can be discerned in the changes under way in the world of broadcasting, by first isolating the contributory factors and then analysing their collective impact. To simplify this analysis, the environmental developments have been divided into two chronologically distinct phases: a destabilisation phase followed by one of reconfiguration.

Phase one: destabilisation

During the 1980s, a blizzard of change (Blumler, 1992; Collins, 1998) swept across the broadcasting landscape, radically altering the established order. A potent combination of deregulation and liberalisation, changes in social structures and attitudes, as well as technological advances combined to redraw the paradigm of broadcasting. Market forces usurped regulatory control; advances in satellite and cable technologies relieved bandwidth scarcity; broadcasting costs escalated; and audiences became fragmented and promiscuous in their viewing habits. A powerful multinational commercial media sector developed, shifting the balance of power between public service and commercial organisations. The market sovereignty, even the very existence, of public service broadcasters, organisations which had long been regarded as the 'natural order of things' (Noam, 1991: 4), was called into question. PSBs found themselves battling for viewers and funding, forcing in turn a rethink of both their mission and their *modus operandi*. In the US, the overwhelming dominance of the three long-established networks was irretrievably damaged by upstart newcomers such as Murdoch's Fox Network and the (government-sponsored) development of a nimble, innovative cable industry.

The following pages analyse these developments, separating them as far as possible into political, economic, social and technological categories.

Deregulation

Regulation bounds the scope of any broadcaster's activities, and shifts in perspective or policy at national or international level can have tremendous implications. During the 1980s and 1990s the regulations governing broadcasting in both the US and Europe were liberalised – creating a much tougher environment for the dominant incumbents. However, although the broad phenomenon of deregulation was common to both continents, underlying causes differ, and therefore the changes in Europe and in the US are reviewed here separately.

Europe

During the 1980s broadcasting regulation was loosened and markets were liberalised. This was in line with the free-market thinking in vogue in much of Western Europe which had replaced the collectivist approach of the 1960s and 1970s (McQuail *et al.*, 1990). There was a desire to introduce market competition into protected public service markets[2] and a changing perception of the function and management of public institutions.[3] At a domestic level politicians hoped liberalisation would allow domestic players to capitalise on the economic opportunities which they believed would be offered in the coming decades by the fast-developing communications sector. New broadcasting technologies were spawning the development of new media industries and politicians wanted to ensure that national economies would benefit, in terms of exports of communications hardware and of giving programme-makers access to international markets. Domestic desires were echoed at international levels. In 1989 the European Community adopted a plan to foster the unimpeded circulation of advertising and programmes within member countries. The aim was to create a new transnational audio-visual space, supporting the idea of economic, social and political harmonisation (Venturelli, 1993). The 'Television without frontiers' directive was introduced, requiring members to admit channels and services originating in member countries, provided they conformed to minimum standards in areas such as advertising and sponsorship, protection of minors, and right of reply (Commission of the European Communities, 1989).

Politicians were also motivated by a desire to rein back public service broadcasters. This arose partly from a growing disenchantment on the part of right-wing politicians with public broadcasting organisations which they suspected had fallen into the hands of the political left (Noam, 1991), and partly from the continuing pressure such organisations placed on over-stretched public purses. PSBs had become accustomed to the high funding levels of the 1970s and showed little inclination to trim their spending. Politicians felt it was time these 'cultural mega-institutions' which had 'gilded the cage of their public service obligations' (Noam, ibid.) learnt to live within their means. Throughout Europe funding levels were frozen and measures introduced to implement cost controls.

United States

The overriding aim of US media policy has always been to further public interest by encouraging competition (Auletta, 1991: 31). In the 1970s, US legislators had also sought to curtail the strength of dominant players, the networks, whose grip on US broadcasting was by then beginning to look like an oligopoly. Their tool was the Financial Interest and Syndication ('fin/syn') Rules. These prohibited the networks from producing much of their own programming, compelling them to rely on studios to produce programming for them, and from participating in the lucrative syndication business (selling re-runs of programmes to local stations).

Further steps were taken with the Copyright Act of 1976, which sought to decentralise television distribution and further weaken the networks. The Act gave the fledgling cable industry the right to distribute network shows to cable subscribers – the networks were obliged to provide their own programmes to cable systems free of charge. At that point cable's only advantage over wireless transmission was that it provided a superior television picture. Many households, seeking to improve reception of network shows, signed up for cable, and the cable companies used the proceeds to finance their own programming growth. By 1985, nearly half of all network viewers received their programmes through a cable system. The Reagan administration continued the policy of supporting the cable industry and introduced legislation to liberate cable companies from state and local price ceilings. This permitted companies to raise subscription rates, and increase profits.

By the early 1990s the cable industry was well established while continuing technological developments had further relieved bandwidth scarcity and limited the networks' power. From the government's perspective it was no longer necessary to ensure diversity and balance via regulation: viewers now had many more options and public interest, it was felt, would be best served by allowing the audience to choose (Auletta, ibid.).

Increases in competition

> We start the decade with the possibility of enormous diversity; with monopoly control blown apart by market forces.
>
> (Murdoch, 1989: 9)

The potent combination of deregulation and the development of new and cheaper communication technologies led to an explosion of competition in what had been a stable broadcasting industry. In Europe PSBs were forced to yield to the commercial players, who until that point had been heavily restricted and circumscribed by regulation (in many countries commercial licences had been allowed for less than a decade). Commercial competition is growing rapidly – the number of channels in the EU nearly doubled in the six years to 1994, rising to 164. The typical European model is now a dual system, where public broadcasters compete with an ever-increasing range of private commercial channels.

In the United States, three network giants, ABC, CBS and NBC, had enjoyed a virtual monopoly of nationwide television for three decades, during which a collective prime-time share of 90 per cent was not uncommon. But government moves to weaken the power of the networks meant that these three, which in the mid-1970s had claimed nine out of ten viewers nightly, had by the early 1990s lost approximately a third of their audience, nearly 30 million viewers, and cumulative profits had dropped from $800 million in 1984 to $400 million in 1988 (Auletta, 1991). New networks had been launched: Fox by Murdoch's News Corporation in 1986, United Paramount by Viacom in 1995, WB by Warner Brothers in 1996 and Pax Net in 1998.

Emergence of powerful international commercial players

The explosion in competition was stimulated in part by the emergence of a number of powerful international commercial media firms[4] with both the will and the wherewithal to expand out of domestic publishing into international broadcasting. The underlying rationale was often that domestic expansion possibilities had been exhausted and foreign print markets were unattractive because of the language barrier. Overseas broadcasting markets were the single option for growth within the media sector.

The development of cable and satellite technology (see below) provided the gateway for their large-scale entry into broadcasting. Public service broadcasters, less well funded than they once had been and in some cases prohibited from moving into the developing broadcasting technologies, were unable to capitalise on such opportunities. Thus the field was left clear for media conglomerates (Siune and Truetzschler, 1992), many of whose leaders had prepared well for this eventuality, having assiduously cultivated friendships with politicians disillusioned with PSBs in order to smooth their way into new international markets.[5]

Competition from substitutes

Competition did not come from new television providers alone. Substitutes, principally the video cassette recorder (VCR), also 'stole' broadcasters' viewers by diverting them away from television. The VCR was launched commercially in the US in the late 1970s. (In 1985 it was present in just 20 per cent of US homes, but by 1991 this figure had increased to 70 per cent). By placing control in the hands of the viewer rather than the scheduler, it arguably represented the first step in the now well-documented shift from the 'passive' 'one-to-many' audience model towards an interactive 'one-to-one' relationship with broadcasting viewers.

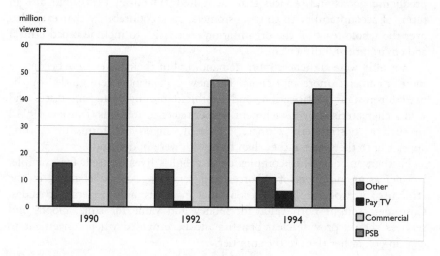

Figure 2.1 Audience share in Western Europe
Source: Goldman Sachs.

New attitudes and demands

Broadcasting's societal context changed too. The closing decades of the twentieth century saw a number of social developments which were to have significant implications. The first of these, termed the 'individualisation' of society, refers to a 'social privatisation' that partnered the privatisation process taking place in many state organisations (Bergquist, 1993). Collectivist and communal ways of living were replaced by individualist and privatised ones, a 'competitive individualism' (Lansley, 1994) took hold, and established sources of authority (the family, schools, the church – and public service broadcasters) weakened.

Further weakening of allegiance to the old structures of political and social control and participation (McQuail *et al.*, 1990) arose from what Samuel Beer termed a 'collapse of deference', a decline in the respect accorded to traditional authorities. There was a discernible dissatisfaction with the old 'official' cultural regulation and establishment control. As these traditional allegiances broke down, institutions which a few decades ago had commanded unquestioning respect now found themselves having to justify their existence to the public.

As traditional structures and old certainties became weaker, new sources of authority and identity developed. Prominent among these was consumerism, resulting in part from greater affluence. This had a significant impact on individual and social expectations and behaviour, leading in particular to the growth of unsustainable demands and expectations (Lansley, 1994).

All organisations, whether public or private, were expected to demonstrate a new customer orientation, expressed not simply in terms of producing goods and services that 'delighted' (Deming, 1986), but also in terms of accountability to those customers, an accountability that extended over the whole reach of the organisation's activities to include broad ethical and environmental dimensions.

Not only were audiences more demanding but their tastes were becoming more ephemeral, more capricious. The new generations were guided by the need for instant gratification, and exhibited rapidly changing tastes and values characterised by detachment, impermanence and fads (Lansley, 1994). In such a 'postmodern' climate, transient, superficial forms of culture, appealing to the senses rather than to reason, were in demand.

Further, an increasing complexity in people's lives (caused, for example, by increasing numbers of divorces and remarriages) and changes in the structure of work influenced consumer patterns and societal attitudes. Customers sought both value for money and value for time. Goods and services should provide clear benefits and be provided when convenient to consumers, rather than to the supplier.

Technological developments lower entry barriers

A number of advances in broadcasting technology also contributed to the destabilisation of the television industry:

- *satellite*: an increase in the number of communication satellites made international programming available to homes that had reception dishes or that were connected to cable
- *cable*: more households were cabled, greatly increasing viewers' exposure to external as well as domestic commercial television
- *cheaper broadcast technologies* were developed which reduced the once prohibitive costs of setting up and running a television channel.

Such developments simultaneously reduced bandwidth scarcity and brought down broadcasting production costs, leading to an increase in viewing options and thereby fragmenting homogeneous markets. They also provided an entry route for commercial players.

The widespread introduction of cable and satellite technology in Europe was often politically influenced. Many European states sponsored the development of rockets and satellites for a variety of reasons; once operational these had to be put to use to justify the effort and expense. Similarly, cable television was actively pushed in some countries by the post and telecommunications monopolies as part of their expansion into new areas. It has even been argued that the ultimate proliferation of new commercial channels triggered by technological developments resulted not from media or cultural policy, but from national economic and development policy in the electronics sector (Noam, 1991).

Implications of environmental 'destabilisation'

This 'redrawing of the paradigm of broadcasting' had a number of implications.

For television supply

Technological progress altered the fundamental characteristics of television supply. Because television had always been a classic example of a public good, policy-makers had treated it differently from other goods and services, and indeed from other media such as newspapers and magazines. An increase in suppliers, channels and methods of transmission and funding, meant that broadcasting ceased to be a public good, becoming instead a private good like any other media product. Technological developments therefore helped move broadcasting step-by-step towards a market-orientated system (Congdon *et al.*, 1991).

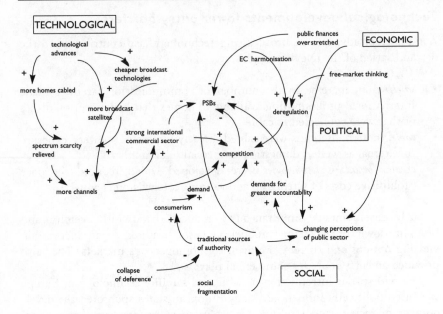

Figure 2.2 Environmental factors and their impact on the broadcasting industry[6]

For national media systems

During this period broadcasting ceased to be a purely national activity and could no longer be analysed, or regulated, from an exclusively national perspective.

> Some people don't understand. When you can hurl down programmes from a satellite with the speed of light to 3.5 billion people simultaneously, you live in a global marketplace. You can't fence off your borders.
> (Jack Valenti, President of the Motion Picture Association of America)[7]

Competition, regulation and technology were ruthlessly imposing an international orientation. Although national governments still sought a dominant voice in the regulation and steering of national and subnational broadcast media, the emergence of international satellite and cable channels meant they had effectively lost complete control over national airwaves – it was no longer feasible to maintain national frontiers against foreign media intrusion and policy-makers were forced to abandon legislation that blocked out overseas channels. A 'national chain reaction' (Noam, 1991) took place, where as one country opened up, its neighbour's viewing options were increased.

For regulation

EC attempts to encourage cross-frontier broadcasting led ironically to a relaxation and fragmentation of domestic regulatory control. EC rules were often less stringent than the national regulations over which they took precedence, and although they contained detailed provisions for 'minor' aspects of media activities, the overall framework was weakened to provide only vague guidelines (McQuail *et al.*, 1990).

The net result was to leave regulation in an ambiguous state ('woolly and open to interpretation', Noam, 1991) and undermine national media policies and regulation. Domestic regulators were faced with the dilemma of seeking to preserve diversity of control at a national level while ensuring they also fostered or allowed the growth of organisations large enough to compete internationally. There was no commonly accepted definition of efficiency or success, and public and private sectors were treated asymmetrically, inhibiting the public service broadcasters' ability to compete in a 'freer' market system.

For audiences

As competition and broadcasting choice increased and allegiances to public sector organisations dissipated, loyalties to long-established broadcasting patterns decreased. Audiences that had once been socially and culturally homogeneous fragmented both socially and spatially. The predominant image of the audience as a large aggregate of passive spectators became less and less accurate. Scheduling became correspondingly more challenging. Viewers wanted variety, entertainment and originality, as well as programmes that focused on their own particular interests. Thanks to the remote control it became easier and easier to surf between broadcasters' offerings.

For public service broadcasters

For Europe's public service broadcasters such developments amounted to a paradigm shift. Their world had once been a nationally bounded, protected market, in which their function was primarily orientated towards 'higher' goals like reflecting national culture, building national identity, enhancing democratic processes and educating and informing. Now broadcasting had joined the free market and was increasingly influenced by factors outside domestic boundaries. Theirs was now first and foremost an economic activity. Television was an industry like any other with customers. Viewers had suddenly become a market.

PSBs found themselves under pressure from three directions: politicians, the public and competitors. Politicians saw PSBs as an aspect of the broadcasting industry in need of reform rather than protection (Forman, 1987). An important repercussion was that the criteria by which public service broadcasters' performance was judged shifted correspondingly. Whereas the critical assessments had once been primarily qualitative, concerned with content, and carried out by peers, financial and economic indicators now became critical. PSBs were expected to meet a whole range of new criteria, primarily concerned with financial management, efficiency and accountability, and performance against these indicators was externally assessed – by auditors, accountants and consultants. This conflicted with long-held industry convictions about where priorities should be placed and what constituted quality.[8] In the sphere of regulation, the introduction of market disciplines meant the primary task became to ensure an optimal and fair market. To place these developments in context, they were, of course, part of a much larger paradigm emerging at that time in Europe and the US (Pollitt, 1990; Power, 1992; OECD, 1995) concerned with the role and management of the public sector. This sought to restructure public service organisations, whatever their function, along the lines of greater cost effectiveness and market orientation, and make this an overt condition of continued public sector funding.

Such developments have been described as a shift in the prevailing 'dominant' political logic towards broadcasting (Blumler, 1992). The 'cultural–educational' logic, which had been the driving force behind broadcasting in Europe and which ascribes to broadcasting a culturally dynamic role in informing and educating the audience to function as full members of an optimal democracy, and the 'state' logic, which holds that public broadcasters should meet national needs, were gradually usurped by an 'economic logic', which had financial performance as a key performance criterion. According to this philosophy, broadcasting is an industry like any other, operating in a competitive market, where the public is arbiter of success or failure.

New attitudes on the part of government were echoed in the public at large. In an era of privatisation, large public monopolies were no longer fashionable, and public service broadcasters were not immune to this trend. There was a reduced willingness to fund collective institutions, whether public health services, public schools or public broadcasting organisations. Further, in addition to castigating PSBs as spendthrift bureaucracies, viewers began to claim that their programming was out of step with the times (McQuail et al., 1990), catering for an old élitist hierarchy that no longer reflected mass tastes.

The third area of pressure was exerted by the massive growth in the commercial sector, which created unprecedented levels of competition. In 1980 Europe's thirty-six public service channels faced commercial competition from just five commercial ones. By 1990, forty public service channels were facing an onslaught from thirty-six commercial ones. By 1994, there were over 164 channels in Europe, the majority of which were commercial, broadcasting via cable and satellite.

The high cost of launching such services meant that their inaugural programme budgets were minimal; as a result PSBs were encouraged to dismiss the threat they posed. However, once a critical mass of subscribers had been established (often through heavily discounted introductory offers) and the high set-up costs swallowed, cable and satellite operators were able to increase investment in programme budgets to a point where the largest cable and satellite providers enjoyed greater programming budgets than PSB players. Their programme quality thus increased steadily and broadcasters whose launch services had been dismissed as risible suddenly emerged as serious competitive threats. This process was aided by a virtuous circle boosting the development of subscription-funded channels – the greater the viewership, the higher the potential advertising a channel can command; the greater its revenues, the more it can spend on improving programming quality, and thus the viewership increases still further.

The continued growth of subscription-funded broadcasting sowed the seeds for what was destined to become an ever more pressing argument against licence-fee funding for PSBs, and by extension against PSBs themselves: if ever larger groups of viewers opt to subscribe to such services, a flat fee for all set owners, regardless of whether or not they use PSB services, becomes increasingly hard to justify.

For broadcasting costs

Increases in market competition normally drive down product costs by stimulating technical innovations which in turn bring productivity gains and consequently cost reductions. In television the opposite is true. Increased competition has increased costs for broadcasters across the board.

An important contributory factor is 'talent inflation', i.e. the fact that one of the largest costs – that of the creative product itself – has risen in line with or faster than inflation in response to increased demand from proliferating media services. In the BBC's words (1992):

> Competition for talent [has] escalated sharply as the number of potential outlets has increased and as the battle for audiences has intensified
> ... Paying for it is also more expensive than it used to be. The immediate imbalance between supply and demand is one factor, but another is the growing recognition among talented people themselves of how much their work is worth ... talented people of every kind ... are discovering that they too have new power in the marketplace.

A second cause is the exponential increase in the cost of rights to broadcast sporting events such as the Olympics or Premier League football. Such programming, reflecting as it does core national interests, was once the undisputed and automatic province of public service broadcasters. However, it is exactly that pan-national mass market appeal that has turned sport into a battleground between public and private broadcasters. For extra-terrestrial commercial broadcasters, such events are invaluable as a means of encouraging potential customers to adopt new services (BskyB referred to them as 'dish drivers', meaning they 'drive' new viewers to buy a satellite dish and subscribe, or as a 'battering ram', forcing hesitant new consumers to 'open up' to new services). They will therefore pay exorbitant amounts for exclusive rights knowing that these will be covered by the numbers of new subscribers who will sign up (Bennet and Carrot, 1995). However, for PSBs such events lie at the heart of their public service mandate, and ceasing to cover them undermines the justification for universal licence-fee funding. They are therefore forced to devote more and more of their capital to acquire such content,[9] but are also increasingly having to surrender key sporting fixtures to commercial operators. In the words of the BBC:[10]

> Sport polarises audiences, so we can't spend more on sport per viewer than can be justified ... We have recognised that the sports budget needed upping and we have upped it ... But you can't just say we'll have test cricket at any price.

Phase two: the digital revolution and convergence

The first phase of environmental changes was characterised by a number of growing pressures which severely distorted the structure of the existing broadcasting system. The second phase, which is ongoing, involves a number of 'discontinuous' (Handy, 1989) developments which are serving to reconstitute fundamentally the world's media and communication industries. These 'change drivers' are analysed in the following pages.

Technology drives change

The underlying drivers of this phase of transformation are primarily technological. A cocktail of closely interwoven developments – including the exponential growth of the internet and World Wide Web, digitisation, dramatic reductions in the cost of computing power coupled with equally dramatic increases in bandwidth capacity – are combining to provoke what has been termed the 'digital revolution'. This has been defined as 'a digital transformation that blends voice, data and video into a seamlessly networked flow of information over public and private networks',[11] and in practice means that the boundaries between the media, telecommunications and information technology industries are becoming more and more indistinct. This phenomenon is termed 'convergence' (see below).

Table 2.1   A paradigm shift for public service broadcasters

	Old	New
State philosophy	Television is a public good, paid for indirectly. Market pressures play no part in the system	Television is a private good with buyers and sellers. Certain vulnerable values (diversity, plurality etc.) need protecting, but television must take its place in the free market
Purpose	To meet national needs, to inform and educate the public to function as members of a democracy, to broaden the public's intellectual horizons, to further the nation's cultural development	To capture audiences ('old' public service values must be realised through a system of extended choice or take their chances in a free-market environment)
Audience role	Aggregate to be educated, informed and entertained in the way that broadcasters, with their specialist understanding, judge most appropriate	Prime arbiter of success or failure whose needs must be met. Increasing potential for needs to be directly expressed.
Nature of audience	Passive, national, undifferentiated	Active, international, fragmented
System	Monopolistic, non-commercial	Mixed
Geographic reach	National	Supra-national
Technology	Terrestrial	Terrestrial, satellite, cable, digital
Programming	Limited number of omnibus channels, homogeneous	Diverse range of channels offering general and niche content
Control via	National regulation	Market forces, national and international (EC) regulation
Financial resources	Generous and guaranteed	Shrinking ('growing poor slowly'), less than leading commercial competitors
Aim of regulation	Ensure pluralism and diversity, guarantee access for and representation of minorities, protect against encroachment of commercial pressures, uphold national standards of decency, taste, fairness etc.	To guarantee an optimal and fair market which will automatically ensure performance and diversity along the old 'public service' lines

Internet and World Wide Web

The exponential growth of the internet and World Wide Web (WWW) is a fundamental driver of the digital revolution. The internet is a loose matrix of interconnected computer networks which enables PCs to communicate globally at low cost. A hybrid between a broadcast and a point-to-point medium, the internet is used for communication, education, entertainment and, increasingly, electronic commerce; driven by the economics of networks it is the world's fastest growing communications medium (US Department of Commerce, 1998).

Before the development of the WWW, the internet was essentially an email service for the academic world (having been created initially for defence purposes as a computer network for defence-related research networks). However, the emergence of the Web, coupled with the open architecture of the internet, means there has been an increasing trend towards commercialisation of these entities. Initially businesses responded to the internet by using it to enhance existing concepts and practices – creating corporate websites as an extension of corporate communications activities or using email to distribute documents which would once have been sent by fax or mail. More recently, however, a panoply of new products and services, ranging from virtual brokers to virtual bookstores, have emerged. Using the internet to transform basic business processes represents significant opportunities for organisations perceptive enough to see them. Included in this group are media organisations, especially US ones, who have been particularly quick to move into the internet arena. One reason for this is that the internet promises to be an important new channel for distributing content. The last 'new' medium was cable television, which is now the most profitable area of US broadcasting. Traditional media players scorned this new conduit when it first emerged, leaving it to newcomers (such as CNN). By the time cable's potential was clear the field was expensive and difficult to enter. They are anxious not to make the same mistake with the internet.

Digitisation of information

Digitisation simply means mathematically reducing all types of information (video, still pictures, audio, text, conversations, games or graphics) into binary form. Once in this format the information can be understood, manipulated and stored by computers, transmitted by networks in perfect fidelity to the original, and used immediately by another party on the network or stored for later use. Recent years have seen an unstoppable trend towards transferring all types of information into digital formats. Once information is digitised immense possibilities for new products and services result. Different forms of information – pictures, sound, text – can be combined to produce new multimedia products which can be stored, transmitted and retrieved instantly from any point on the globe. Furthermore, they can also be compressed. Whereas analogue technology transmits an entire picture, over and over again, digital compression technology allows only the parts of the picture that change to be transmitted, meaning that the amount of broadcasting frequency varies depending on what is being broadcast.

When applied to a broadcasting context, alongside new transmission techniques allowing more bits per second to be transmitted, this has two significant implications. Firstly, many more channels, with improved picture quality, can be broadcast in the same frequency spectrum, thus relieving spectrum scarcity once and for all. Secondly, when combined with addressability and interactivity viewers can send digital commands back to the broadcaster by telephone line or cable.

Computing power – faster, cheaper and ubiquitous

Constant improvements in computer performance, coupled with falling prices, are another enabling factor in the digital revolution. This results from what is known as 'Moore's Law' (named after the founder of Intel, Gordon Moore), which observes that every eighteen months processing power doubles while the cost holds constant. When personal computers were introduced in 1985 they cost $3,000; by 1998 they cost under $1,000 and were significantly more powerful (Downes and Miu, 1998). In the decade between 1996 and 2005 the price per million instructions per second of a microprocessor is predicted to fall by 99 per cent (Henzler, 1998). This means that the cost of participating in the global networked electronic platforms that are developing (see below) is falling dramatically. At the same time the potential performance and benefits for users are growing exponentially, meaning in turn that the extraordinary potential of computing power can be applied across a much broader spectrum of uses, can extend out of the workplace into domestic environments, and makes feasible the extension of digitisation of information beyond data to include audio and video.

Increases in bandwidth capacity

In parallel to the advances in computing power, technological developments in wireless technology, coaxial and fibre optic cable, routers and software compression mean that telecommunications bandwidth, the speed at which data can be moved through the phone network, is also increasing rapidly. The phenomenon here is 'Gilder's Law' (named after George Gilder of the Discovery Institute, a futurist and economist), which states that the total bandwidth of communications systems will triple every twelve months, with the result that data storage and communications bandwidth will, like computing power, also become faster, cheaper and more powerful.

Standardisation of network architecture

Increasing agreement on standards for network architecture is improving the exchangeability of signals of all kinds. This represents a progression from the era of proprietary systems (1950s–1990s), which featured closed networking standards (such as IBM's System Network Architecture) and which was followed by a stage of standard platforms (1980s–2000s), typified by the IBM PC or DOS/Windows. In the era of standard network computing which is developing, each computer is autonomous and functions as a peer of its 'colleagues'. This is characterised by the open public standards of internet protocols such as TCP/IP, programming languages like HTML and internet browsers such as Netscape or Microsoft Explorer.

Convergence

> Television and the computer have been different in nature, television viewing a broadly passive activity, computer use far more active. Changes in technology are now bringing television and computers together into a merged technology. The converging of these two technologies is no futuristic concept. It is just around the corner.
>
> (House of Commons, 1998: v)

Convergence is a huge topic, rendered complex by jargon and acronyms, and clouded by uncertainty and untested assumptions. Full discussion is outside the scope of this book, but it is necessary to understand the broad nature of the changes it will bring and to grasp some of the potential repercussions for the industries concerned. The term 'convergence' itself, although ubiquitous, has no commonly agreed definition. One of the simplest comes from the House of Commons (1998), which defines convergence as 'the ability of different network platforms to carry essentially similar kinds of services'.

The impact of convergence can be understood if one considers that, in crude terms, before convergence each of the converging sectors had traditionally transmitted its own type of communication (media programming, telephone conversations, data) on a dedicated conduit or transmission system, to be received by a dedicated user interface (TV, telephone or PC). Each of these industries operated in a neatly segregated environment, in some cases a monopoly environment, the boundaries of which were enforced by legislation.

Now, as a result of two technological developments in particular the boundaries between what were separate universes – content, communications and computing – are gradually eroding. The first catalyst is the digitisation of information. Once in this format it can be manipulated by computers and transmitted over electronic networks. The second is the emergence of high-

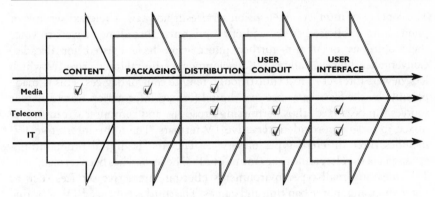

Figure 2.3 Spheres of activity before convergence

speed open digital networks, for example the internet or high-speed cable TV or telecoms systems, to replace the once discrete delivery systems for the telephone, television, and PC industries.

Convergence will not happen overnight. For the immediate future, the media, telecommunications and IT sectors look set to retain their individual identities, although consolidation is clearly taking place within the various segments and new 'crossover' areas are emerging, such as internet telephony, which defy categorisation into any one segment. However, in the long term they are increasingly expected to merge into a mammoth new 'media and communication' sector, the implications of which are limitless. Shopping, voting, banking will all be affected by the development of hybrid products that combine the features of a TV and PC. From a managerial perspective the new sector will represent an entirely new context for organisational strategy.

From the perspective of broadcasting organisations, two developments in particular stand out.

Digital television

The chief response of the broadcasting industry to convergence has been digital television, which offers significant improvements in terms of reception, sound and picture quality, the number of channels which can be transmitted over the same bandwidth, and enhanced potential for the interaction between broadcasters, other media and consumers. Digital television developments are taking different forms in different countries and launches are being carried out across all the different distribution platforms: satellite, cable and terrestrial.

Interactive television

The advent of interactive television will transform the broadcasting industry.

The concept of interactive television services is not new – Teletext services or phone lines publicised at the end of programmes that allow viewers to voice their opinions or obtain further information have existed for decades. Convergence, however, allows the development of digital interactive TV, which lets viewers interact in real time through remote control devices. This is made possible by the fact that, once in a digital format, information from different sources can be mixed, thus permitting broadcast and computer streams to be mixed in order to provide interactive TV formats. The term 'interactive TV' includes three different types of service. The first is digital programming accessed via the electronic programme guide. The second has been termed 'non-TV', meaning mall-type environments offering interactive services such as home shopping, home banking and games. The third is enhanced TV or bridge TV – interactive overlays integrated with TV programmes.

Corporate restructuring: take-overs, mergers and alliances

Convergence cuts across many technologies and sectors and has profound implications for organisations in the converging industries. It both creates massive opportunity (new products and markets) and poses significant threats (that players from other industries will move in and take away their markets, or that in the complex and fragmented disaggregated value chains that are developing (see below), they may be locked out of core products or core markets).

Such thinking has provoked a flurry of mergers, acquisitions and strategic alliances between different communication industry entities such as IT companies, cable companies, broadcasters and telecoms organisations. Organisations may be seeking to ensure they are not 'locked out' of technology, skills, content and distribution capabilities that do not fall within their core businesses, or to position themselves to gain access to geographical markets outside their current reach, or, for those with large traditional businesses under regulatory or technological threat, to move into new areas to compensate for the actual or expected decline in their core businesses.

Dennis (1994) points out that such moves are primarily driven by a combination of fear and uncertainty, a suspicion that 'not being in the game could be disastrous'. In addition to this, two underlying assumptions are at work. The first is that in a multi-channel environment, a hierarchy of value is created in which content, the scarcest commodity, rises to the top, triggering the so-called 'race for content'. The second is that whoever controls the conduit controls access to the customers. Thus those failing to anticipate developments in technology standards or to forge agreements with conduit suppliers could become 'locked out' of their current markets.

For the media sector, the smallest of the converging industries, corporate level activity of this type is viewed as critical to securing future survival –

going it alone is not an option ('No organisation has the skill level or the balance sheet, except maybe Bill Gates', then Chairman of TCI Inc, John Malone[12]). They can no longer hope to control all stages of the new disaggregated processes, but they must ensure they have access to three stages within it: content, delivery system (cable, satellite, telephony or even online services) and user conduit. (It is true, though, that the ability of media organisations, particularly broadcasters, to produce content evens up the balance between them and the telecoms and IT giants which are stronger in terms of financial resources and market muscle.)

Much of the first round of corporate activity focused on the 'race for content', and was characterised by attempts to integrate content and distribution vertically. Such moves ranged from the outright acquisition of companies to equity investments, partnerships and joint ventures[13] (e.g. Walt Disney's purchase of Capital Cities/ABC Inc., Time Warner's agreed bid for Turner Broadcasting Systems, Viacom's purchase of Paramount and Blockbuster Entertainment, and NBC's link up with Microsoft). This led to the development of a 'super league' of global media organisations, with activities ranging from TV production and motion pictures, through music, print media publishing, theme parks, TV networks, TV stations, cable networks, cable and satellite systems, to home video and retail stores. Even before its merger with AOL, the largest of these was Time Warner (1997 revenues, $24.6 billion), followed by Disney (1997 revenues, $22.5 billion). Significant players in Europe include Bertelsmann (1997 revenues, $14 billion) and News Corporation (1997 turnover, $12.9 billion).[14]

At the level of joint ventures and alliances, activity is equally frenetic. A complex and often incestuous network of alliances, either within the same industry but in different geographic areas, or across converging industries, or between players active at different stages in the value chain, is being formed which is at once bringing all players closer and increasing competition.

Disaggregation of media processes

For media organisations, these developments have combined to remodel basic media processes (as well as media vocabulary), a phenomenon normally referred to as rebundling or disaggregation. Fundamental to this is a concept of all such businesses (broadcasting, feature films, newspapers, software) as a single process stretching from content originator to consumer.

Significant players in the broadcast media sector tend to have monopolistic or oligopolistic roots, particularly in Europe. A strong regulatory framework combined with dominant national players and a relatively stable technological base gave rise to a straightforward broadcasting process that comprised three stages: (1) acquiring or producing content (programmes); (2) packaging (scheduling programmes into channels); (3) distributing the packaged content to the end-users (transmission). As a rule, traditional broadcasting organisations controlled all these stages. Thus public service broadcasters in Europe and the US networks originated or commissioned their content, packaged it and transmitted it over a national broadcast network which they either owned or to which they had guaranteed access. They could expect to produce or commission the bulk of their content, package it themselves, and have unlimited access to distribution and thus to viewers.

In the new converged world these stages have been disaggregated, or 'unbundled', into five discrete stages. Thanks to digitisation, convergence and deregulation, both the number of options and the number of players offering such options at each stage in the process have multiplied.

1   *Originating the content or programming.* Content in this context includes the output of production companies, movie studios, news organisations, record companies and software houses.
2   *Packaging, scheduling or otherwise integrating the content.* Packaging or integrating the media content into a 'metaproduct' designed to meet specific consumer needs. In the broadcasting sector this involves scheduling.
3   *Distribution or delivery.* Wide-scale distribution – the element in the broadcasting system known in the US as the 'conduit'. Distribution or delivery can be via traditional systems such as terrestrial television transmitters, cinemas and telephone lines or via digital networks such as cable television systems, satellite carriers and cellular carriers.
4   *User conduit.* This is essentially domestic distribution, the conduit by which the ultimate consumer receives the content. It includes traditional electrical cable, telephone cable, local area networks, modems and set-top boxes.
5   *User interface.* Also termed user conduit, this is essentially domestic distribution, the means by which the ultimate consumer receives content in a domestic or business environment (PC, TV etc.). This stage is being revolutionised by technological developments and is subject to the same

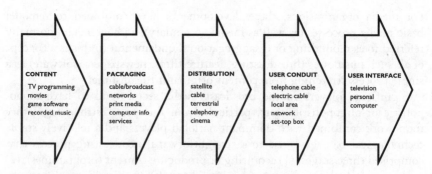

Figure 2.4 Steps in 'disaggregated' media processes

forces of fragmentation that are evident elsewhere in the value chain. New types of interface that slot in between the stages of user conduit and the end-user are constantly developing. An example is the conditional access system which was developed initially as a means to enforce payment of subscription fees, and which plays a major role in enabling the delivery of interactive services to TVs and PCs and also provides a bridge to electronic commerce (Peled, 1998). More radical examples are intelligent schedule assistants or electronic programme guides (EPGs), which are enhanced remote control devices.

Implications for broadcasters

Such developments herald the onset of a multi-channel broadcasting environment. Omnibus channels, characterised by cleverly scheduled offerings designed to appeal to as many different groups as possible, will be increasingly supplanted by a wide range of niche channels, themed to appeal to specific interest groups (for example comedy, music, golf, cookery). The majority will be commercially funded, via advertising and subscription. By extension, the 'bottleneck' in the broadcasting system will cease to be transmission frequency but the problem of acquiring sufficient content to fill channel capacity.

PSBs, as integrated factory producers with analogue transmission systems, have traditionally focused on content and packaging, and have enjoyed assured distribution to mass audiences. The developments outlined here have put them at a disadvantage in distribution, user conduit and user interface. In order to remain a broadcaster to mass audiences, they must ensure access to all emerging distribution platforms, and thence to the viewers. An extreme reaction to this situation mooted by some analysts is that they may opt out of delivery activities entirely so as to concentrate on content production.

Because it relieves spectrum scarcity, the digital revolution heightens the pressure on PSBs which has been growing since the commercial sector began to strengthen. When spectrum capacity was limited, it was acceptable to argue that one broadcaster, dutifully fulfilling a mandate of diversity and choice, financed by a universal licence fee, should control the majority of airtime. As digital television multiplies the number of channels available, audiences will shrink, and with it the rationale for universally funded public service broadcasters.

Battle for eyeballs

There is widespread concern that although the range of media opportunities will increase exponentially, media consumption itself is likely to remain static. Thus the same amount of time will be devoted to a wider range of activities, with consumers 'hopping' between them, or perhaps undertaking two simultaneously. Players will become engaged in a 'battle for eyeballs', a fight for consumer attention against an ever increasing array of media-related alternatives from internet chat rooms to home banking. Spending on media and communications products is also predicted to remain constant (McCombs and Shaw in Dennis, 1994). While convergence, therefore, theoretically makes a panoply of new services and products possible, there is no guarantee that these will be attractive to customers.

Uncertainty about consumer response

One reason for this is that these new products and services emerging as a result of convergence are primarily driven by technology, rather than by the customer. Organisations are seeking to seize the opportunities presented by convergence (to expand into potentially lucrative new business areas) and to avoid the threat that it poses (of missing the bandwagon and being left with out-of-date products for minority ageing audiences), assuming all the while that the mass market will embrace new products and services as it did television broadcasting when it began, or VCRs. There is, however, a high degree of uncertainty over how consumers really will react. A number of issues cause concern.

First, although the new products offer many benefits to customers, they will be, initially at least, technologically complex. Benefits will be difficult for salespeople to explain and for prospective customers to understand. The risk is that confused buyers either ignore the new products and services or simply wait until the situation is clearer. Second, many of the new services are led by demand rather than by the supply side. It does not automatically follow that there is demand for a new service, simply because it can be developed.

Conclusion: the status quo is not an option

The combined impact of the digital revolution, convergence, corporate restructurings and the disaggregation of basic media processes means that all broadcasters, whatever their commercial or programming orientation, now find themselves in a 'looking glass world'. Long-held assumptions no longer believed implicitly, long-standing definitions of activities are no longer relevant, while long-lived business processes are being superseded, circumvented or entirely redesigned. The rules of the game, even the very game itself, have changed. To borrow a term from the BBC, 'the status quo is not an option' – broadcasters have no alternative but to change.

Chapter 3

The mass paradigm fragments

The changing nature of the broadcasting activity

It is now commonplace to describe the changes that have taken place in the broadcasting arena over the past decade in terms of a 'decline of the mass paradigm'. This chapter argues that a more correct description is perhaps a 'fragmentation' of the mass paradigm. It considers how changes in transmission, funding, programming and scheduling, in the nature of audiences and the means of interacting with those audiences, are fragmenting as the activity of broadcasting moves along a continuum from the universal to the individual.

The chapter also acts as an explanatory backdrop to the analysis of the BBC and CNN by describing and defining the broadcasting sector from an international perspective. Because the potential scope is vast (extending from social scientific theories of mass communication through broadcasting policy into information and transmission technologies), rigorous selection criteria have been applied. The material provided here either provides context (because it has significant and direct bearing on the management and strategic direction of broadcasting companies, including the BBC and CNN) or supplies insight into various industry and professional cultural groupings which exert influence on broadcasting organisations.

This section therefore covers the essential characteristics of broadcasting as a cultural industry: an overview of funding and technology options; an analysis of the structure of the broadcasting industry in Europe and the US, covering key actors such as public service broadcasters, networks, network affiliates and cable operators; a discussion of the structural options for the broadcasting organisation, as well as its role as an institution and as a mediator between social reality and personal experience; a typology of broadcasting products, that is, programming; a description of the culture of a dominant professional group in broadcasting – journalists – and, finally, a discussion of regulation and its impact on the industry.

Broadcasting is an industry in transition. Radical and discontinuous environmental changes are reshaping it fundamentally, meaning that analysis is out of date almost before it is written, and certainly before it is published. This is unavoidable, but I hope does not diminish its value. The terms and concepts discussed represent a common body of knowledge that has shaped the world view of those currently working in the industry. They therefore serve as a 'baseline' from which the strategic and management challenges facing the BBC and CNN can be analysed.

The broadcasting industry and its products

The broadcasting commodity has been defined as:

> the total set of broadcasting outputs that results from the interaction between the set of audience needs which broadcasting attempts to satisfy and the historically given set of production resources which the broadcasting industry has at its disposal for the fulfilment of that task.
>
> (Garnham and Locksley, in Blumler and Nossiter, 1991: 10)

Broadcasting is part of the media sector. Like book and magazine publishing and the music and film industries it can also be classified as belonging to the cultural industries. Such industries produce consumer goods, but these goods have traditionally shared a number of distinct economic characteristics that separate them from other sectors:

- *Essential features: immateriality and novelty*. The essential feature of broadcasting products is 'immaterial', being the symbolic meaning contained in the products. The essence of this meaning, from which the value of cultural products derives, is novelty.
- *Pressure for constant product innovation*. For cultural goods, where the commodity is immaterial and value derives from its novelty, constant product innovation is a fundamental requirement. Each product is effectively a prototype or one-off, and there is limited scope for duplication. Competition between suppliers is normally on the basis of product attributes, rather than price.
- *Labour-intensive*. Because cultural goods cannot be mass-produced they are inherently labour-intensive. The 'labour' is performed by knowledge-workers, who tend to be educated, intelligent, creative, articulate and challenging to manage, requiring high levels of autonomy.[1]
- *Public goods*. Broadcasting products are public goods, characterised by non-competitive consumption and the impossibility of excluding individuals who have not contributed to their provision from enjoying their benefits (Samuelson, 1954).[2] The cost of reaching an additional consumer is low to zero, and because cultural goods are immaterial they are not destroyed by the act of consumption.
- *Economies of scale create pressure to expand market share*. Because the cost of providing the commodity to additional consumers is very low in absolute terms in relation to the cost of the original prototype, and in terms

of the value to the new consumer, the potential returns to economies of scale are virtually continuous. This creates constant and heavy pressure to expand market share.

Realising value from broadcasting products

The unique nature of the broadcasting commodity has given rise to two distinct strategies for realising value from the industry's products:

- *Economies of scope.* Producing a range of products for a range of market segments and thereby maximising chances of finding programme 'hits'. This can be achieved in two ways. An 'editorial strategy' means assembling a 'list' of products with a distinct editorial identity, which can then be marketed as a whole. CNN, with its innovative and individual style of covering news, adopted this approach. A 'flow strategy' involves assembling a range of items appealing to a range of possible needs and tastes and packaging or scheduling these into a constantly renewed stream which is sold to consumers as a complete service. This has been the traditional approach of PSBs and the US networks. Success according to this strategy depends on ensuring a constant flow of novel new products (thus the launch of 'summer' or 'Christmas' schedules, creating the need for constant consumption and leaving no time for others to exploit the same market).
- *Control of distribution.* Both editorial and flow strategies depend on guaranteed access to audiences. Thus control of distribution is critical.

Paying for broadcasting – funding options

The means by which the broadcasting activity is financed, and the relative merits and demerits of the various funding options (licence fee, government grant, advertising, subscription, pay-per-view, even transaction fees), have been the focus of much recent attention. The combined influences of market liberalisation, the digital revolution and convergence have combined both to increase the number of funding options available and to alter the relative attractiveness of the business models they underpin.

Broadcasting funding is in an era of transition. The once dominant scenario, whereby PSBs were funded by a universally levied licence fee (which in most countries was supplemented by advertising income) and commercial broadcasters by earnings from advertising is gradually being eroded. In a digital, multi-channel environment, new sources of funding, such as subscription and pay-per-view, are set to become primary means of paying for broadcasting, meaning that in future, consumers will be able to exercise a far greater level of personal choice over what they want to watch and when, and to pay for these choices directly.

Broadcasting funding is fragmenting. The typical European situation whereby the majority of national households paid a universal fee for a portmanteau monopoly product, regardless of their viewing preferences and habits, is gradually being diluted by the increasing presence of subscription funding, whereby viewers purchase a package of channels matching their own specific interests. Personal discretion will increase further as pay-per-view systems become more widespread, allowing viewers to purchase only the channels, or even individual programmes, they wish to view, to be viewed when they wish to view them.

A broadcaster's means of funding exerts a decisive influence on that organisation's strategic and editorial options, that is, on the content and style of its output. Thus while virtually all broadcasters define their mission in terms of the Reithian trio – to inform, educate and entertain – the way in which a broadcaster is funded will affect how that broadcaster weights these elements.

Finance options

Because the means of finance exerts such a strong influence on the activities of a broadcaster, the sector is often segmented according to funding model. Current funding options include the following.[3]

Licence fee

This is essentially a tax, a universal levy paid by all households owning a television. It is the traditional means of financing for public service broadcasters, although most supplement licence-fee income with commercial revenues of some type. Only the UK, Sweden and Japan have public broadcasters whose domestic operations are supported only by licence-fee funding.

Licence-fee funding provides a direct fiscal relationship between the service provider and the consumer. However, it supplies no direct mechanism for viewers to express choices. Ensuring output matches consumer demand is difficult, and history indicates that, especially under monopoly conditions, licence-fee funded broadcasters display a tendency to impose élitist tastes on their audiences (Garnham and Locksley, in Blumler and Nossiter, 1991).

Recent technological developments threaten to make licence-fee funding increasingly anachronistic. Broadcasting services allowing the direct purchase of television products are now not only technologically feasible, but have already been introduced in Europe and North America. Combined with the trend towards subscription payments, these undermine the acceptability of universal payments. Resistance to universal licence fees is likely to increase in step with the amount that viewers are paying directly for alternative services. Thus even if politicians remain committed to the concept in principle, there is a risk that in practice consumers who are paying an increasing amount for alternative commercial services might balk at paying licence fees.

Licence-fee funding brings benefits in terms of the permitted scope of content broadcast. Public service broadcasters, with funding that does not derive directly from (although is indirectly highly influenced by) crude viewer numbers, can afford – and in some cases are formally required – to appeal to significant audience numbers, but also to cater for pluralistic tastes. This provides the freedom to experiment, take creative risks and produce programmes catering for minority or specialist tastes.

Advertising

Advertising revenue is the traditional means of funding commercial broadcasters. From an economic perspective, its benefit is that it circumvents the problem of realising the cost of production from the consumer. However, advertising finance has drawbacks. Because revenue levels do not correlate with consumer demand for broadcasting, but rather with the health of the economy, corporate profitability and levels of consumer demand, advertising-financed broadcasters are sensitive to swings in domestic economy.

Advertising finance also has implications for programming options. The system depends on 'delivering' specific audience profiles to the advertiser consistently and reliably. Under competitive conditions there is pressure to maximise audience size within certain demographic groups and as a result limit diversity in programming. Crudely put, commercially funded broadcasters must seek to attract the largest number of viewers in the categories most attractive to advertisers, forcing them to concentrate, at peak viewing times at least, on pleasing as many as possible and not offending.

Subscription

Subscription funding was for many years the 'poor relation' of broadcasting finance. However, the fragmentation of broadcasting supply, and the long-term advantages inherent in subscription-based revenue models, have combined to make this both the fastest growing and one of the most attractive means of broadcasting finance.

In subscription systems, revenue is generated when viewers pay directly to receive the entire output of a channel or package of channels. While prohibitively expensive to develop and install, once a critical mass of viewers has been created and set-up costs covered, subscription broadcasting systems offer many advantages over other models.

First, they enjoy a dual income stream: a regular 'base income' of subscription fees which provides some 'insulation' from economic fluctuations, which is 'topped up' with a second income stream from advertising revenues. In addition, subscription broadcasters are creating valuable subscriber lists and have access to valuable information about subscriber preferences. Further, although a subscription management infrastructure is expensive, once established it can function as a powerful entry barrier.[4]

Interactive payment systems – 'pay per view'

This is a fast developing type of funding which has arisen as a result of the convergence of the media, telecommunications and IT industries, specifically, developments in cabling, addressability and PC interactivity. 'Pay-per-view' systems allow viewers to watch programmes (often recent feature films or key sporting events) of their choice at the time of their choice and pay directly only for those they watch. In recent years trial pay-per-view services have been launched in many European countries and the US (offering coverage of live events such as sport, pop concerts and recent film releases). Important developments associated with pay-per-view include:

Near-video-on-demand (NVOD)

This offers customers a choice of a limited number of feature films or sporting events (key football matches), which are broadcast continuously on a number of channels, each scheduled to start about 15 minutes after the last. NVOD services have been launched by a number of broadcasters, but a successful business model for NVOD remains to be found: revenues tend to be low, concentrated on a handful of programmes, and promotional investments are significant.

Video-on-demand (VOD)

Unlike NVOD, video on demand is not broadcast but delivered via the telephone line. Viewers call a cable operating company and order an individual programme to be sent to their homes; the programme can then be handled in the same way as a VCR – paused, stopped or rewound. Eventually households will be able to access full libraries of television programmes and films. There have been many US trials of VOD, the largest being Time Warner/US West's in Orlando, Florida.

Delivery options

Broadcasting has been defined as 'the one-to-many transmission of information' (OECD, 1992). Currently the means by which that transmission takes place, just like funding options, are undergoing rapid change. Whereas a few decades ago all television was transmitted via analogue signals over terrestrial networks to mass audiences simultaneously, a whole palette of delivery options now exists and a future where television involves the

Table 3.1   Television funding options

Funding type	Typical for	Example
Advertising	All commercial broadcasters (also extra revenue source for PSBs)	RTL, Carlton
Subscription	Cable, satellite	BSkyB, Canal+
Pay per view	Cable, satellite	DFI
Licence fee	PSB	BBC, NHK
Voluntary donation	PSB	PBS (US)
Government grant	PSB	CBC
NVOD	Cable, satellite	Telepiu, DirecTV, Canal Satellite

transmission of information to an audience composed of one is not hard to envisage.

The transmission options currently available include the following.

Terrestrial

Land-based broadcasting transmission networks were the first means of television distribution and still account for the bulk of today's global television viewing. These are wireless communications networks which transmit signals through the free-space environment using microwave rather than by using a coaxial cable or other physical conduit. Their advantage is that anyone can receive the signal in the broadcast area, their disadvantage that the frequency is used up for the entire transmitting zone.

Satellite

Direct broadcast communications satellites (DBS) or direct to home satellites (DTH) are orbiting antennae which receive signals beamed up from earth and then re-broadcast them across a 'footprint' thousands of miles wide to receiving dishes owned by individual households or to cable networks which then distribute the signal further. DBS is widespread in Europe, and growing fast in the US. Because the signal travels vertically through the atmosphere, reception is almost always clear and unaffected by atmospheric conditions or weather. A satellite costs a fraction of the cost of terrestrial systems and offers greater reliability and better signal quality. The industry classifies such services as indigenous (that is, broadcasting to one national market) or transnational (broadcasting to many different national markets simultaneously).

Cable

Cable in a broadcasting context denotes a broadband television system that redistributes programming from satellite, terrestrial and cable-only networks. Cable offers particular advantages in areas where geography makes terrestrial transmission difficult. Further signal quality tends to be uniformly high because of the size and quality of satellite dishes used by cable operators and their expertise in maintaining picture and sound quality.

Increased competition from satellite-delivered signals has put great pressure on cable systems to increase the number of signals carried. In analogue form, the bandwidth requirement for cable has limited the best systems to seventy-five channels or less. This is not competitive with direct-to-home satellites which may have two hundred digital channels.

At the start of the twenty-first century, cable systems are adopting digital formats to gain a six-fold increase in channels, and thus compete with satellite. At the same time, satellite is expanding its cable capacity in order to carry local signals on a 'spot beam' basis.

An additional driver for cable system expansion and improvements is the use of the wiring infrastructure to carry telephone signals and compete with the once monopolistic local phone companies. Internet bandwidth requirements are also well served by the increased bandwidth and speed offered by cable systems.

Broadcasters as organisations

New options for funding and transmission have led to a new diversity in the type of organisations operating in the broadcasting sector. For decades this was dominated by integrated factory producers (see below) such as the networks or PSBs, but there is now a rich array of different types of organisation operating in the sector:

Public service broadcasters – PSBs

When national television services were launched in Europe in the early 1950s they were mostly included in the activities of state radio broadcasting companies. This led to the development of public service broadcasting organisations which were responsible for the provision of national television and radio programming. They functioned on a monopoly basis and were financed by universal licence fee, often supplemented by advertising income.

The European PSBs have always had a complex relationship with national political institutions – an interdependence whereby both sides are simultaneously scrutinising and being scrutinised. The potential of PSBs to shape public opinion, coupled with their funding basis, meant they were always closely supervised and regulated, both in terms of output and of management. Conversely, political control over them was restrained by the fact that their remit represented effective monopoly of broadcast coverage, comment and analysis of current events.

In their heyday during the 1960s and 1970s, PSBs were powerful and influential institutions. They held the dominant position within national broadcasting systems, enjoyed high levels of guaranteed funding and were seen as playing an important national role, in terms of strengthening democratic values, fostering national identity and encouraging national cultural life. They were successful in their core task of creating high-quality programmes and generously financed in comparison with other cultural institutions (Noam, 1991).

Defining characteristics

There is no commonly held definition of public service broadcasting (Barnett and Docherty, in Blumler and Nossiter, 1991). However, until the onslaught of liberalisation in the 1980s there was an identifiable consensus as to the typical characteristics and core principles of Europe's public service broadcasters (Brown, 1991):

- *Protection from all-out competition.* All PSBs began life as highly regulated public monopolies. Domestic broadcasting systems subsequently loosened into duopolies or mixed systems, but some form of competition-decreasing measure was always present.
- *Close regulation of commercial elements.*[5] PSBs were to serve cultural and political rather than commercial or economic functions; market forces were not allowed to dominate or distort programme-making (McQuail et al., 1990). Financial factors were taken into account, but were never decisive (Blumler, 1992). Programme budgets were structured in line with programme needs rather than marketplace performance (in contrast, advertising-financed systems tend to allocate resources in proportion to audience size).
- *Public accountability.* PSBs operated under an elaborate system of public accountability. Their activities were scrutinised, discussed and debated by the public, press and academia. They were also subject to periodic intensive reviews by independent public committees.
- *Support from public finance.* PSBs were financed by a universal licence fee on television and radio. In many cases this was supplemented by income from advertising or sponsorship.
- *A national scope.* PSBs served audiences and social institutions within the national territory and were expected to protect national language and culture and (however implicitly) to represent the national interest.
- *Political neutrality and non-partisanship.* PSBs were ultimately creatures of the state and as such highly politicised, either via enforced political neutrality, or via enforced balanced representation. Journalists had

effectively taken 'vows of objectivity' (Tunstall, 1993), meaning that editorially they automatically sought to 'balance' opposing political views.

- *Semi-autonomy.* PSBs were run by a semi-independent board (normally seven to thirteen members) appointed by the government. These boards were part of the structure of the organisations and were supported by a staff responsible for the day-to-day running of the organisation. They enjoyed much latitude in determining what the 'public interest' required in policy terms at any given time.
- *Broadly worded mandates with much flexibility of interpretation.* PSBs had considerable freedom, provided they observed political sensitivities.
- *Provision of an omnibus service.* PSBs had multiple goals of education, information and entertainment, range, quality and popularity, too (Nossiter, 1986). The rationale for this was the fact that their revenue derived wholly or predominantly from a licence fee levied on each household. Because funds came from equal payments made by considerable numbers of the public, a public broadcaster had a clear obligation to meet the common denominator of broadcasting demand. In practice this meant most majority channels incorporated some demanding materials in their schedules, and minority channels had some large audience attractions in theirs.
- *Pluralism.* Pluralism of many kinds – regional, linguistic, political, cultural, and at all taste levels – was a hallmark of public service broadcasting; there was something to suit every type of audience group.
- *A cultural role, offering an enriching experience.* Public television was seen as a cultural enterprise, responsible for generating and disseminating society's linguistic, spiritual, aesthetic and ethnic wealth. Fundamental to this was the belief that viewing should be a worthwhile experience and could even enhance the quality of life. These ideas fused into a concept of programme quality as 'enabling an enriched viewing experience' (Blumler, 1992).

Networks

A network is an office building where executives package programs they do not own and sell them to advertisers and local stations they do not control.

(Auletta, 1991: 4)

The networks are an American phenomenon. Described as 'programme and audience delivery wholesalers' (Vogel, 1994: 139), the US networks offer a full schedule of entertainment, news, special events and sports to both the television stations they themselves own and their network affiliates (see below), effectively leasing the advertising time and signal distribution capabilities of their affiliates. The US has three long-established networks, ABC, CBS and NBC, and four newcomers, Fox, established in 1986, United Paramount (1995), WB (Warner Brothers, 1996) and Pax Net (Paxson Broadcasting, 1998).

For the most part these are integrated factory producers, spanning the whole range of broadcasting activities: production, news bureaux, technical and administrative services and advertising sales offices. Resolutely part of the private sector, and in comparison with their European counterparts relatively free of government regulation, the networks have profit maximisation as their chief goal and their products are designed to attract the maximum possible number of buyers. The sale of advertising time has always been their principal source of revenue (Willis and Aldridge, 1992).

Affiliates

These represent a powerful multiplier of the activities of network or cable broadcasters. A cable company that offers a particular programming service to subscribers of a particular cable service is an affiliate of that service; a television station carrying the programming of a broadcast network is an affiliate of that network. The US has hundreds of independent stations, the majority of which are affiliated with one of the national networks. The rationale for this arrangement is that viewers receive higher quality programming, because networks are able to spend significantly more money on their products than local stations would be. Each of the three major networks (or 'webs') has approximately two hundred affiliates which it pays to carry the scheduled programming that is provided free by the networks.

Satellite and cable broadcasters

Such organisations have emerged as a result of technological advances in broadcasting transmission. Cable and satellite broadcasters offer packages of channels made up of programming acquired from a variety of sources – in-house, independent producers, cable television companies etc. In return for a monthly fee, two types of 'package' are typically offered:

- *Basic.* A mixed package of channels, including news, weather, financial news, natural history, children's programming, sports, education etc.
- *Premium.* A la carte channels for which viewers pay extra, carrying special programming such as feature films, cartoon channels, key sporting events.

Niche cable broadcasters

These are 'narrowcasters', offering special interest channels for small audiences.[6]

Their channels are included in the packages distributed by satellite and cable broadcasters. Examples include Eurosport (sports), MTV (pop music) and Nickelodeon (children's). Niche broadcasters enjoy many advantages over their larger peers which seek to cover a far wider spectrum of programming. Although in aggregate the niche channels produce a broader range of programming, each niche channel is exactly that, totally devoted to a single genre of programming, be it by theme or style. This creates a virtuous circle: specialisation allows close concentration on particular viewer segments; successful channels can deliver a precisely targeted set of viewers to advertisers; production costs are generally lower; as young organisations they tend to be unbureaucratic and fast-moving, and, as newcomers to the broadcasting field, they can often avoid union involvement. However it is calculated that fewer than one-third of such channels break even financially, partly since by definition narrowcasting is watched by few people and therefore unattractive to advertisers.[7] It should also be noted that many of these niche players belong to well-heeled parents – Viacom, for example, owns MTV and Nickelodeon.

Organisational options

The broadcasting organisation has traditionally been involved in three separate economic activities: production, scheduling and distribution. The typical broadcasting organisation has been a monolithic entity delivering portmanteau packages to restricted markets. However, the fragmentation observable in the fields of funding and transmission applies to organisational structures too. The industry now contains a diverse range of types of organisation, a fast-growing sector of which is highly focused organisations with minimal overhead structures and great flexibility of operation.

Four main types of organisational style can be discerned, and these are discussed below. However, it should be noted that in the current turbulent environment new hybrid forms are emerging. BSkyB, for example, started life primarily as a packager but is now originating a substantial proportion of its programming itself.

- *Integrated factory*. This refers to vertically integrated broadcasters which make the bulk of their programmes themselves in their own studios ('factories'), assemble these into a schedule and transmit this over a national network over which they have control. They are characterised by high degrees of central control, high levels of own production, an integral link with distribution and, as a consequence, a high proportion of fixed to variable costs. This is the traditional model for European PSBs and US networks. A typical example is the BBC.
- *Publisher*. This means a publisher/broadcaster which assembles and transmits programming commissioned and acquired from producers

outside the organisation. This model is growing in popularity since it enables organisations to offer a broad spectrum of programming with maximum flexibility and creativity, while minimising the fixed cost base. An example is the UK's Channel 4.

- *Packager*. This is the predominant model for cable and satellite broadcasters. Such organisations assemble channel 'packages' out of programming acquired in bulk from suppliers of news, sport, movies and so on. An example is the UK's Flextech.
- *Independent producer*. Such companies make programming for sale to broadcasters of all types (public service, commercial, terrestrial or satellite/cable). Industry trends, such as 'unbundling' (the separation of functions) and outsourcing on the part of integrated factory producers, the increasing popularity of the packager model, and the increasing differentiation in cable and satellite television between programme providers and channel management, have led to growth in this sector. In the UK it was given a significant boost by a government requirement that the BBC commission 25 per cent of programming from independent sources.

Broadcasters as institutions

This study analyses broadcasters as organisations from a management perspective, but they are also important societal institutions, responsible for the cultural transmission of a nation-state's traditions and for helping to form the dominant consensus in society (Stevenson, 1995). Their output enables us 'to make sense of experience, shapes our perceptions of it and contributes to the store of knowledge of the past and continuity of current understanding' (McQuail, 1987: 37).

Mass media organisations have been extensively studied by communications and media studies theorists. While academic constructs have not on the whole permeated far into the organisations themselves (media practitioners tend to dismiss such concepts as impractical (Dennis, 1994)), their work provides valuable insight into media organisations' wider context and serves to deepen understanding of their broader function. Such approaches identify a number of characteristics particular to media organisations, which carry with them organisational and strategic implications (McQuail, 1987):

- *Their core product is knowledge*. Media organisations' primary task is the production, reproduction and distribution of 'knowledge' in the form of information, ideas and cultural products.
- *They act as channels of communication*. Media institutions create and deliver messages that people want to receive. In the purest sense they provide channels for relating certain people to other people: senders to receivers, audience members to other audience members, everyone in the society

to its constituent institutions. This creates a heightened sensitivity to its wider context and implies close communication with its various stakeholder groups.

- *They operate in the public sphere.* Media institutions are open institutions in which all can participate as receivers and increasingly as senders. The media institution also has a public character: it helps to shape public opinion in that its products deal with matters on which public opinion can be formed. It is because of this potential to influence public opinion that its activities are closely scrutinised and stringently regulated.
- *They are associated with political life and the power centres of society.* Media institutions serve purposes that are at once popular and political, heightening both the importance of their function and the scrutiny applied to their affairs.

Broadcasting products: programming

Television programmes fall into a number of categories (Tunstall, 1993). Each has its own requirements and working cycles, and as a result its own genre-specific subculture ('private world' (Tunstall, 1993)). These classifications cut across the sector:

- *Documentary.* An expensive genre which achieves modest audiences. In terms of cost per viewer it is one of the most costly of the factual genres.
- *News and current affairs.* A fast-paced genre. Immediacy and exclusivity are increasingly important since, partly due to CNN's influence, a growing proportion of programming is live or near live. An élite professional area whose proximity to political power makes it highly attractive to educated and ambitious journalists.[8]
- *Sports.* A complex area, technically (involving many live outside broadcasts, video replays etc.) as well as commercially and legally. It was once one of the cheapest genres but its capacity to attract mass audiences, coupled with the recent (and directly associated) explosion in the cost of exclusive broadcasting rights to key sporting events, has turned it into a high profile and contentious area.
- *Edinfotainment.* A clumsy term for magazine-style programmes involving several short items ranging over a mix of genres – interviews, mini-documentary, plus an element of entertainment. This is a growth area since it appeals to a wide range of diverse audiences (thus increasing plurality) and is relatively cheap to produce.
- *Drama/fiction.* One of the most glamorous areas of television, involving high investment in a relatively small volume of output. Programming ranges from one-off dramas, through serialisations to soap operas. Interesting is the inverse correlation in the industry between audience

size and prestige, or alternatively, the positive correlation between production costs and prestige.

- *Comedy*. This is an expensive area of programming, with costs comparable to studio-based drama.
- *Light entertainment*. This genre embraces quiz shows, game shows and chat shows and is popular with commercial operators, being both inexpensive to produce and popular with mass audiences. Defenders of 'traditional' television values are critical of this area – seeing programming as formulaic, exploitative and trivial.

Industry culture

It is widely assumed that the social background and outlook of those responsible for media production will influence the content of those media products. Consequently the culture of media workers has been frequently investigated. Key findings include:

- *Social background*. Those in charge of mass communication tend to share similar backgrounds to those in control of economic and social systems (Johnstone *et al.* in McQuail, 1987). Although engaged in a middle-class occupation, media employees tend to be less professionalised and well paid than those in comparable professions such as law or accountancy.
- *Dominant role of journalists*. Within broadcasting organisations, journalists are a dominant professional group, helping to set industry norms, shape the prevailing value orientation and sway how reality is perceived.[9] The culture of journalism is a complex subject which has been extensively studied (although usually from the perspective of media studies). What follows is an attempt to extract from such research a flavour of the strength and complexity of value orientations present in this key occupational community.

Influences on journalism

Journalism is a highly interactive industry sector, acting as a channel of communication between all groups in society. It has been termed an 'uninsulated profession' (Schudson, in McQuail, 1987), one which simultaneously shapes, and is shaped by, successive 'layers' of influence (Wilke, 1987):

- The outermost layer of influence is the *national media system*, which is governed by a series of variables including the societal, legislative and historical infrastructure, national media policy and prevailing professional and ethical standards.

- Next are the *media organisations*. This layer is shaped by the economic, political, technological and organisational imperatives governing such organisations.
- The third layer is the *media message* itself. This is influenced by variables such as the type of media – broadcast or print – available sources of information, editorial policy and the presentational style.
- The innermost layer of influence comprises the nature of the *media actors* (or journalists) themselves. It reflects variables such as demographic profile, education, social and political attitudes and the public image and perception of the role.

Plurality of roles and role perceptions

At an individual level a journalist is fulfilling many different roles at once, and each of these exerts influence on attitudes and behaviour. These include the roles of:

- *the individual*, with private personal norms
- *the member of a media organisation*, sharing norms particular to that organisation, relating, say, to editorial policy and audiences served
- *the member of society*, subject to prevailing national societal norms
- *the member of a professional group*, sharing norms common to journalists as

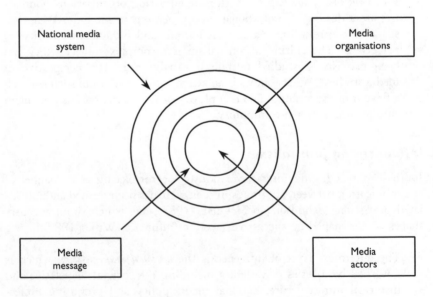

Figure 3.1 Journalism as an industry sector – layers of influence
Source: Wilke, 1987 (adapted).

a profession, relating to journalism's wider societal function, the ethics of investigative journalism, perceptions of quality etc.

Although all journalists mediate between objective social reality and personal experience, the way in which they do this, the approach they adopt, is governed by their underlying perception of their function as journalists. McQuail (1987) has produced a valuable typology of journalists' differing perspectives which can be applied equally at organisational level, i.e. to explain broadcasting organisations' differing perspectives on their role:

- *window on experience*: the essential function is to extend the audience's vision, enabling them to see what is going on for themselves, but without the interference of bias
- *interpreter*: explaining and making sense of fragmentary or puzzling events
- *platform*: acting as carrier for information and opinion
- *signpost*: actively pointing the way, giving guidance or instruction
- *filter*: selecting parts of experience for special attention and closing off other aspects of experience, whether or not deliberately and systematically
- *mirror*: reflecting back an image of society to itself – usually with some distortion – by accentuating what people want to see, or sometimes what they want to punish or suppress
- *interactive link*: relating senders to receivers by way of different kinds of feedback
- *screen or barrier*: concealing the truth in the service of propagandist purposes or escapism.

National differences in role perception

Interesting research has been carried out into national differences in how journalists perceive their role. The findings provide useful, if somewhat contradictory, background to the investigations of the cultures of the BBC and CNN.

In broad terms a journalist can be passive (a neutral reporter, informer and interpreter) or active (a critic, advocate and policy-maker) (Cohen, 1963, in McQuail, 1987), and strong national similarities have been detected in which of these roles journalists adopt. German journalists prize the opportunity to influence public opinion and help shape important public decisions, and to work with like-minded individuals. They prefer to act as advocate, critic and policy-maker. British journalists by comparison see the watchdog role as important, but less so than communicating new ideas and entertaining the public (Donsbach, in Wilke, 1987). Professional ethical standards also vary according to nation. British journalists exhibit fewer scruples than their German counterparts about 'creative' methods of garnering information, such as paying informants or pretending to be someone else. Whereas German journalists see their primary role as drawing attention to potential dangers or threats and communicating their personal interpretation of events, their UK peers feel their professional role is to report neutrally on events, even ones they privately judge as alarming. US journalists adopt an adversarial approach towards government and see their primary role as protecting the interests of the public they claim to represent. Their dominant professional motives include the need for power, fear of that same power, and narcissism (Kumar, 1975, in McQuail, 1987).

Köcher (1985) reported that UK journalists are orientated primarily towards research, as opposed to their German peers who place greater priority on analysis, and that UK journalists display a greater willingness than German ones to publish information that conflicts with dominant norms and may generate controversy, justifying such actions with 'the public's right to know'.

From the perspective of organisational strategy, a number of related implications can be drawn from these findings. The first is simply that media organisations seeking to establish a global presence need to bear in mind the potential impact of such strong national–professional cultural assumptions. Journalists in 'foreign' countries will not automatically share the motives, priorities and underlying assumptions of domestic journalists. Attempts to impose homogeneity, or to impose domestic approaches in an international context, may backfire in surprising ways. Second, assessments of quality in terms of broadcasting are highly subjective nationally: 'neutral' journalism might be considered to be of high quality in one country but simplistic in another.

Regulation

> Stories, songs and images are among the principal means by which human society has always transmitted its values and beliefs ... If we fail to use [movies] responsibly and creatively, if we treat them simply as consumer industries rather than complex cultural phenomena, then we are likely to damage the health and vitality of our own society.
>
> (Puttnam, 1996)

Regulation at national and international level influences the activities of all broadcasters (who are far more stringently regulated than their print media peers (McQuail, 1992)) and is a significant external determinant of strategy.

Instruments to regulate broadcasting

These can be divided into two broad categories (Hoffman-Riem, in Blumler, 1992):

Structural controls

These establish a general framework for the indirect control of broadcasting organisations, normally via the awarding of broadcasting concessions. Once such a licence has been awarded, the state remains largely uninvolved. Structural instruments typically seek:

- to protect the external diversity of media by ensuring the market contains a variety of competing broadcasters and by preventing concentration
- to maintain internally pluralistic programming by guaranteeing that various interest groups have access to programming, so that the widest range of programming may be provided
- to control the scope or span of broadcasting organisations by limiting cross-media ownership and the number of television stations owned.

Imperative controls

These are prescriptive instruments which set forth specific requirements, normally in the form of codes of practice or guidelines. Such 'negative controls' safeguard values which are normally protected under the standard legal system, but which are possibly threatened by broadcasting. They include:

- prohibitions on advertising
- rules to safeguard the moral development of juveniles
- protection from defamation, breaches of privacy
- quotas to protect national production resources.

Regulatory challenges

For decades the European broadcasting industry was nationally orientated and regulation relied on processes of public accountability that were narrow but effective. Television was a nationally bounded activity, focused around easy-to-monitor public service monopolies which competed with a limited number of closely regulated commercial competitors. The dominant players – public service and commercial – were largely self-regulating, subscribing more or less voluntarily to public service codes of conduct. Against a backdrop of stable competitive activity, regulators were free to concentrate on issues such as diversity and pluralism – guaranteeing access and representation to minority interests, upholding national standards of morals and decency, and protecting against the encroachment of advertising (Euromedia Research Group, 1992). However, liberalisation has created aggressively competitive television markets in Europe which have become a battleground for multinational commercial players, who do not always subscribe to the old principles of self-regulation. This has created a new set of concerns for regulators:

Concentration

> Deregulation is likely to lead to oligopoly at both the national and international level ... optimal allocation is likely to be achieved, both for society in general and the individual consumer, under regulation, whatever the technological developments.
>
> (Garnham and Locksley, in Blumler and Nossiter, 1991: 22)

From an economic perspective, large conglomerates of uncertain nationality, whose activities span many continents, pose problems for regulators.[10] The majority of commercial channels in Europe belong to such organisations. These tend to be transnational, operating networks in several countries (for example Canal+ which has companies in France, Germany and Spain) and multimedia, with interests in print as well as audio-visual media (e.g. News International), and sometimes with interests in industries other than communication (e.g. Berlusconi's Fininvest). These groups are skilled at fashioning and interpreting regulations and finding loopholes by which to advance their interests. The national perspective of domestic policy-makers and Europe's mosaic-like structure means that regulation processes are complicated and slow (Siune and Truetzschler, 1992). This allowed transnational media companies to grow rapidly, highlighting in the process the relative weakness of legislation to prevent concentration of ownership (for example, measures to regulate the cross-ownership of media are not included in the EC directive). Regulators fear that without adequate countervailing powers EC broadcasting may jump from a system based on regulated public monopoly to one based on unregulated private monopoly. However, the European media conglomerates themselves complain that inconsistent cross-ownership legislation is hindering the development of European players big enough to compete with the largest US players.

Adequate supervision at an international level

This is a particular problem in Europe, where, in spite of the internationalisation of broadcasting, neither of the European directives provides any real mechanism for pan-European supervision. The supervision of trans-frontier broadcasting is still a national matter but, as a result of new EC legislation, national governments have less ultimate power.

Increasing commercial influence

This is also primarily an issue in Europe, where dislike and mistrust of commercialism has been a strong historic influence on the development of broadcasting systems. The strengthening of the commercial sector has led, not surprisingly, to increasing commercial orientation, despite the regulatory attempts to curb it. Regulations are frequently violated in many countries, partly because supervisory bodies have difficulty in interpreting the rules in practice, and also because advertisers are inventive in devising ways to circumvent the controls, using techniques such as product placements, concealed advertising and sponsorship, none of which are dealt with effectively in existing regulation.

Quota issues

The increase in channels in Europe during the 1980s and onwards led, not surprisingly, to a corresponding increase in demand for content. To the dismay of many Europeans, this failed to trigger an increase in European television production, but rather an increase in US imports which are cheaper than home-grown content (since by the time such programmes are sold to Europe, the bulk of production costs have been written off in the home market). European regulators, fearing that US products would swamp European markets, began to demand national production quotas.

Conclusion: fragmentation of the mass paradigm

> In the past, television threw information out to viewers when it wanted to; in the future it must reel viewers in to participate in discussions they can join in when they want to. Welcome to the world of broadcatching. The one-to-many, centre to periphery model is being overturned, as a less hierarchical, many-to-many model develops.
>
> (Wyver, 1996: 35)

Social scientists reviewing the changes taking place in the world of media frequently speak of 'the decline of the mass paradigm'. Used in this way the term refers predominantly to developments in the uses of and responses to media, that is, to the way these are shifting along a spectrum that extends from universal, one-way messages from powerful and centralised message sources to the small-scale local exchange of ideas and information about familiar things (McQuail, 1992).

The concept is, however, strikingly applicable to the wider economic, technological and organisational changes taking place in the industry. In terms of funding, the act of purchasing television products is moving along a continuum from the universal to the individual. The boundaries of media institutions are becoming less monolithic as production ceases to be concentrated within large integrated factory producers and is increasingly transferred to 'unbundled' organisations concentrating on publishing, packaging or niche areas. Transmission, too, is being decentralised, as supply and choice move from the hands of omnibus service producers to outside agencies controlling transmission and ultimately into the hands of the consumer. As technology allows greater flexibility in form, content and use, scheduling too becomes an increasingly individual issue.

The term 'mass media', it would appear, is becoming less and less appropriate for television. Observing the changes at work in the sector in their totality, a more appropriate term is perhaps not 'decline', but 'fragmentation'. Product, audience, payment and transmission are all in the process of fragmenting, as the universal is replaced by the individual.

Table 3.2   Decline of the mass paradigm

Provider	PSB	Commercial	Commercial/PSB
Transmission	Terrestrial	Cable/satellite	Cable/satellite/ telephone line
Funding	Universal flat fee	Subscription	Pay per view
Programming	Omnibus service	Package of channels	Individual programmes
Audience	Entire national population	Small select groups	Individual
Market	Mass	Specific	Niche
Interaction	One-way	Two-way, but media organisation dominant	Interactive
Organisation	Integrated factory	Publisher or packager	Focused
Paradigm	Mass	General/selective	Individual

Chapter 4

'Serving the nation'

The BBC and its unique place in the UK's broadcasting ecology

The BBC, or 'Auntie', has always been Britain's 'national instrument of broadcasting' (Blumler, 1992: 11), regarded with trust and affection by its devoted audience. Its uniquely broad range of programming – a blend of liberal and conservative, high-brow and low, mass market and élitist – was once famously compared to the English breakfast (something which shouldn't work but somehow does). Even in an era of ever growing competition it still dominates British broadcasting: in 1994, 96 per cent of all households watched and listened to the BBC for at least two hours a week and the average household watched or listened to BBC programmes for forty-eight hours a week.

It is also an organisation with tremendous national cachet and influence. One factor behind this is its recruiting pattern. The BBC has always been the institution of choice for the best graduates from the best universities. Until relatively recently (say the late 1970s) jobs at the BBC were still viewed as gentlemanly occupations, somewhat akin to the senior echelons of the civil service, and, like the civil service, reserved for applicants from Oxford and Cambridge (Holland, 1997).

Historically, the BBC's recruiting style owed much to Britain's gradual decline as a world power. While the British Empire was dissolving, the BBC's scope, programme reach and influence were growing. Graduates who might once have joined the Foreign or Colonial Services turned instead to broadcasting and the BBC as a career (Blumler, 1992); furthermore, creative talent, particularly from the Commonwealth countries, was drawn to London. As a consequence, there has long been a conviction that the BBC is connected to a privileged upper stratum of British life (Burns, 1977), and thanks to its position and recruiting policy, BBC staff are formidably articulate, intelligent, well educated and often well connected – perhaps helping to explain why the organisation has such strong support among national opinion-formers.

Range of activities

The BBC was the world's first public service broadcaster and for over seventy years has operated on the integrated factory model, producing a very high percentage of its own programming (in 1993/4 this was over 70 per cent, just about the highest figure globally for a PSB). It owned its own transmission system until 1997 when it was sold off (the corporation was allowed to keep the proceeds of the sale to invest in digital technology).

Among public service broadcasters the BBC is unusual in having a licence fee as its dominant source of revenue. In 1998 its income was approximately £2,000 million and it employed around 21,000 staff, engaged in a broad range of broadcasting activities:

Domestic broadcasting

- two national television channels, BBC 1 and BBC 2 (market shares in 1998 were 31.8 per cent and 4.7 per cent respectively)
- five national radio stations and thirty-five local radio stations.

Digital services

- a range of five free-to-air digital channels available on each of the UK's three digital platforms (including BSkyB's digital satellite package): BBC News 24, BBC Choice, BBC Parliament, BBC Learning, BBC 1 and BBC 2 in digital widescreen format
- BBC Text (successor to analogue Ceefax)
- digital radio
- BBC Online – a non-commercial internet operation.

Commercial activities

Through its subsidiary BBC Worldwide, the organisation is engaged in a range of commercial activities including:

- UKTV – a series of five pay-TV channels produced through a joint venture with Flextech: UK Arena, UK Gold, UK Horizons, UK Style, UK Play
- joint venture with Discovery Communications (DCI) to create BBC Channels around the world, including BBC America, Animal Planet and People and Arts. This involves a £12 million ($20 million) investment in BBC programmes by Discovery
- two subscription/advertising-financed international satellite networks, BBC Prime (55 million homes) and BBC World (6.5 million subscribers)
- UKTV in Australia (275,000 cable subscribers)

- Beeb@theBBC – a commercial internet site
- non-broadcasting commercial media activities: videos, books, magazines, programme-related merchandise and programme formats.

BBC World Service

- international radio news service broadcasting in English and other languages to 140 million people (partly funded by the Foreign Office).

Founding circumstances

The British Broadcasting Company was founded as a monopoly radio broadcaster in 1922. The organisation now called the British Broadcasting Corporation (BBC) dates from 1927, when, after extended and heated parliamentary discussion about how the organisation should function (an activity which was to be taken up at regular intervals over the next seventy years), the 'Company' was relaunched as a 'Corporation' and given a Royal Charter, to last initially for ten years. Then as now, the BBC was financed by a licence fee, could carry no advertising and was closely regulated by government, the prevailing sentiment being that radio had unprecedented power to reach mass audiences and was too dangerous a medium to be left to unregulated commercial interests (Burns, 1977). This arrangement continued without basic changes until 1955. A pilot television channel was launched in 1936 (at that point viewers were termed 'lookers').

Television broadcasts were discontinued during the war (to resume in 1946) but radio activities continued throughout. These were to sow the seeds of current national attitudes towards the organisation. The BBC's wartime domestic and foreign radio services were a trusted and welcome source of comedy and entertainment, as well as of reliable and impartial news (Scannell and Cardiff, 1991). The organisation emerged from the war immensely strengthened at home and abroad, having become a major influence on the social, cultural and political affairs of the nation (Blumler, 1992). In 1962 a second national television channel was launched.

John Reith

> Reithian. Of, pertaining to, or characteristic of Reith and his principles, especially relating to the responsibility of broadcasting to educate and enlighten public taste.
>
> (Supplement to the Oxford English Dictionary, 1982)

The BBC has a rich and well-documented history which has left a clear imprint on today's organisation. Discussion of its founding circumstances inevitably focuses on its extraordinary first Director General, John Reith (1889–1971), a visionary leader by any modern management standards – certainly equivalent in stature and influence to contemporary media moguls such as Turner and Murdoch. His vision of the role and responsibilities of public service broadcasting shaped not only the BBC but also its continental PSB peers from their inception to the present day.

Reith was an outstanding and energetic administrator, and, in public at least, deeply religious and a model of moral rectitude (he once insisted that a colleague should resign because he had divorced his wife), although he is also said to have had hidden and exotic romantic depths (McIntyre, 1994). Reith imposed his personal code of ethics on the organisation and under his leadership the broadcaster was consistently seen and heard to occupy the 'high moral ground' (Blumler, 1992: 63).[1]

Early mission and programme policy

> It is the BBC's responsibility to carry into the greatest number of homes everything that is best in every department of human endeavour and achievement.
>
> (John Reith, cited in Blumler, 1992: 11)

Reith developed a clear vision for the BBC and its services. Broadcasting should be a public service which should not simply entertain, but inform and educate as well. The defining characteristics of Reith's philosophy of broadcasting were, firstly, a distinct élitism:

> Few [listeners] know what they want, and very few want what they need.
>
> (Reith, cited in Congdon, 1992: xvii)

Second came a belief that broadcasting should direct public taste rather than follow it. The BBC's task was to train its audience to digest material it might not otherwise attempt, to provide a service somewhat ahead of what the public would demand were it able to articulate its demands. Simply responding to market needs was ruled out from the beginning:

> He who prides himself in giving what he thinks the public wants is often creating a fictitious demand for lower standards which he will then satisfy.
>
> (Reith, cited in Briggs, 1961: 334)

By the time television services were launched in 1936, Reith had fleshed

out his ideas into a rich concept of public service broadcasting. That programmes should improve and elevate those who listened was a guiding principle. Viewing should be a worthwhile experience, one that could even enhance
the viewer's quality of life. The BBC would have to carry easily digestible information and act as a means of relaxation for those not up to its more taxing fare,
but it should aim to challenge the rest of its audience with more stretching
material, programmes which would broaden their cultural knowledge and
perhaps even question their basic assumptions. Such a dictatorial approach was
made possible by what he shamelessly called the 'brute force of monopoly',
which had enabled the BBC 'to make out of broadcasting what no other country
in the world has made of it' (Blumler, 1992: 64).

Broadcasting in the UK

The UK's broadcasting system displays a number of features which are
unique. One particular characteristic is the extent to which commercial
forces have been severely constrained until relatively recently. When radio,
and later television, services were introduced, they were perceived by politicians as far too important to be handed over to uncontrolled commercial
interests (McNair, 1996). Instead, British broadcasting was to be a 'utility to
be developed as a national service in the public interest' (Scannell and
Cardiff, 1991: 8). As a result, competition was either entirely absent (until
1954), or, until relatively recently, present only to a very limited degree.
This allowed the development of a strong indigenous television industry
with a track record of producing high-quality programming in all genres,
and also meant that the longer-established organisations, such as the BBC,
had almost no experience of full-throttle competition.

Until the Broadcasting Act of 1990 the BBC led a sheltered existence. It was
generously funded and protected from domestic competition, especially in
comparison with its West European counterparts. Its schedulers were required
to deliver prestige as much as ratings (Tunstall, 1993) and had been relatively
untouched by the commercialisation of the television sector under way at that
time in much of Western Europe (Euromedia Research Group, 1992).

The BBC enjoyed a broadcasting monopoly until 1954, when ITV
(Independent Television), the national supplier of commercial television, was
launched. The BBC, with its two channels, was funded by the licence fee
paid by every household with a television set, while ITV enjoyed an advertising monopoly. Thus a highly complementary system was created whereby
the two broadcasters competed for audiences but not for funding.

This system functioned smoothly for nearly four decades. Competition
was limited to programmes and did not extend to revenue sources. Public
and private broadcasters were officially in separate camps but exhibited a
high degree of similarity, in organisational as well as programming terms.
Both were considered to be serving a public function and accountable to

parliament (Blumler, 1992). Private companies were required to meet the same regulatory standards as their public service peers, and had anyway voluntarily adopted many public service values (Euromedia Research Group, 1992). This led to the development of a stable and unchallenging competitive environment. Both organisations were dancing to similar strategic tunes in a neatly divided, nationally bounded television market.

In 1982 a second national commercial channel, Channel Four (C4), was launched. It was designed to be a 'minority channel', concentrating on the type of programming that mainstream providers might avoid. It thus fitted neatly into the existing situation and enabled the BBC and ITV to concentrate, as before, on mainstream programming. Channel 5, the UK's newest terrestrial channel, was established in 1997. This was designed as a popular channel whose biggest innovation was 'stripping', a form of scheduling whereby specific genres of programmes (soap operas, news etc.) are scheduled at the same time each day each week.

A distinctive characteristic of British television is the tradition of covering a wide range of programme types and of carrying this range into peak-time evening viewing. News and current affairs programmes were 'protected' from market pressures and both public and commercial broadcasters were required to schedule these programmes during prime time. Regulation dictated that both popular and less popular programming should be scheduled in prime-time viewing hours, therefore ensuring that the purposes of information and education did not become subservient to those of entertainment. It was further typified by a 'principled pluralism' (Blumler, 1992), whereby programme schedules were deliberately skewed to reflect the range of interests represented in a diverse society and to enable each sector to come into contact with the opinions and ways of life of others.

Industry culture

> One of the strongest traditions in British media is under-estimating the intelligence of the British public whom they allegedly serve.
>
> (Wyver, 1996: 34)

Although Britain's television industry is split into two sectors – public service and commercial – the industry culture, which is homogeneous, strong and lively, is dominated by public service values. This reflects the BBC's commanding position within the sector, as a result of which a great many of those working in the industry gained their formative experiences at the BBC (the BBC invests heavily in training its staff, seeing this as part of its public service mandate to help create a strong UK audio-visual sector), and indeed probably grew up watching the BBC and ingesting, albeit unconsciously, the organisation's broadcasting philosophy. The founders of the UK's commercial companies were ex-BBC broadcasters, and today employees switch frequently between public and commercial sectors. The same applies to 'suppliers': many actors, presenters and independent production houses get their first broadcasting experience with the BBC. Thus the majority of those working in the industry have been deeply influenced by the public service mindset.

The industry has been described as producer-dominated, meaning that individual producers enjoy significant leeway in producing programming (it has been said that the British tradition of PSB would stand more accurately for 'Producer Self-Service Broadcasting' (Tunstall, 1993)), and by extension that the creative skills of broadcasting are valued more highly than commercial ones. In public and private organisations, senior decision-makers have often risen through the ranks of producers, and therefore share creative rather than commercial backgrounds. (Former producers have gone on to run the BBC's two national television channels and also the entire BBC.)

A number of latent attitudes are present in the industry culture. The first is a deeply rooted anti-commercialism, a belief that commercial considerations should play no role in quality television. This view can be traced back to the beginnings of radio broadcasting; strains of anti-commercialism are evident in the parliamentary debates of the 1920s about how the BBC should operate, when discussions of broadcasting in the US, which had been left in private hands, were characterised by a tone of 'virtually permanent disapproval' (Blumler, 1992). (However, although sometimes scathing about the quality of American TV, the industry has traditionally looked to the US rather than to Europe for inspiration and innovation – the 'Eyes West' phenomenon.) Even today, working in the UK broadcasting sector, particularly the BBC, represents 'a trade off between creative opportunity and lower salary levels' (Barnett and Curry, 1994: 7). Those who choose to work in the industry do so principally for creative rather than commercial reasons and hold a social rather than commercial view of the purpose of broadcasting (Barnett and Curry, ibid.).

The second is a certain arrogance about the quality of UK television. The prevailing assumption is that the mixed environment of competition and protection has prevented Gresham's Law (the bad driving out the good) from applying to British broadcasting (Blumler, 1992), and enabled the BBC to thrive compared to its peers overseas (BBC, 1993c). The UK, argues the industry, might have fewer channels, but what is shown on those channels is more varied and of higher quality than that available in multi-channel environments where, in the words of Bruce Springsteen, there are '57 channels – and nothin' on'.

According to many indicators of quality in television, British television, led by the BBC, scores highly (Tunstall, 1993). However, some alarmist critics feel that the UK has an enormously inflated view of its own media worth, and is dangerously uninterested in or dismissive of large media conglomerates outside its own boundaries.[2]

Organisation culture

The culture of the BBC has been extensively studied over the years. This book contains its own analysis of the organisation's culture, but the findings of previous studies provide valuable background for this.

Schlesinger (1978, in Stevenson, 1995) describes the disposition of the organisation as 'democratic pluralism', arising from the unique culture of public service broadcasting, which presumes that there are no predominant interest groups in society. He also draws attention to the 'stop watch culture', that is, an event-driven orientation that values immediacy, speed and accuracy, and which arises, no doubt, from the specific nature of the task of news journalism.

A celebrated ethnographic study of the BBC from the same era conducted by Burns (1977) finds three main attitudes to the occupational task. First is a deep commitment to the traditional goals of public service broadcasting as something that makes a unique contribution to national cultural and social life and that maintains broadcasting standards. Second is a deep commitment to the task and craft of making good television. Third is an overriding professionalism, which favours, in extreme cases, 'television for television's sake'.

Regulation

The UK's public and private broadcasters are regulated by different bodies. Authority over the BBC is held by its Board of Governors (see below). Authority over commercial broadcasters is held by the Independent Television Commission (ITC), a recent body dating from the 1990 Broadcasting Act, whose role is to grant licences and attempt to influence the quality of programming by its choice of licensees. Unlike its predecessor, the Independent Broadcasting Authority, this body cannot influence commercial broadcasters' schedules or enforce impartiality, an issue some would argue is becoming increasingly relevant in an era of cross-ownership of media. Both these bodies are staffed by amateur regulators – professional men and women from different backgrounds, appointed to their roles by the government.

National media policy

The BBC was created at a time when the scarcity of technical resources, specifically wavelengths, was seen as necessitating a monopoly, and thus a collectivist system of support. By the 1980s collectivism was seen in Downing Street as synonymous with communism and so the BBC was a hotbed of reds, QED. What was needed was the firm smack of market forces to bring the BBC into line.

(*Financial Times*, 11 August 1995)

Until the Thatcher era, British media policy was languorous and cautious, characterised by gradual change after extensive consultation with affected groups (Euromedia Research Group, 1992). Channel space was scarce and the medium considered highly influential. Television was therefore closely regulated, with governments seeking to safeguard the rights of the viewer and control the activities of broadcasters.

However, the Conservative 'monetarist revolt' (Barnett and Docherty, in Blumler and Nossiter, 1991) meant the BBC was forced to live under a cloud of uncertainty with the threat of privatisation (partial or total) constantly present (Curran and Seaton, 1997). This represented a fundamental change in political attitudes towards the BBC in particular, and to public broad-casting, and indeed public service organisations, in general (McNair, 1996).

For many Conservative politicians the BBC had long exhibited the worst sins of British business: complacency, excessive trade union power, weak management and inadequate entrepreneurial spirit (Blumler, 1992). The Peacock Committee (1985–6) was asked to investigate whether the BBC should carry advertising. Surprisingly, although 'packed with free marketers' (Euromedia Research Group, 1992: 241), it recommended against this, since in a wholly commercial broadcasting system advertising budgets would be spread too thinly, and, since the BBC held a stable of very strong programmes, the chief casualty of such a change would be the commercial channels, thus reducing rather than increasing market competition.

The proposal to introduce commercial funding may have been quashed, but the Committee was highly critical of the sector's 'comfortable duopoly', as a result of which neither the BBC nor ITV was under sufficient financial disci-pline to keep its costs down. It made the recommendation (subsequently accepted) that both the BBC and ITV should be required to commission at least 25 per cent of their programming from independent producers.

This report was a turning point in UK media policy. Until then it had been tacitly understood by politicians and opinion-formers that market pres-sures and quality in television are mutually exclusive, and that regulation is the best means of ensuring that standards of quality are upheld. This prin-ciple had now been discarded; official policy was that 'the public are best served if able to buy the amount of the service required from suppliers who compete for custom through price and quality. In addition, the stimulus of competition provides further benefits to the public through the incentive given to offer new and improved services' (Peacock, 1986). From now on, viewer choice rather than regulatory imposition would be increasingly relied upon to secure the programmes that viewers wanted (Blumler, 1992). For the industry, placing competitive and financial criteria equal to or above creative ones constituted 'an inversion of priorities in terms of what consti-tuted quality in television' (Siune and Truetzschler, 1992).

The government kept the BBC in a state of uncertainty until 1994, when it published a White Paper on the future development of broadcasting and the role it would like the BBC to play in these developments. This amounted in effect to a complete retreat from the Thatcherite preoccupations which had thrown the future of the organisation into doubt. The Royal Charter was to be extended for ten years, the universal licence fee was assured for a further five years (although comments about its permanent existence were guarded). The direct threat of privatisation was withdrawn, though it also stated that 'the BBC will not continue for ever in its present form'. The organisation would remain Britain's public service broadcaster and retain its current wide range of programming, offering choice for majority, minority and special groups. Its mission would continue as before, to inform, educate and entertain, and to reflect the national cultural identity and enrich it by sponsoring music, art and theatre. In addition, through long-term investment in production and training, it should play a leading role in developing the nation's creative potential. At the same time, it should ensure that public funds were used efficiently and responsibly, continue with its programme of radical reforms and change initiatives, make further efficiency gains, and comply with tighter requirements to be introduced about feedback to parliament and the public. As a result of its efforts to improve accountability and efficiency, in 1995 parliament reported itself happy with current financing arrangements.

In 1999 a further review of the future of BBC funding was announced. By this point the government had become fully aware of the increasingly important role played by the media, communications and technology sectors in promoting economic health. Keen that the UK should remain a player in the race to develop new communications technologies, government attitudes towards the BBC shifted once again, seeing the organisation as representing one of the UK's strongest candidates in an important and emerging global sector. It therefore required the BBC to take on a dominant role in developing global multimedia industries. It should retain its traditional vertically integrated span of activities, acting as both producer and transmitter of a broad range of programmes, but also broaden its commercial applications and secondary uses. It specified that the licence fee would remain as the dominant method of funding, but not whether it would increase. It also appointed a committee to explore how this could be supplemented.

Ironically, therefore, the turbulence in the world's media industries which has caused the organisation so many headaches has relieved government pressure on the organisation and may well help to ensure its survival as a licence-fee funded public service broadcaster. The government wants to boost a strong indigenous media sector and recognises that along with Pearson and BSkyB, the BBC is one of only a handful of UK candidates with the critical mass necessary to compete globally. Chapters 6, 8 and 10 of this book explore whether the BBC is organisationally and culturally equipped to take on this task, to expand its dominant role in the UK media ecology into an international arena.

Chapter 5

The 'Mouth of the South' and his 'Chicken Noodle Network'

Ted Turner and the beginnings of CNN

> I mainly did CNN to see if it could be done.
>
> (Ted Turner[1])

CNN's early days were characterised by a maverick opportunism and a great deal of luck. Both of these characteristics can be traced directly back to its founder, the heretical and charismatic Ted Turner, known variously as 'Captain Outrageous' and 'The Mouth of the South'. This chapter looks at CNN's turbulent early history and at Turner's struggles in a highly sceptical industry to establish his vision of a 24-hour global news service. These developments are reviewed within the resolutely commercial free-market context of the US broadcasting system.

The beginnings of CNN

Cable News Network (CNN) is a niche broadcaster concentrating on round-the-clock news reporting. It was founded in 1980 as a subsidiary of Turner Broadcasting Systems Inc. (TBS), a diversified communications company with interests in entertainment, news syndication, licensing, sports and real estate. In 1996[2] Time Warner, a 20 per cent shareholder in Turner Broadcasting, bought the remaining shares of the publicly traded company, describing the acquisition as a merger.

The two organisations created the largest media and entertainment company in the world (1997 revenues were $24.6 billion), in the process realising powerful synergies between Time Warner's distribution capabilities and TBS's strength in content (cable television products, cartoons and an extensive film library). Ted Turner, who ended up with around 12 per cent of the merged entity, became Vice Chairman of Time Warner Inc. and head of its cable networks.

The CNN News Group, a division of Time Warner Inc., is engaged in a wide range of broadcasting activities across a variety of media:[3]

- *Cable News Network*: 24-hour news and current affairs; available in 80 million homes
- *CNN Headline News*: complete newscasts every thirty minutes, day and night, with 67 million subscribers
- *CNN International*: channel transmitted via international satellite network; available in 150 million households in 210 countries and territories
- *CNNfn*: all-digital television network carrying business and financial news; coverage to 9.5 million US homes
- *CNN/SI*: 24-hour sports news service produced in partnership with Time Warner's *Sports Illustrated*
- *CNN en Español*: independently produced 24-hour Spanish-language cable channel for 4 million subscribers in Latin America
- *CNN Airport Network*: news channel for domestic airports
- *CNN Radio*
- *CNN Radio Noticias*
- *CNN Interactive*: seven Web sites with 2 billion page impressions in 1997
- *CNN+*: a joint venture with Sogecable in Spain for a national 24-hour news channel which began broadcasting in January, 1999
- *CNN Turk*: a joint venture with Dogan Group, publisher of Turkey's biggest newspapers, for a 24-hour news channel to begin broadcasting in late 1999.

CNN has two major sources of income: subscription fees (cable operating companies make a payment to CNN for each subscriber who receives CNN) and advertising (carried predominantly on its domestic networks). Since its merger, unconsolidated figures are not available, but CNN's revenue for 1998 has been estimated at $676.5 million and this is anticipated to increase to $713.4 million in 1999.[4] 1997 revenues for the entire Turner Broadcasting System (which include such entities as the Atlanta Braves and Hawks, the Goodwill Games alongside the TBS Superstation, TNT etc.) were $2.9 billion, up from $2.47 billion in 1996.

In 1996, CNN had around 3,300 employees world-wide, their ranks swelled by several hundred freelancers, also world-wide. (Turner International and the rest of the Turner group employed around a further 3,000.)

Core concept

The inspiration behind CNN was to concentrate completely on news and to cover that news in an entirely different way from anyone else. First, it would be a 24-hour service broadcasting news non-stop. Second, the orientation would be global – CNN would report news from all over the world to all over the world. Third, it would be live – CNN would cover news as it happened, rather than report after the fact. The network underlined the 'differentness' of its news product by presenting it in a radically different way to the slick, groomed approach of the US networks. The guiding principle was to create 'a role in the process for our viewers' (Peters, 1992: 33); 'ragged edges' would be on display, creating an impression of immediacy and authenticity, of real news stories evolving as viewers watched.

Overcoming widespread industry cynicism, CNN's unconventional approach proved to hold real attraction for viewers, ultimately revitalising what had become a stale and tired field. It is even claimed (Peters, 1992) that CNN redefined news from something that *has* happened to something that *is* happening.

Behind this unorthodox approach is an unorthodox organisation, displaying an originality, dynamism and speed of response that has made it a magnet for management researchers (including Hamel and Prahalad, 1994 and Peters, 1992), and which no doubt reflects its core business, since news is by definition a highly time-dependent commodity.

In terms of structure and process, CNN is somewhat paradoxical. First, it is simultaneously centralised and decentralised. Despite the merger with Time Warner, activities are centralised at Atlanta, with senior decision-makers a few yards apart, but at the same time, the organisation represents a far-flung international network and has a policy of decentralising as far as possible. Second, day-to-day management style is simultaneously loose and tight. This is euphorically described by Peters as:

> A carnival: a well-oiled underpark below, madness on the surface ... always dynamic ... hurry is the normal style ... meetings are open, free and easy, side conversations are rife ... an over-riding emphasis on action, action ... immersion ... a premium on moving fast and keeping pace, without careful industry analyses and broad-ranging strategic plans. Being simultaneously in control and out of control is the key to making it work at CNN ... committee meetings – there are no committees to have meetings! ... It never takes more than three or four folks, all located within a few yards of one another, to make any decision – which they seem to do, with no fuss, on the spot, and often on the run.
>
> (Peters, 1992: 34)

Founding circumstances

> Perhaps the only really global television player that had no media presence 25 years ago.[5]

CNN was created in 374 days. Its founder, Ted Turner, a larger-than-life businessman (known as 'The Mouth of the South') announced its launch at a press conference on 21 May 1979, saying it would go on air on 1 June 1980. It duly did, with access to 1.7 million subscribers, although the minimum number of subscribers required to cover 50 per cent of operating costs was 7.5 million (Whittemore, 1990).

Turner became involved in the media world when he inherited his father's billboard advertising business. He moved into television by acquiring a small local station in Atlanta. His business style soon became clear: a combination of inspired risk-taking and bravado, with a particular skill at exploiting existing industry practices to his advantage. A minor but typical early example was his trick of scheduling programmes for his local Atlanta station at five minutes past the hour, rather than on the hour, thus ensuring they got a stand-alone place in the crowded newspaper TV listings. His first big coup, foreshadowing future developments, was to create the world's first satellite 'Superstation', by placing the signal of his minor Atlanta station on a satellite which distributed the signal to cable systems around the country, thus turning a small local station struggling to find an audience into one with a domestic audience of millions as well as additional viewers in Canada and Mexico (Willis and Aldridge, 1992: 117–18). Such irregular moves have enabled Turner in a short space of time to create a business empire that includes the largest news-gathering organisation in the world, the largest library of motion pictures anywhere, one of the largest collections of animated films, and more individual programming networks than any other broadcaster.

The network's early days were characterised by a maverick opportunism and a great deal of luck. The industry was scathing about 'The Chicken Noodle Network', and considered it a gamble in virtually every respect. However, Turner was convinced that a 24-hour news channel had potential, and this conviction was endorsed by a series of scoops beginning within the first half-hour of service, demonstrating the value of his concept and enabling CNN to establish itself as a major international broadcaster.

The link between environment and strategy is particularly strong at CNN. Turner founded the organisation because he saw the potential implication of a number of simultaneous environmental changes (Hamel and Prahalad, 1994) in lifestyle (ever longer and more unpredictable work hours), in technology (handicams and suitcase-size satellite link-ups) and in the regulatory environment (government attempts to boost the development of a cable television industry).

Both the US television industry and US television news had traditionally been dominated by the networks. Their approach, cemented in the 1960s and 1970s, was to provide a fixed news broadcast at 6.30 p.m. and news on the morning breakfast shows. Local television affiliates provided news at both 6.00 p.m. and 11.00 p.m.

By the mid-1970s the news departments of the three networks had grown to more than 1,000 staffers. Yet these news departments had only limited

time in the broadcast schedule and when networks compared news department operating costs with the revenue generated by the advertising time
within the news programmes, they concluded that news departments lost
money (although on a consolidated basis the networks made significant
profits).

This situation – losing money on news – was justified by the networks on
the basis that news was part of a broadcaster's duty, reflecting the public's
'right to know' (Bibb, 1993). However, during the late 1970s, the desire to
inform was tempered with a need on the part of broadcasters to boost
ratings. Competition between the networks had intensified and a recession
had cut advertising spending. This had two results. First, budgets were cut.
Resources were concentrated on feature programmes that were cheaper to
produce and more popular with advertisers, rather than on core news
programmes that were often unprofitable. (At the time there was even spec-
ulation that the networks would get out of the news business altogether.)
Use of footage from affiliates and agencies increased and coverage of routine
White House press briefings was pooled. Second, networks realised that by
approaching news differently, they might even be able to boost ratings and
thereby profits. This marked the start of 'infotainment' – current affairs
coverage with less hard news and more carefully presented stories designed
to appeal to audiences (Bibb, ibid.).

CNN itself discerns three distinct eras in its past. First came the struggles of Turner, amid much scepticism, to establish with CNN his concept of
24-hour news. Second came CNN's coverage of the Gulf War in 1990,
which established CNN as a global player which could compete with any
other news organisation. The third era, the current one, is concerned with
issues of growth – new products and services, further globalisation, but
further regionalisation as well.[6]

Ted Turner

Turner (also nicknamed 'Captain Outrageous') is a charismatic and heretical
figure. It is impossible to over-stress the role his personality has played in
shaping CNN, and the influence he exerts, even today, on the organisation.
Much has been written about Turner, largely characterised by hyperbole (as
the quotes here demonstrate). Reportedly an 'enormous bundle of contradictions'[7] (Bibb, ibid.: ix), Turner is widely viewed as a true visionary, someone
'who does more than simply identify trends and find innovative ways to
seize niches, but goes a step further to create trends and develop new niches
… a methodical, deliberate creator of systems' (Wallace and Marer, 1991).
He shares this view of himself: 'I've always thought several moves ahead. I
pride myself on being able to look into the future and say, "What is the
future going to look like? What can we do to be in the right place at the
right time?"' Turner's 'vision' was idealistic and technologically driven, as

he explained in 1990: 'I want to look to the future, not to the past. We need more cultural exchanges, scientific exchanges, satellite exchanges' (cited in Rosenstiel, 1994: 28).

Turner is a skilled businessman, reported to possess a 'visceral' sense for strategic deals, and a knack for corporate finance: 'making acquisitions, always trying to use the other guy's money, that was Ted's genius' (Bibb, 1993: 64). He is open to opportunities everywhere: 'We do business with everybody in the entertainment business, and from time to time we talk with just about everybody' (Bibb, ibid.: 416).

In all areas of his life he is a 'fiercely competitive, risk-taking opportunist' (Bibb, ibid.: 147). In 1977 he won the America's Cup race in a yacht named 'Courageous' despite the fact that, as he later admitted, he hated sailing ('I got wet and I got cold'). Believing that his father committed suicide because he had achieved his limited goals in life, Turner has ensured that the personal goals he sets himself are as formidable as possible:[8] 'I'm trying to set the all-time record for achievement for one person in one lifetime, and that puts you in pretty big company: Alexander the Great, Napoleon, Gandhi, Christ, Mohammed, Buddha, Washington, Roosevelt, Churchill.'

Indeed, his appetite for risk is said to be insatiable; he is always 'ready to roll the dice. Willing to lose everything'. His style is to 'keep looking for the next challenge. Try anything, if the odds against you are long enough. Keep moving. Fall down, get up, and fall down again, until you suddenly find yourself running with the wind' (Bibb, ibid.: 61). Turner himself views risk-taking as the key to his entrepreneurial success:[9] 'If you are going to try to change things in a big way, you have to be willing to go against the odds and sacrifice everything ... you've just got to keep trying, fight the obstacles, and maybe you will win in the end.'

In recent years much of his competitive drive has been focused on his antagonism towards Rupert Murdoch. On hearing that Murdoch planned to launch a 24-hour news service, Turner threatened to 'squish Rupert like a bug'. His decision to sell out to Time Warner was framed in terms of this feud: 'Time Warner was the best place for us to go. I didn't want to get run over by a car and have Rupert Murdoch, God forbid, end up with CNN.'

Balancing his aggressive nature is an equally extreme strain of idealism, which some credit to the influence of his wife since 1991, Jane Fonda. In 1997 he pledged $1 billion to the United Nations for humanitarian causes. In the same year he called on CNN to report more upbeat stories to even out its coverage of gory or tragic events. Turner himself claims that he has changed in recent years from 'a man of war to a man of peace', whose greatest concern is 'the fate of a fragile planet'.[10] However, he does not dismiss rumours that he is considering a presidential bid: 'I don't rule it out. I didn't get where I am by ruling out rumours.'[11]

When the idea of merging Time Warner with CNN was mooted, much scepticism was expressed about the ability of flamboyant Turner to work within the corporate confines of a media monolith and to co-operate with the low-key Gerald Levin. These doubts even extended to Turner himself, who referred to the merger as 'the biggest compromise I made'.[12]

Such concerns appear unfounded. Indeed, Turner appears surprisingly to have been a restraining influence on the merged entity, claiming, 'I needed my company to be an example of cost cutting to gain credibility for financial scrutiny within Time Warner as a whole'.[13] Analysts credit Turner's emphasis on reducing costs, eliminating duplication and maximising group synergies with significant improvements to Time Warner's balance sheet. Indeed, in 1998 Time Warner made a profit for the first time in five years and its stock almost doubled in value, outperforming its traditional broad-based media company peers in the entertainment sector.

Broadcasting in the US

> Dreamers who hope that broadcasting will become a force for education and cultural enrichment overlook the fact that it is a business and as such must seek to maximise profits in order to exist. Thus programming must appeal to the largest audience possible so that advertisers will be interested in buying commercial time.
>
> (Willis and Aldridge, 1992: 445)

US broadcasting is resolutely commercial – the product of the free market economy in which it exists. Apart from the PBS networks, which play a marginal role in the larger broadcasting system, all US broadcasters are privately owned and have profit maximisation as their goal. Marketing perspectives dominate: viewers are a market – an 'aggregate of potential consumers with a known socio-economic profile at which the medium or message is directed' (McQuail, 1987: 221) – television is described as 'just another appliance – a toaster with pictures',[14] and programmes as 'scheduled interruptions of marketing bulletins' (Vogel, 1994: 152).

The underlying ethos, therefore, is that although viewers may not always watch what experts judge to be the 'best' programmes, they, rather than regulators, should remain the final arbiter of their own tastes. The market's job is to provide a rich menu from which people can choose the options that best meet their wants, so that those programmes offering the highest quality in terms of value to the customer will automatically dominate. Television's primary aim should be to produce programmes which will tempt the type of audiences advertisers want to attract, and those advertisers are 'guests of honour' rather than 'tolerated visitors' as in Europe (Setstrup, 1989: 9). The critical aspect of audiences is their attention-giving behaviour, expressed via viewing patterns (ratings), which are the fundamental criteria of programming success. The consumer–broadcaster relationship is therefore calculative from the consumer perspective and manipulative from that of the sender. Non-fiscal goals common to public service broadcasting – for instance, educating viewers to function as informed members of a democracy or promoting and disseminating national culture – are, if they exist at all, subordinate to those of maximising audiences and therefore commercial revenues.

Within such a commercial broadcasting ethic, public service broadcasting has a minor role. PBS, the public service network, was launched in 1969, about twenty years after the first commercial channels, in response to a market gap for high-quality programmes (BBC, 1993c). From these origins, it has developed into a niche channel with an élitist image, 'an island of welfare in an ocean of commercialism' (Blumler, 1992). It fills whatever gaps are left untended by private broadcasters, serving relatively small audiences with cultural and artistic programming.

Like public service broadcasters everywhere, PBS is frequently the target of right-wing politicians who see it as élitist and liberal-biased. However, in 1994, 85 per cent of Americans indicated that they found commercial broadcasting vulgar and violent because it is driven by ratings and revenues, and felt that PBS should receive increased government subsidies.[15]

Whereas Europe's broadcasting industry is divided along public service versus commercial lines, in the US, as a result of the Fin/Syn Rules, the industry has traditionally been divided between content (the production of films and television programmes) and conduit (providing channels of distribution for televisual products). Which side of this schism mattered more was always fiercely debated, with content providers claiming that viewers pay for entertainment not distribution, while conduit suppliers argued that distribution was critical, since even the best programmes would die if they failed to reach the right audiences. However, such arguments have been rendered irrelevant by the repeal of the Fin/Syn legislation, which gives broadcasters more leeway to own some or all of the programming they transmit, and has also resulted in a wave of industry mergers, ending this artificial division.

CNN is therefore a paradox in many respects – at once an upstart maverick that disregarded industry conventions to develop an entirely new broadcasting concept, and at the same time a successful business drawing on traditional and deeply entrenched elements of the US media and business scene, namely, dynamism, opportunism and strong commercial instincts. Chapters 7, 9 and 11 explore the organisational and cultural characteristics that have enabled the 'Chicken Noodle Network' to develop into a leading player in global broadcasting.

Chapter 6

Continuous revolution

The BBC as a business

> Some degree of deconstruction may well be the only way that the BBC
> can compete in the media wars of the new century.
>
> (Robert Heller, 1996)

The BBC is a complex organisation operating in an equally complex environment. In postmodern management terms it is an 'intersect' organisation
(Bergquist, 1993), that is, one which is required to be many, often
conflicting, things at once. In the case of the BBC this means to be public
and private, profit- and non-profit-making, a respected and responsible
national institution as well as a nimble entrepreneurial entity.[1] This chapter
focuses primarily on the BBC as a business, rather than as the UK's premier
broadcaster. It uses management, not media, terms and tools of analysis to
examine its competitive environment, its mission and strategy, its stakeholders, its core competencies and its distinctive strengths and weaknesses.

Financial pressure – growing poor slowly

> Until ten years ago the BBC enjoyed constant rises in its income, 4%
> compound a year. There was expansion, everything was in hand. It was
> very comfortable. The second the Government indexed the licence fee it
> had to learn to expand its services ... on a frozen income. It has done so
> brilliantly. But it has affected every single individual in the organisation.
>
> (John Birt)[2]

Since the 1960s and 1970s, the BBC's finances have been negatively transformed. For decades it had been cushioned by, and accustomed to, regular
real rises in income. During the 1960s and 1970s the number of households
in the UK grew, bringing consistent increases in licence-fee income. As
large numbers of households each year traded up from black-and-white to
colour sets with more expensive licences, fee income grew further, boosted
by periodic increases in the licence fee. But increases in the licence fee

reached a ceiling in the 1970s. In 1991 it was cut by 3 per cent and it has since been pegged to inflation. Low growth in UK households coupled with drop-off of homes upgrading from black-and-white to colour mean that its income is effectively flat while its costs are escalating for a number of reasons:

- real programming costs (wages, broadcast talent, scarce professional skills) have risen faster than inflation and new entrants such as BSkyB have bid up the price of sporting events (in 1993 these cost over £250 million a year, in 1994 £310 million)
- convergence and the shift towards digital technologies are necessitating expensive investments in new technology and retraining
- the organisation is attempting to cut its borrowing requirement to zero
- the government's requirement that 25 per cent of programming must be commissioned from independent producers means that overheads must be spread over fewer programmes
- the BBC is pledged to an ambitious programme of new products and services including digital channels, the development of its brand internationally, 24-hour news operations and internet sites.

The BBC is 'growing poor slowly' as its financial base is being continually hollowed out. Meanwhile, commercial competitors' income is increasing[3] and their range of services becoming broader and more ambitious. The BBC's financial options are limited. Since it is prohibited from financing growth via risk capital it can generate extra revenue only via efficiency improvements or by increasing revenues from commercial activities. Its international activities must be financed via joint ventures with other organisations who can supply the necessary capital. In 1998 the government allowed a £6 increase in the annual licence fee (increasing it to £97.50) to help finance the corporation's digital plans, but even so, the financial pressure that has become a fact of life in recent years represents an almost unconscionable *volte face* in terms of the BBC's traditional role and original remit. In recent years its ability to realise its public service goals has come to depend as much on its financial, managerial and strategic skills as on its programme-making abilities.

Competition

Until the mid-1990s broadcasting in Britain was still, by American or continental European standards, a protected market. In 1994 the combined market share of BBC 1 and 2 and the two terrestrial commercial channels was 93 per cent, of which the BBC's share was around 40 per cent. Cable and satellite programmes had a market share of only 7 per cent.

In recent years, as a result of the technological and regulatory changes outlined in previous chapters, the BBC has been faced with an enormous increase in competition. Not only has commercial satellite television become entrenched, but digital television is bringing a range of new digital channels to UK households via digital satellite, digital cable or digital terrestrial transmission systems. The BBC plans to be present on each of the new digital platforms, but UK consumers can nonetheless now receive over 250 channels from a multitude of providers. This constitutes a clear threat to all established television networks and particularly to the BBC, which has traditionally enjoyed a dominant position in the UK market.

The advent of multi-channel television means that the market share of all incumbent networks is likely to fragment and the launch of interactive services will exacerbate this trend. Further competition comes from the exponentially growing internet, which offers an ever increasing array of content, which will grow inexorably closer to TV content as broadband distribution becomes widespread.

Instability and an increasingly complex business model

> What I'm saying is that there is uncertainty in the air. For fifty years we've owned our own transmission, pumped out pictures that effectively everyone in the UK had free and open access to. That will not be so in the future.
>
> (BBC interviewee)

The environmental developments described earlier mean that the structure of the world's television markets, including that of the UK, are changing. The BBC, like all established players, finds itself in a very different world from the one it has traditionally known.

Against such a backdrop the business model that has served the BBC and its commercial network peers for so long is becoming increasingly inappropriate. Broadcasters such as the BBC have traditionally commissioned programmes (from internal or external sources), packaged these into coherent schedules to meet general audience needs, and transmitted them over its own networks, to be watched by viewers who could choose between the two BBC or two commercial channels. Now, however, the BBC's channels must take their place alongside hundreds of others. It no longer owns its own means of transmission with the consequent guaranteed access to viewers. Like its commercial peers, it must jockey for position, forming alliances as necessary with the various organisations offering distribution and user conduit – a sector which has shown huge growth in the UK thanks to a relatively relaxed regulatory regime which allows cable companies to offer an array of telephone services, thus attracting a host of foreign cable operators to the UK.

Stakeholders

> The BBC occupies a unique position in the British social and economic structure and, by its nature, all its actions are subject to very public scrutiny.
>
> (Cloot, 1994: 3)

The increasingly complex strategic challenge facing the BBC during the 1980s and 1990s was reflected in the growing complexity of its stakeholder picture. Until the early 1980s, the BBC's stakeholder task could be broadly described as meeting and balancing the needs of three interest groups: the public, the government and its own employees. This was not overly difficult. Audiences were relatively homogenous and passive (and for many years had had only one other channel with which to compare the BBC's output), and the organisation enjoyed substantial and increasing revenues, meaning it could offer good conditions of employment, invest in a range of programmes at a level which would satisfy both viewers and employees, and offer staff freedom of expression, creative licence, top-quality facilities and protection from commercial pressures.

However, the far-reaching environmental changes discussed in Chapter 2 disrupted this peaceful scenario. As government policy, society and competition changed and as technology advanced, the BBC's stakeholder picture became ever more complicated. New groups emerged with new demands. Existing groups fragmented. Loose uncoordinated coalitions transformed themselves into pressure groups skilled in the art of lobbying. Professional media monitoring by interest groups of all types became commonplace, as did expensive legal challenges to programming construed by the groups as critical (Tunstall, 1993). As a result the BBC found itself confronted with a broad range of different stakeholder groups with which to contend, ranging from 'old' ones such as the public and the national government, to 'new' ones such as joint venture partners and the European Union.[4] The following pages review the organisation's key stakeholder groups and the nature of their demands on the organisation.

The public

Until the late 1980s the UK public formed a homogenous group with two basic sets of demands. As an audience it wanted entertainment, unbiased information and programmes that did not offend their morals or standards of decency. As a group of licence-fee payers, it was concerned with the responsible use of public funds.

However, changing social attitudes caused this solidly uniform group to

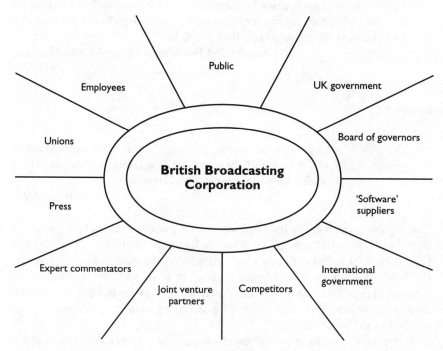

Figure 6.1 The BBC's stakeholder groups (NB: the segments are not
proportional)

fragment into special interest and minority groups with stronger individual
identities and individual and eclectic demands:[5]

> The face of the UK is changing rapidly ... traditional values and alle-
> giances are breaking down. There is less consensus in the established
> political, religious and social spheres ... institutions and figures who a
> few decades ago commanded almost universal and unquestioning
> respect – politicians, church leaders, the press, the police, the monarchy
> – now find they have to justify themselves to the public virtually from
> first principles ... regional and local identity and pride are more evident
> than they used to be and seem likely to grow further.
>
> (BBC, 1992)

In the UK, payment of the BBC licence fee is mandatory for everyone
owning a television. This places an obligation on the organisation to ensure
that it provides something for every viewer, and that it is accountable for
what it does. The organisation's assumptions are that viewers want to know
how their money is spent, and to receive something directly in return for
their contribution.[6]

A public broadcaster cannot become obsessed with audience share (though it cannot afford to ignore it); it must devote as much attention to the proportion of the population which is reached.

(Barnett and Docherty, in Blumler and Nossiter, 1991: 28)

Employees

The BBC's success depends on its relationship with two key groups of people: those who watch and listen to our programmes – the audience; and those who make our programmes – the creative talent.

(BBC, 1992)

The organisation regards its employees[7] as a priority stakeholder group. A dominant element of this group is the programme producers. They, and the skilled craft base that supports them, determine the quality of the organisation's broadcast output, and hence its market share and ability to meet its Charter obligations. Therefore their bargaining power is high: producers' continued artistic flair and talent play a central role in guaranteeing the survival of the organisation.

However, the organisation's counter-bargaining power *vis à vis* this group is also relatively high because of its national and industry position. Working for the BBC has always been considered special – more of a vocation than a job (Horrie and Clarke, 1994). There is a long-standing acceptance that the kudos of the organisation, combined with the calibre of its projects and staff, the size of its audience and the dominance of its national voice, compensates for modest salary levels (considering the prestige of the organisation) and long hours. Turnover levels are traditionally low – 86 per cent of BBC employees in 1989 had been with the organisation for all their broadcasting work-careers.

Creative staff are primarily motivated by the opportunity to exercise and develop their professional skills, to have creative and editorial freedom and to contribute to the country's national debate. Important to them are freedom of expression, creative licence, the facilities, funds and managerial support to produce top-quality programmes, a secure work environment and freedom from commercial pressures (Barnett and Curry, 1994).

National government

The broadcaster's life has to be one of continuous political ingenuity.

(ex-Director General Charles Curran, in Blumler, 1992)

The BBC has a complex, contentious and in some respects incestuous relationship with the UK government, due in no small part to the fact that television has usurped parliament's role in creating a forum for national debate (Curran, in Holland, 1997). In principle, politicians place two basic requirements on the organisation. As media policy-makers they seek compliance with regulations governing the media. As politicians they seek balanced, impartial programming and accountability. However, occasional conflict is inevitable – if the organisation fulfils its public service mandate of providing balanced coverage of current affairs there are bound to be certain programmes which politicians do not like. However, although their relationship can be combative, these two groups are closely linked, often sharing similar backgrounds and education and having a close professional involvement with each other.

Via the Royal Charter and accompanying Licence the government holds considerable power over the organisation. It sets the licence fee, specifies its sphere of activities, whether and how additional finances may be raised and the extent to which commercial activities may be undertaken, and appoints the BBC's Board of Governors. Many feel this forces the organisation into a supplicatory role in its dealings with the government:

> The BBC adopted the position of a spaniel with its legs in the air – vaguely hoping for a benevolent tickle, more likely to get a wallop from a handbag.
> (Alan Yentob, then Controller of BBC 2, *Guardian*, 19 November 1996)

Theoretically the government has wide powers over programming: it can require a programme not to be broadcast and the BBC is precluded from broadcasting its own views on matters of public policy. But in practice these are seldom exercised. Although the Thatcher era saw a number of high-profile disputes about specific programmes (Barnett and Curry, 1994), in general the relationship between the two institutions in this area is subtle, depending more on the BBC's Governors' judicious exercise of influence on the organisation and on ministers' restraint, than on the precisely enforceable letters of agreement.

As a counterweight comes the BBC's perceived ability to shape public opinion, to set the agenda for political debate and to determine the public-relations approach of political parties. This means that appointments to the independently constituted Board of Governors are closely scrutinised and that its output is closely monitored. Criticism of programming, by politicians of all persuasions, is a long-standing tradition extending back to the organisation's origins. For some this antipathy is inevitable:

> The reason why prime ministers, of whatever political complexion, always resent the BBC is that, in their eyes, it represents an altogether too powerful, non-elected citadel within a democratic state ... an autocratic centralist institution, [which] could not [be easily manipulated].
> (Anthony Howard[8])

International government

In addition to responding to domestic government policy, the BBC must monitor, interpret and comply with European broadcasting initiatives. In this it goes further than simple passive compliance. It has adopted a pro-active role towards the EU, seeking to ensure that the BBC's interests and arguments contribute to the shaping of the policy debate, and to provide a counterweight to the extensive lobbying activities undertaken by its competitors in Brussels.

Press

The media, including the 'talking heads' who prognosticate on its channels and in its pages, are an influential, some would say over-influential, group in British society:

> Within Britain, much of the talents appear to have been siphoned off into a culture of commentary of journalists and pundits, a kind of groaning Greek chorus on the edges of the stage, bewailing the folly of the actors. Commentators are individuals referred to as 'chattering classes' usually by that class itself.
>
> (Hampden-Turner and Trompenaars, 1993: 298)

The media can be divided broadly into print and broadcasting sectors. As a business, the BBC is primarily concerned with broadcast media (although it has a successful magazine publishing division) but it is closely involved with print media, particularly newspapers, which form an important stakeholder group. The BBC's relationship with the press has been described as a 'multi-faceted dependence' (Tunstall, 1993), whereby newspaper coverage of television plays an important role in shaping public opinions about the organisation and its output, and the BBC plays an important role in building or extending press journalists' careers.

Over recent years the importance of this stakeholder group has grown. The organisation has come under criticism from many quarters – from Conservative political circles, from the public, and from an increasingly powerful and vocal commercial sector. Virtually every move made by the organisation, therefore, is subject to extensive public scrutiny.[9] This is made additionally complex by the fact that because of the BBC's dominant position in the UK media sector it is almost impossible to write about it objectively:

> Those who write about the BBC either work for the BBC, or have worked for the BBC, or want to work for the BBC, or have been refused work for the BBC or want to topple the BBC.
>
> (Melvyn Bragg[10])

Further complexity stems from the fact that as a result of the liberalisation of the UK media sector, the BBC's critics in the press can also be competitors: News International, the parent of the UK's leading satellite provider, BSkyB, is also owner of five national newspapers.

Expert commentators

There is a great deal of overlap between expert commentators and the press, since the latter often provides the channel by which the former express their views. However, for simplicity's sake, the term 'expert commentators' is used here to refer to those who have a professional interest in television, predominantly media academics and media policy-makers. This stakeholder group, concerned as it is with issues such as diversity, pluralism, balance and impartiality, and with matters of decency, taste, fairness etc., has to some extent seen its influence wane in recent years as a commercial, free-market paradigm has come to dominate UK broadcasting, meaning in turn that policy debate has come to be dominated by issues such as market access, financial performance and efficiency.

Board of Governors

On a day-to-day basis the BBC is run by a Board of Management, a regulatory body within the organisation comprising thirteen people (the executive heads of departments – ranging from broadcasting and publishing to corporate areas such as resources and finance) who report to the Director General. However, final authority over the organisation is exercised by the Board of Governors, a group of twelve individuals from different professions and backgrounds who have within their gift senior appointments and who are responsible for remuneration for key positions and audit (they are accountable for the proper use of public money). The Governors oversee all senior management activities, with five distinct responsibilities: to stay closely in touch with public opinion; to ensure that the BBC's overall strategy reflects public needs and interests; to monitor and review performance against agreed objectives; to ensure compliance with statutory requirements and BBC guidelines; and to guarantee regular reporting to the licence payer and to parliament.

The Board of Governors thus has the power to 'intervene, chide or even discipline' the BBC (Blumler, 1992: 177). Janus-like, it faces in two directions at once: on the one hand it is responsible for protecting the organisation's autonomy, while on the other it is charged with ensuring that its output serves the public and is accountable to viewers and listeners (BBC, 1993a). The buck for the BBC stops with the Board of Governors; it is their job to ensure that all stakeholder groups are satisfied. Because press interest in the organisation is so great, and because critical coverage can have serious repercussions, BBC governors are seen by some to be particularly concerned with relations with the press:

> When you have a public board ... you have the great and the good on those boards; they're hyper-sensitive to the agenda of the press, and to rows, manufactured rows, stoked up by the press.
>
> (BBC producer quoted in Tunstall, 1993: 197)

Competitors

The heightening of competition in what were once settled and protected home markets has turned the BBC's competitors from a marginal and fraternal stakeholder group into a ferocious and politically acute one. Players such as BSkyB claim the BBC has an unfair advantage in UK markets and are skilled at aggressively promoting this view to politicians and the public alike,[11] in some cases using their extensive newsprint interests as a vehicle for doing so.

Joint venture partners

This is a new but increasingly important set of stakeholders. Like all major players in the converged media world, the BBC's strategy depends on the support of a wide range of external partners to ensure that it has access to every stage in the disaggregated media process. The BBC has extensive experience in working with external content suppliers and with foreign production partners, but traditionally its reputation, expertise and, in the case of independent producers, financial muscle, meant that it normally had the upper hand. What is new about the current set of strategic partnerships, with, say, Discovery Communications Inc. or Flextech PLC, is that these are alliances of equals, whereby each side brings something of equivalent value to the table.

Suppliers

This group includes creative performers, independent producers and outside facility and service providers. This group has grown, firstly as a result of the government requirement that the BBC commission 25 per cent of its programming from outside sources, and secondly because the organisation's efficiency measures have encouraged the contracting out of non-specialist services. As a result of 'talent inflation' (see above) this group has come to exert a growing influence on the organisation.

Unions

During the late 1970s and early 1980s unions exerted considerable power over the organisation. The restrictive practices that ensued led to large and unwieldy crews, extreme overtime payments and the blacking of new technical equipment. However, the very public financial pressures on the organisation, coupled with changes in legislation, mean that the power of this group has diminished greatly. The BBC is still heavily unionised lower down in the organisation and must take union reactions into consideration when restructuring or introducing new technology, but this group no longer has the power to block strategic initiatives.

Mission and strategy

The Director Generalship of John Birt (1993–2000) was marked by a series of radical strategic initiatives embracing process, structure and programming, designed to ensure the BBC's survival as Britain's premier broadcaster, with a full public service mandate and funded by the licence fee.[12] The concepts underlying these initiatives were expressed in catchphrases such as, 'The status quo is not an option', 'Get lean and fit for the telecoms world of convergence' and 'Serving the nation, competing worldwide' (Wegg Prosser, 1996). During this period, the Burke Litwin Model (Warner Burke, 1994) was adopted as the basis for the organisation's management development and organisation development activities. This describes the external environment as:

> any outside condition or situation that influences the performance of the organisation – marketplace, world financial conditions, social pressures, and political, governmental circumstances,

and strategy and mission as:

> what staff believe is the central purpose of the organisation and the means by which the organisation intends to achieve that purpose over an extended period of time.

Mission

Underpinning the BBC's strategy is a threefold mission concentrating on serving the needs of the UK:

Table 6.1   BBC stakeholder demands

Group	Seeks	Key issues
General public	*As viewers*: entertainment, unbiased information, high-quality broadcasting of high moral standards. *As licence-fee payers*: responsible use of public funds, accountability. *As special interest groups*: access, programmes that speak to individual interests	Choice, diversity, objectivity, originality, credibility, 'shared experience'. Value for money, growing consumer awareness, schedules that fit busy lifestyles. Growing eclecticism, growing awareness of minority identities
Employees	Opportunity to develop professional skills, stimulating work environment, opportunity to set national agenda, glamour/peer and public recognition	Quality of technical and technological infrastructure, adequate resources, creative licence, freedom of expression
Board of Governors	To protect the organisation's independence, to ensure output serves the public	Support of organisation and of government, quality of internal and external communication
National government	*As regulators*: compliance with regulation, fair competition at a national level. *As politicians*: balance, impartiality, accountability, that the BBC becomes leading global media player	Diversity and pluralism, development of market alternatives, investment in organisation, efficiency. Editorial independence, journalistic bias
International government	Compliance with EC directives	Protection of EC production resources, concentration of ownership
'Software' suppliers	*Performers*: maximum financial return for creative content. *Independent producers/outside service providers*: 'level playing field'. Fair trading practice	Talent inflation. Shift to outsourcing
Competitors	Equal access to UK market	BBC's 'protected' position, 'structural' regulatory controls on competition
Press	Opportunity to set broadcasting agenda	Co-dependency (develop stories in tandem, part of same industry group), also competitors
Joint venture partners	Access to BBC's professional experience and brand name	Control over BBC's ability to develop into new products and territories
Unions	Job security, new technology, new working patterns, outsourcing	Power has declined steadily since 1970s
Expert commentators	Regulatory and 'quality' issues (balance, impartiality, levels of violence and bad language, diversity)	Involvement in media debate

TO UNIFY A FRAGMENTING SOCIETY

[To] ensure, in the brave new world of choice, that programmes of the widest range and ambition are still available to the public. If we succeed, the BBC really can be a unifying creative force in an age of complexity and fragmentation.

(BBC 1995b)

TO COMPLEMENT COMMERCIAL SCHEDULES

[To] provide distinctive, high-quality radio and television, offering something for everyone, but paying special attention to those areas of broadcasting most at risk in a purely commercial marketplace ... to provide distinctive, high-quality services that complement, rather than emulate, commercial schedules.

(BBC, 1994a)

TO MEET THE NEEDS OF DIVERSE AUDIENCE GROUPS

The BBC's audience is made up of many distinct and diverse groups. We have an obligation to serve them all and to recognise their differing needs and the expectations they have of the BBC ... We are committed to reflecting national and local identities in every aspect of our programming, not solely in regional programmes but also in those made for the whole network audience.

(BBC, 1994a)

In 1998 the BBC's mission was re-formulated to summarise these points:

We aim to be the world's most creative and trusted broadcaster and programme maker, seeking to satisfy all our audiences in the UK with services that inform, educate and entertain and that enrich their lives in ways that the market alone will not.

(BBC, 1998)

Strategy

Strategy processes at the BBC are perhaps inevitably complex, reflecting the demands placed on the organisation by stringent government requirements and a converging globalising environment, coupled with the organisation's own ambitions to hold on to its position as one of the world's premier broadcasters. Significant numbers of staff are involved in strategic activities.

Many aspects of the BBC's strategy, including its product range, its sphere of operations, how it finances investments, its income, how much of its programming it buys from outside, are determined by the government. Within this framework, it is the BBC's task to find the optimal means of ensuring these goals are met within the context of its own strategic aims. Strategy-making takes the form of a policy duet with government. An agenda is set, normally via a White or Green Paper, and the BBC launches a strategic response, either beforehand to influence the drawing up of the policy, or afterwards, to explain how it may be implemented.

During the Birt era, the BBC developed a set of five strategic priorities derived from the government's espoused goals for the organisation:

INNOVATIVE QUALITY PROGRAMMES

Content has always been the organisation's first priority and strategic goal number one. Irrespective of new activities in developing media fields, the BBC has always remained focused on its traditional activities and strengths – the development of high-quality, innovative programmes over a wide range of subject areas:

> While good broadcasters must respond to what audiences already know and say they want, they must also innovate and offer the surprising and even the perplexing.
>
> (BBC 1995b)

The emphasis on high-quality innovative programmes was to be extended to cover the raft of new non-commercial channels and services launched by the BBC (including its new free-to-air digital channels, BBC Text, digital radio and BBC Online) and a clearly articulated Programming Strategy (see below) was developed to support this strategic goal.

EFFICIENCY

Efficiency savings are, apart from commercial activities, the only way in which the BBC can raise the additional funds needed to finance its ambitious plans for the future. Efficiency became strategic goal number two, and the organisation launched a successful series of initiatives in this area. These include property disposals, improved cash management and a programme of cost cutting which freed £180 million (involving over 4,000 jobs lost) between 1989 and 1993. In future cost cutting will be more challenging. As a premier content producer in a competitive market, programme budgets are sacrosanct, so the most promising – but controversial – options include eliminating duplication in creative staff and repurposing.

COMMERCIAL ACTIVITIES

Increasing its revenues in the commercial areas in which it is permitted to operate (e.g. television channels in the international marketplace, subscription services in the UK secondary market, publishing activities derived from its programming) has long been the BBC's primary means of raising additional funds. It has extensive experience of selling its programmes internationally and is a successful publisher of magazines, books and audio and video tapes. It is now seeking to develop these activities into a coherent commercial portfolio, spanning music, magazine and book publishing and channel creation:

> Public service broadcasters must realise that they are likely to receive a falling share of broadcasting revenues. If the BBC's licence fee remains stable, its share of industry revenues from that source will fall from 25% to less than 20%. The lion's share of the growth will go to subscription based services. We must expect, therefore, a gap to develop between rising costs – sports rights and the cost of talent in particular – and our revenues. It is for this reason that we have no option but to pursue vigorously the efficiencies and savings that can be achieved by embracing new ways of working in the digital environment. We will work to increase the commercial earnings of BBC Worldwide, and we are already making good progress on that front ... I believe it will be possible for us to achieve these aims, as well as to continue to uphold our traditions of public service.
>
> (Phyllis, 1996)

The catalyst for achieving its commercial goals is branding. The BBC plans to unlock the hidden potential of the BBC's brands in music, children's, education, factual, and drama and entertainment. The strategy is straightforward:

> Build the brand, get it on TV, exploit it internationally, and make it happen over a wide range of formats.[13]

WORLD DEVELOPMENT

Digital technologies, interactive broadcasting and the proliferation of international cable and satellite channels all offer opportunities for the BBC to increase revenues from commercial sources. The UK government, anxious to ensure that the UK remains a player on the world media stage, and also to lighten the BBC funding burden, is keen that in addition to maintaining pole position in the UK, the BBC becomes a major global media player. A number of assumptions underlie the government's global intentions for the BBC.

First, if the market for television products can be increased sufficiently, it may be possible for the BBC to maintain its present resource commitment to its programmes, despite the rise in the number of programmes. Second, if the UK's domestic market is saturated it makes sense to seek a larger foreign market for the BBC's UK products. Third, because English is the national language, the BBC's products have an inherent advantage over television production companies in the non-English speaking world.

The net result is that world development became an important element of the BBC's strategy:

> The BBC intends to become a major international broadcaster in the satellite age. For the BBC and for the United Kingdom, the cultural and economic stakes are high ... Over the next couple of years the BBC will launch satellite services in Europe, the Americas and Far East.
>
> (BBC, 1994a)

As with commercial developments, the BBC hopes its brand will serve as the 'motor' to drive its world development, that the high levels of brand recognition enjoyed by the BBC worldwide will give it an advantage versus its peers:

> What channel presence outside this country does Carlton have? Nothing. Granada? A bit. Pearson? Next to nothing. Sky? A bit. But who is forging the way in getting British products on screens? We are in a different league.
>
> (Rupert Gavin, Controller, BBC Worldwide, 1998[14])

ALLIANCES AND PARTNERSHIPS

The BBC's funds are stretched and it cannot raise risk capital. It therefore has no option but to turn to private partners to finance its ambitious commercial ventures. The forming of alliances and partnerships is thus a strategic goal:

> The BBC does not have huge amounts of cash to invest ... But we also have formidable strengths and skills. Working with our partners, we believe we shall achieve our objectives. And let me make clear how important to us, in all these ventures, are our partners. Without their participation – both financial and in terms of commercial skills and experience – the strategy I am describing would be even more difficult than it already is.
>
> (Phyllis, 1995b)

The organisation has already closed two large deals. The first is for $565 million with Discovery Communications Inc., the US cable network operator, to produce and package programmes around the world. This brings the BBC additional revenue from the broader distribution of its products, as well as revenues from advertising on new channels created as a result of the agreement, including the BBC America channel. The second deal is with Flextech of the UK for the production of new pay-TV channels using BBC archive material.

Separation of commercial and public activities

One of the most challenging aspects of the BBC's strategy is the intrinsic and inevitable conflict between the expansion of its commercial activities and its publicly funded status. Is it right for UK licence-fee payers to subsidise new channels they may not be able to access without further payments? If the organisation is competing squarely against full-blown commercial players, should it receive licence-fee funding?

The BBC's strategy attempts to resolve these issues and deflect criticism from commercial competitors in two ways. First, it has a clear policy of separating its commercial and public service activities:

> Commercial activities will be linked closely to the public service programming values and objectives and kept clearly separate from our core publicly funded services. Commercial activities will not be funded by public money, and licence fee funds will not be used to subsidise our commercial activities or to support any operating losses made by such activities.
>
> (BBC, undated)

Second, it is seeking to link commercial and public activities in a virtuous circle whereby both activities, public service and commercial, benefit: commercial earnings will be invested in domestic services and thereby improve the public service offering. The resulting programme assets can then be exploited globally by the organisation's international commercial services.

Programming mission and strategy

The BBC is primarily a creative organisation whose first priority is upholding its track record of innovative high-quality programming. Accordingly this area has its own mission and strategy with 'four defining programme purposes' (BBC, 1992). These are:

TO INFORM THE NATIONAL DEBATE

The BBC seeks to provide comprehensive, in-depth and impartial news and information coverage across a range of broadcasting outlets in order to support a fair and informed national debate:

> Of all its responsibilities to its audience, the BBC's duty to provide viewers and listeners with access to regular and authoritative news and information is perhaps the most fundamental ... the BBC plays an important role in the informing of British democracy.
>
> (BBC, 1995b)

TO EXPRESS BRITISH CULTURE AND ENTERTAINMENT

The BBC's programming should support and stimulate the development and expression of British culture and entertainment:

> Arts and entertainment is also the area where the forces of audience choice and competitive change will apply most strongly ... the BBC will have two distinct roles: working as a patron, collaborator, commissioner and producer to guarantee that arts and cultural forms of limited commercial appeal continue to thrive on radio and television, but also bringing a commitment to quality, originality and diversity to the most popular forms of broadcast entertainment.
>
> (BBC, 1995b)

TO CREATE OPPORTUNITIES FOR EDUCATION

The BBC seeks to guarantee the provision of programming and services that create opportunities for education:

> Every area of the BBC will be transformed by the social and technological revolutions that are leading us towards a new broadcasting age. But of our main programme aims – to inform, to educate and to entertain – education faces arguably the greatest challenge and presents one of our greatest opportunities.
>
> (BBC, 1995c)

TO COMMUNICATE BETWEEN THE UK AND ABROAD

The BBC seeks to be a primary source of communication between the UK and other countries, bringing credit to the UK and promoting understanding of British culture and values:

> For the first time, broadcasting is becoming a truly international industry
> ... The BBC can and should work as a major force within this expanding
> market. It is a natural outlet for British talent and creative skill.
>
> (BBC, 1992)

Competencies, strengths and weaknesses

This section reviews the distinctive attributes that contribute to the BBC's
performance, specifically its competencies, strengths and weaknesses.

Core competence – broadcasting creativity

> The BBC is one of the twentieth century's great inventions, enjoyed by
> its audiences at home and admired around the globe for the quality, the
> originality, the wit and intelligence of its programmes.
>
> (BBC, 1998)

The BBC's outstanding competence is its ability consistently to produce
excellent and original programmes over a wide range of genres and subject
areas that appeal to a broad cross-section of taste and interest groups.[15] This
competence rests on the bundling together of a number of individual organisational attributes:

CREATIVE MASS

The BBC is a large bi-media organisation. This enables the cross-fertilisation
of staff and ideas between television and radio, between regional and
network units.

PROTECTED STATUS

For many years the BBC has had the luxury of a significant and guaranteed
income and relatively little competition. This allowed it to experiment, to
invest in the long term, to learn and to develop an extensive repertoire of
skills and a solid base of experience.

TEAM-WORKING SKILLS

An important component of its core capability is the organisation's long-
standing expertise in forming multi-skilled teams made up of internal and
external staff to meet the requirements of specific types of programming:

The best values of the BBC lie in a dedication to programme quality – to stylish, original broadcasting that holds an audience enthralled, to the crafted programme, on the face of it effortless, but in fact the product of infinite teamwork and care.

(BBC, 1994a)

ELITE PROFESSIONAL SKILLS

There has been a dedication in the BBC to craft excellence, ensuring that the many skills and technical and support services that contribute to programme making ... are themselves provided to the highest quality.

(Birt, 1993b)

The BBC has always has been a creative and technological pioneer. Perhaps the best objective measure of the standard of the Corporation's professional and technical skills is the quantity and range of awards, national and international, it receives. In 1993/4 it won forty different awards (television only), including an Oscar for the best animated film.

TOP CALIBRE INTELLECTUAL AND ARTISTIC INPUT – 'APPLIED INTELLECT'

This skill has its roots in the organisation's élitist recruiting patterns and has been reinforced by its long-standing tradition of excellence. An employee describes this skill as follows:

It's the ability to shape something, shape a subject ... phenomenally bright people and the whole range of skills around what is basically the shaping of ideas ... on the whole when the BBC's worked, it's worked because it's been able to apply brainpower to a subject in a variety of ways ... there's a whole range of competencies and skills that you need to make it work in process terms.

LONG HERITAGE AND REPUTATION

The organisation's long heritage means it has great reservoirs of experience upon which it can draw. Its reputation for quality means it can attract leading creative talent worldwide to work on its projects – often for moderate compensation.

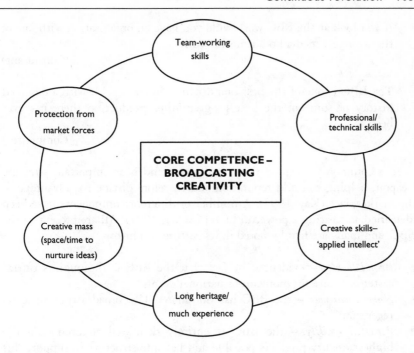

Figure 6.2 The BBC's core competence

BBC brand

Chief among the organisation's distinctive attributes is the BBC brand:[16] a powerful competitive asset and a valuable addition to its organisational equity. In an era of proliferating media supply channels and cross-media fertilisation, a strong brand image is essential. The BBC ascribes the following properties to its brand:

> The BBC Brand ... reflect[s] the BBC's reputation for independence, integrity and quality. Our brand is underpinned by our skills, expertise and our vast programme archive. As such it is a vital and invaluable asset.
>
> (BBC, undated)

> ... original entertainment, intelligent news and current affairs, a comprehensive service of education and the full reflection of our national culture. These are the BBC's historic broadcasting strengths.
>
> (BBC 1994a)

This view is widely shared by external commentators:

If you look at the BBC worldwide you have an organisation with one of the strongest media brands in the world.

(Consultant)

The BBC is one of the best brand names in the world, with a deserved history of some of the best programming production there has ever been.

(Competitor)

It is commonly accepted that a premier brand is an important strategic weapon, helping to build reputation and therefore distinctive advantage in the marketplace (Kay, 1993). A number of different components have been identified as creating a powerful brand (Aaker, 1991). All are present in the BBC, and many are firmly rooted in its culture and history:

- *Brand loyalty* – evidenced by fact that the BBC is the public's broadcaster of choice for momentous national events
- *Name awareness* – the BBC has dominated UK broadcasting since its inception
- *Perceived quality* – the BBC is entirely dedicated to producing the highest quality products possible and has infrastructure to support this goal
- *Brand associations* – the BBC brand has a long history of serving the nation in various ways, ranging from morale building during wartime to amusing its children to educating its adults
- *Other proprietary brand assets* – BBC magazines, books, audio cassettes and videos all sell successfully, and some are market leaders.

Stakeholder complexity

As an 'intersect' organisation required simultaneously to be public and private, profit- and non-profit-making, large and small, the BBC's role is ringed with ambiguities and conflicts. By virtue of its heritage and its funding it is committed to the production of a wide spectrum of programming, far wider than that of many of its competitors, although unlike its competitors its revenue levels stay constant, irrespective of viewer numbers. Partly at the government's behest, it has undertaken an ambitious programme of commercial activities and world development. Meanwhile, the industry itself is changing beyond all recognition, from one characterised by civilised competition between a limited number of domestic channels to a global battle based around bits, bytes and digitisation.

Stakeholder complexity is the direct result of its unique position and a significant strategic burden on the organisation. In comparison with its commercial peers the BBC has many stakeholder groups – often with conflicting interests – with demands that are both vociferous and hard to prioritise. This poses a serious competitive constraint. Viable strategic options are ruled out while others, questionable from a purely strategic perspective, must necessarily be included. The decision-making process is slowed, and a significant proportion of stretched organisational resources is diverted away from programme-making into massaging relationships with stakeholder groups.

Bureaucracy

The organisation's tendency towards bureaucracy is well documented (see, for example, Burns, 1977). This is said to date back to Reith's departure, after which, it is reported, 'the BBC became more and more like an extra-mural department of Whitehall: decorous and slow-moving – having lost much of its original *élan* but also much of its roughness' (McIntyre, 1994: 251). For General Director John Birt, bureaucracy was still a problem in the 1980s:[17]

> Alongside its creative and craft cultures of excellence, the BBC developed an administrative, not a managerial, ethos of safety and solidity ... The BBC has always been awash with memos, a byword for obfuscating detail ... Auntie ... became a vast command economy ... obstacles lay in the path of programme makers. Territorialism stifled initiative. Nothing was transparent, everything opaque. It was Byzantine in many of its structures.
>
> (Birt, 1993b)

Weak marketing skills

That the BBC should have only recently begun to make marketing a priority is logical considering the organisation's history. As the dominant player in a protected national sphere, where audiences had few alternative viewing options, the BBC was 'an organisation that did not have to "market" its products or existence in day to day terms' (Saxer, 1989: 67).

The recent exponential growth in broadcasting alternatives, coupled with an increasingly challenging remit from the government, means, however, that marketing has recently become a high priority. Over the past few years the organisation has learnt to market itself with greater success, despite opposition from its commercial competitors, and programme-makers who suspect that the principles of marketing may be incompatible with those of broadcasting creativity.

A formidably difficult management task

The BBC's unique situation creates a rare and complex management task. As a business, the BBC confronts a powerful and at times conflicting set of pressures placed on it by its outside environment. These include declining revenues, steadily increasing competition, and a 'permanent impermanence' in respect of many important issues ranging from government intentions to media technologies. Chapter 8 explores how the organisation's culture reconciles these challenges with its primary role as Britain's premier broadcaster.

Chapter 7

Reinventing the news
CNN's business model

Underlying CNN's unorthodox approach to news broadcasting is an equally unorthodox organisation. As with the previous chapter's analysis of the BBC, this chapter looks at the many unique aspects of CNN as a business in the competitive national and international arena. Using management rather than media concepts it examines CNN's environmental challenges, competitive environment, mission and strategy, stakeholders, core competencies and distinctive strengths and weaknesses.

Environmental challenges

Increased competition

US broadcasting is intensely competitive. In part this is a reflection of national values, in part also a function of a regulatory environment which has, since the 1980s, relied on competition to ensure diversity (Blumler, 1992).

Competition between the scheduled television services, the networks, has always been fierce, and during the 1980s some industry observers feared that weaker network players might even be forced to leave the sector. For many years CNN was outside the fray – compared to the terrestrial networks it was a marginal player delivering a niche service using what was widely perceived as an inferior delivery system. Neither cable nor news were considered attractive by the industry's dominant players, so that CNN was not viewed as a threat (the networks at this point were scaling back their investment in news). This meant CNN had the field of 24-hour international news coverage to itself for fifteen years.

However, from the mid-1990s onwards, CNN's competition intensified. A raft of new entrants entered the 24-hour news field, creating a 'gold rush for news services'[1] and giving the network its first taste of full-blown direct competition:[2]

- *FNC*: The Fox News Channel, a 24-hour news service, drawing on the Fox Television network
- *FNN*: The Financial News Network. A financially focused network which broadcast from the middle to the end of the 1980s, when it was sold to NBC and relaunched as CNBC, a business channel
- *MSNBC*: 24-hour news joint venture by NBC and Microsoft. One of the first significant attempts to realise commercially the potential offered by convergence and combine the PC and the TV. MSNBC offers a 24-hour cable news channel combined with an internet service
- *BBC World*: a commercial international satellite network offering news and current affairs. This has a smaller reach and is less well known internationally as a news provider than CNN but benefits from the BBC's strong brand and monumental newsgathering capability, encompassing 250 correspondents in 42 bureaux worldwide.

Further competitive uncertainty surrounds the growth of the internet and the development of interactive TV. It is not clear how these developments will affect the traditional news broadcasting activities of businesses like CNN. However, the organisation has a strong toehold in the emerging interactive arena through its seven web sites, which it claims make up the number one news site on the internet.[3]

It may well be that if broadcasting supply fragments in response to the huge increase in the number of channels, many broadcasters, whether on cable, satellite or the internet, will simply find themselves unable to afford what has been described as the 'budget-bending business of serious news reporting' (Cronkite, 1996). During the late 1990s, a period of violent 'talent inflation', where prices for 'killer content' escalated dramatically, the major networks were forced to scale back their news operations in response to higher costs for entertainment and sports programming. Throughout this period, CNN retained its strategic focus on news and invested heavily and consistently in news services, upgrading digitally and opening more bureaux. As a result, in late 1998, CBS, ABC and NBC were all reportedly in discussions with Time Warner about outsourcing their news operations to CNN. Environmental developments, it appears, may well bring new groups of customers or joint venture partners to CNN's door.

Industry instability

While the domestic cable market, which has carried CNN since its inception, shows signs of maturity (Vogel, 1994), satellite broadcasting is growing dramatically in the US. Direct broadcast satellite (DBS) services, offering direct-to-home transmission via satellite dish, were slow to take off, but have since enjoyed fast growth ('only the satellite dish market has significant growth potential'; Turner Broadcasting Systems, 1995). By the year

2005 a domestic subscriber base of 28 million is anticipated. Growth will come at the expense of cable – it is anticipated that cable's share of the domestic multi-channel television industry (excluding traditional terrestrial broadcasters) will shrink from 91 per cent in 1996 to 77 per cent by 2000.[4]

Further and more radical turbulence is being generated by the same trends of liberalisation, convergence and globalisation that are affecting broadcasters in Europe, and which are discussed in earlier chapters. In the US such changes have led to a widescale industry restructuring and consolidation of the industry. CNN, which merged with Time Warner during this period, was intimately involved in such developments.

Stakeholders

The following discussion covers CNN's stakeholders and the demands they place on the organisation, which reflect its unusual business model.

Employees

A defining characteristic of CNN is its unusual approach to human resources. A happy combination of unplanned elements have combined to

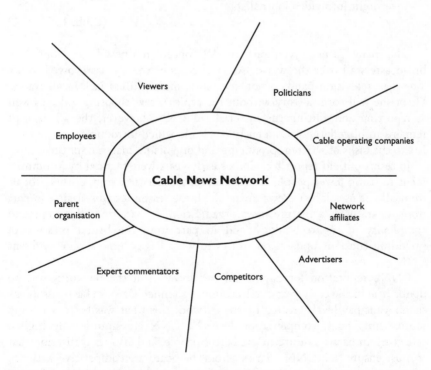

Figure 7.1 CNN's stakeholder groups (NB: the segments are not proportional)

create a system that is not only highly motivating for employees but also engenders great organisational flexibility.

Employees are a critical stakeholder group for CNN, but as a result of its distinctive origins, a number of factors balance their potential influence over the organisation. The first is that many staff are attracted by the unusually open, decentralised style of management. They enjoy considerable autonomy (provided they have demonstrated that they understand the concept and vision), and are encouraged to take initiative as they see fit (there is a concomitant tolerance for errors (Peters, 1992)). A key advantage for journalists is that because staffing is lean they have more opportunities for on-air exposure than is the norm at traditional broadcasters (reporters usually air two or three packages a day, where one is typical for a network journalist).

Second, CNN has overturned many established broadcasting role definitions to create new categories of jobs. Chief amongst these is the video journalist, 'VJ', which was developed out of necessity during CNN's frenzied run-up to its on-air launch in 1980:

> Graduating journalism students were offered the chance of a lifetime, at $3.50 an hour. Nearly one hundred wildly enthusiastic, totally inexperienced young collegians soon descended on Atlanta to be converted overnight into video journalists.
>
> (Bibb, 1993: 176)

Like many Turner inventions, the VJ concept has now been adopted by broadcasters all over the world. At local stations the VJ has evolved into a 'one-man television band', a non-specialist, multi-skilled jack of all trades. He or she will cover a story without the typical crew, shooting video as well as reporting and editing the material. At CNN, however, the VJ concept remains in place largely as an entry level role which introduces new journalists to the tasks of writing, producing and organising material for broadcast.

In terms of field reporting, CNN's early years were marked by a commitment to using fewer people than its unionised network competitors. Today, ironically, it uses larger crews in the field, the reason for this arising in part from its status as a mature news organisation, in part from the scope and complexity of the technology, and in part from the brutal pressure of providing constant updates on stories to what has become several different CNN networks.

CNN's reputation for paying salaries lower than the networks was no doubt true in the early years, reflecting not so much CNN's cheapness as the flamboyant pay levels created by the networks for what was basic television journalism. Today, compensation levels at CNN are significantly higher, reflecting in part its desire to get better people, and also its realisation that it must ensure that CNN salaries across the board are competitive with the networks in order to keep its staff.

Third, further flexibility is created by limiting union involvement (there are union members, but they are a small minority), and making much use of freelance labour in technical jobs, thereby further avoiding union involvement and allowing CNN to control costs by expanding and contracting personnel as needed (Bibb, ibid.). Periods of retrenchment have been few, if any, due to the constant growth in channels and company size.

CNN's approach to human resources involves a specific style of recruiting. Journalists are hired on the basis of their enthusiasm for and love of the news – CNN believes it can teach any technical skills which may be missing. Unlike many broadcasters, it does not restrict applications to arts graduates from leading universities, but prefers dedicated, determined highly self-motivated individuals who will fit into the culture, are 'desperate to tell their stories and don't mind hard work' (Bibb, ibid.). The organisation looks for team players rather than potential star personalities, its philosophy being that the news is, or should be, the star.

The needs of CNN employees as a stakeholder group differ little from those of journalists in public sector broadcasting organisations. They seek airtime and the opportunity to use and develop their television skills (and, where possible, their own reputation), things CNN is well positioned to provide. Key issues are the newsgathering infrastructure and technology, and CNN is equally well placed with respect to these.

Cable operating companies

These are important customers: CNN has 'must carry' agreements with its cable operators, meaning operators must include CNN in the package they provide to domestic subscribers. In 1998 Turner adopted a more aggressive strategy towards its affiliates, converting TBS from a super-station that collected no affiliate revenue to a basic cable web that charged a fee per subscriber per month. This added a new income stream from affiliate revenues but also alienated this stakeholder group, who have responded by not launching some of Turner's smaller networks, for example CNNfn, on systems that had originally planned to carry them.

In more regular circumstances, cable operators' concerns centre on the quality of programming – the more attractive CNN's output is, the higher the subscriptions they can demand from viewers paying for cable access. A key issue for them is the controls recently introduced on the price of the basic package they offer; this means revenue growth can only come from premium-tier special-interest channels for which they can charge more.

Advertisers

CNN's twin income sources, subscription fees and advertising, make it less dependent on advertisers than its network competitors. However, advertisers are nonetheless an important stakeholder group, not least because ratings are still the definitive indicator of media success in the US television industry.

Advertisers are basically interested in consistently reaching large numbers of 'attractive' viewers, where attractiveness is determined by factors such as disposable income. CNN has traditionally had problems in this respect. For one thing, a large proportion of its audiences fall into categories that are unattractive to advertisers, being either elderly or on low incomes.[5]

CNN's satellite infrastructure means it is uniquely placed to offer international TV advertising, and international advertising sales have been centralised within TBS to encourage this. Advertisers can promote their brands to a worldwide audience of over 150 million homes, regionally targeted to Asian, North American, European or Latin audiences if necessary. Although this business has been growing steadily for the past few years, it is still fledgling, in 1997 representing only 10 per cent of total advertising income,[6] with about half that coming from US-based clients with multinational marketing campaigns. It is still not clear whether significant demand exists – very few products are marketed consistently on a global basis (although the product itself may remain constant in different international markets, the advertising message promoting it tends to be tailored on a country-by-country basis).

Network affiliates

Part of CNN's unique infrastructure is a network of over 600 affiliate television stations worldwide. The traditional affiliate relationship is one-way, from channel or network to affiliate. CNN has characteristically redrawn this. Its affiliates, the majority of whom are affiliates of a terrestrial network as well, act as news clearing houses: it feeds news to them, and they deliver local footage back to CNN in return. As with many elements of the CNN system, its 'reciprocal deal approach' with a web of national (and now international) affiliates stem from its cash-starved start in life. It was a lateral, and for the industry unorthodox, response to weaknesses arising from *ad hoc* beginnings. First, there was the need to cover the entire country without adequate regional bureaux or reporters. CNN's answer was to establish arrangements with stations in every state whereby they would give their national and international material away, in return for free video and audio coverage of local events (Whittemore, 1990). The second problem was a chronic shortage of revenue. Here, CNN saw an opportunity to sell the mass of footage it did have to the hundreds of local news operations around the country. In doing so, it once again benefited from developments in its wider environment. In the mid-1980s a rash of new independent stations were licensed which needed to establish news programmes. The three networks had traditionally kept their footage exclusive, seeing their news coverage as a competitive advantage. For Turner, in contrast, 'selling on' CNN's footage brought only benefits: it had already broadcast the news stories as they happened, and repeats on local stations a few hours later would only provide advertising for CNN and underline its immediacy. Such arrangements have been replicated worldwide and have enabled CNN to build a global presence quickly and spread the cost of gathering footage:[7]

> We have spent a lot of time cultivating our relationships with our affili-
> ates and that's a large revenue-sharing business for us. We provide
> affiliates with coverage, so for example on the Oklahoma City story,
> rather than local channels having to dedicate resources to cover it, they
> can just air CNN. We have several hundred similar contracts around the
> US. So the affiliates are very important to us.
>
> (CNN interviewee)

Affiliates are therefore an important stakeholder group. They are looking for a long-term, profitable relationship, and high-quality material.

Politicians

Receiving no public subsidy, CNN is not answerable in the way public service broadcasters are to political forces, apart from needing to comply with national regulations governing broadcasting. Further, because it is only one arm of a much larger entity it does not have to devote resources to regulatory lobbying – this is the responsibility of the parent organisation. This means CNN's relationship with politicians is relatively straightforward, and in many respects the organisation could be viewed as having the upper hand.

> Politicians need *us* because they need to communicate with people.
>
> (CNN interviewee)

Politicians are an important stakeholder group, but primarily as performers or pundits, rather than as a pressure group. In the US politicians are skilled users of television airtime. They are looking for positive exposure and the opportunity to set the agenda (and therefore frequently prefer talk shows where they can better control discussions). The key issue for them is the attitude and goodwill of the journalist concerned. This makes them well disposed to CNN, with its emphasis on action and short soundbites, as opposed to the networks which favour lengthy analysis. Indeed, a poll in late 1987 showed that many political professionals preferred CNN over the broadcast networks by nearly two to one.[8]

It is even claimed that CNN's unique ability to cover breaking news in hard-to-reach parts of the globe has turned it into an adjunct of government. CNN is reportedly available in all state department offices – Madeleine

Albright, US Secretary of State, is said to have described it as 'the 16th member of the Security Council'.[9]

Viewers

CNN cares about its viewers, but about their volume rather than their diversity, and about its attractiveness rather than its accountability towards them. For CNN, viewer volume dictates its advertising income, which in turn contributes to the bottom line. US audiences, like those everywhere, are becoming more idiosyncratic and fragmented in their tastes, needs and wants (Tiven, 1994). In terms of news they are seeking relevancy, immediacy, drama, speed and accuracy, as well as flexibility of scheduling (something that CNN realised before its network peers).

Expert commentators

Expert commentators in the US, like those in Europe, concern themselves with topics such as the effects television has on society, the function of news in a democratic society, and the moral, ethical and intellectual impact of the programmes shown, particularly on children.

They are, for the most part, critical of current trends in television in general (television has been famously charged with changing 'the American child from an irresistible force to an immovable object'), and of news in particular, seeing a trend towards opinion and interpretation over hard reportage, a 'Dallasification', whereby news is trivialised and stereotyped rather than analysed, a blurring of the lines between information and entertainment, and an increase in levels of sex and violence, under the guise of 'reality programming' (the depiction of true-to-life chronicles of personal tragedies). Such criticisms are frequently directed at CNN in particular:

> CNN's contribution is almost entirely technological, a linking of video sources, newsrooms, foreign ministries. That linkage has changed the nature of diplomatic communication, and provided a voice for tinpot foreign dictators, but it hasn't done much to improve the way we get our news. In certain ways it has had a pernicious effect on the rest of journalism: it has accelerated the loss of control news organisations have over content, which in turn has led to a rush to sensationalism and an emphasis on punditry and interpretation at the expense of old-fashioned reporting.
>
> (Rosenstiel, 1994: 28)

As a stakeholder, therefore, this group seeks in essence greater responsibility from broadcasters and a shift in focus from entertainment towards information. It is in general critical of mainstream US television (acerbically distorting the famous marketing dictum to remark that 'the vast wasteland of television is not interested in producing a better mousetrap but in producing a worse mouse').

Competitors

CNN's main competitors are the news operations of the US networks and the 'new' news competitors such as the BBC and MSNBC. CNN's recent discussions with the US broadcast networks about sharing the resources of CNN (which have not reached any conclusion) suggest that CNN's relationship with its US network competitors appears to be shifting from competition to co-operation.

Parent organisation

Time Warner views its cable programming activities, which include CNN, as holding great potential for revenue growth, since cable is one of the fastest growing areas of the entertainment business and Time Warner is one of the largest players in the cable arena. As part of Time Warner, CNN is therefore required to deliver consistent and growing earnings. Prime concerns are that CNN develops stronger scheduled programming to smooth out its rating patterns (see below), that it continues to develop the CNN brand, and that it continues overseas expansion. Time Warner is also looking for CNN to conform with initiatives to build synergies and leverage between the various businesses under the Time Warner umbrella and cut costs.

Mission and strategy

CNN is not an organisation which places great emphasis on producing public statements of its strategies, goals and philosophies, preferring to leave such activities to its parent. In fact, the most succinct and accessible source of such information is its oft-repeated programme trailers. The published literature that does exist is generally produced for marketing purposes – to attract new subscribers or distributors. This may reflect the competitive nature of US broadcasting (CNN does not wish to disclose its goals to competitors) and perhaps also the organisation's pragmatic stance (CNN does not waste resources on activities which will bring in little direct return), as well as the immediacy of its informal internal communications (which means it has no need to communicate with employees via 'official' publications).

Table 7.1 CNN stakeholder demands

Group	Seeks	Key issues
Viewers	News – immediacy, accuracy, drama; general programming to meet individual interests; fit with personal schedules	Fragmentation of audiences; increasing competition for news
Employees	Opportunity to develop professional skills; opportunity to set international news agenda; peer/public exposure	Quality of news infrastructure; reputation/brand name; glamour/recognition
Cable operating companies	Attractive programmes which justify higher subscriptions	Restrictions on basic cable packages
Advertisers	Large numbers of 'attractive' viewers	Programming that attracts consistent viewing patterns
Network affiliates	Long-term profitable relationship; high-quality material	Reciprocity deal
Politicians	Favourable exposure; opportunity to set agenda	Editorial independence; goodwill/mistrust
Expert commentators	Less sensationalism, less entertainment, more information, more analysis	'Tabloid television'; 'Dallasification' of US television
Competitors	US networks – co-operation? New players – piece of CNN's action	Cost of establishing international infrastructure; value of brand
Parent organisation	Growth in earnings; consistency in earnings; brand development; overseas development	Continued global expansion; leverage of infrastructure

Mission

CNN publishes no formal mission statement. However, its publications summarise its conception of its basic function in society:

THE WORLDWIDE COVERAGE AND DELIVERY OF BREAKING NEWS

CNN's signature is its unparalleled ability to bring the most thorough and immediate live coverage of the world's news to its worldwide audience. In the pursuit of timely, unbiased and in-depth news reporting, CNN has pioneered innovative techniques and broken new ground for the television news industry. The network has demonstrated a unique ability to cover news comprehensively, reacting quickly to crises by going live to, and staying with major stories as long as necessary.

(CNN, 1994)

TO INFORM THE WORLD ABOUT THE WORLD

CNN's achievements reflect a determined effort to keep the public well-informed about the intricacies of today's world.

(CNN, 1994)

TO BE A UNIFYING GLOBAL FORCE

The spark, the central thread of CNN has been the delivery of a non-stop signal. In the case of a major event, this signal ties the globe together.

(Tiven, 1993)

Espoused strategy

Formal strategic planning has never been part of the CNN culture[10] ('Ted Turner is the strategic planning department. Period.' (Bibb, 1993: 345)), and it is not an organisation that places emphasis on industry analyses or broad-ranging plans. TBS, in contrast, has always been a tightly managed and highly integrated conglomerate, and systematic strategy-making activities for CNN were concentrated at that level. This approach is echoed by CNN's new parent, Time Warner.

During the time that research was taking place at CNN, the organisation had no published strategy document (indeed it had very few 'official' corporate publications in general). CNN's strategic goals at the time of this research are listed below. These were taken from TBS publications (as with the BBC, these are given in the organisation's own words where possible).

STRENGTHENED DOMESTIC PROGRAMMING

Continued expansion of CNN's franchise, particularly in the United States, requires the addition of new programming that will increase daily viewing, regardless of the day's news.

(Turner Broadcasting Systems, 1994)

CNN has always been highly dependent on big international news stories and periods without the adrenaline of a big breaking story can create problems in attracting and keeping viewers. Its strategic priority therefore was to find ways to smooth out its viewer level by improving its 'non-news', 'appointment-based' programming.

The subsequent merger with Time Warner has provided an important boost towards achieving this goal. Cross-fertilisation between key magazine properties and the news network enabled CNN to launch a series of prime-time news magazine shows in 1998. These included CNN & Time, CNN & Fortune and CNN & Entertainment Weekly. The explicit goal was to build appointment viewing and lure an audience even when there is no big news breaking.

> For CNN, the Time Inc. magazines will contribute to the creation of great network programming, and we add a little magic.
>
> (Ted Turner, cited in Time Warner, 1997)

DEVELOPMENT OF NEW BUSINESSES

CNN's response to fast-paced change and the ensuing uncertainty in media industries worldwide has always been bullish. It saw the potential of new media products and services early on and aggressively sought out new applications and outlets for existing material, as well as new material for its existing outlets:

> The exploration of interactive applications for news and information is a major area of interest that the company intends to pursue for new business opportunities ... seeking hardware partners that can match its own brand ... the Company plans to market CNN International to government and educational institutions, multinational businesses, overseas travellers and others interested in news with an in-depth international perspective.
>
> (Turner Broadcasting Systems, 1995)

CONTINUED GLOBAL EXPANSION

CNN has long judged its real growth opportunities to lie outside the US. One strategic goal therefore was significant expansion in underdeveloped markets such as Latin America and South East Asia, while increasing the amount of 'own language' programming (although this can pose problems for CNN's signature coverage, breaking news):

> The international television markets are expanding with the growth of cable and satellite distribution ... cable penetration will grow between 15 and 20 percent annually in Europe, Asia and Latin America over the next five years ... This growth translates into billions of dollars of new

subscription and advertising revenue for the Company to pursue.
(Turner Broadcasting Systems, 1995)

In addition, CNN was under orders from Turner himself to upgrade CNN International (CNNI)[11] and increase its strategic investment in international bureaux:

Ted Turner has instructed us to open more [than 33 bureaux] ... in fact he has instructed me to open a bureau in every country in the planet [and] we are headed in that direction.
(CNN's President of Global Newsgathering[12])

It was also told to establish more strategic alliances with other global cable operators or global broadcasters:

[We are] looking at opportunities in Europe and elsewhere to produce part channels, opt-out channels or channels in the vernacular, stepping down all the time to get closer and closer to our audience.[13]

Competencies, strengths and weaknesses

This section reviews the distinctive organisation attributes that play a part in CNN's performance, specifically its competencies, strengths and weaknesses.

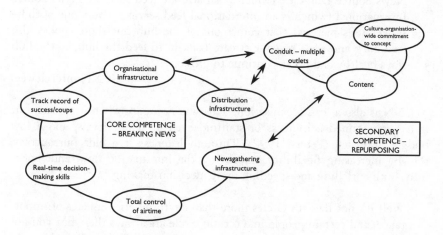

Figure 7.2 CNN's core competencies

Core competence – breaking news

CNN's core competence is its ability both to cover and to transmit breaking news, as it happens, from just about anywhere in the world. This rests on the following 'bundle' of skills or technologies:

ORGANISATIONAL INFRASTRUCTURE

CNN's structure is driven by the demand of its newsgathering and broadcasting activities. Basically, it is a geographically diffused network. Headquarters are in Atlanta, Georgia, and it has production facilities there as well as in Washington, London and Hong Kong. It has news bureaux in twenty-one countries outside the US, as well as nine national bureaux (in addition to Atlanta and Washington). It has, moreover, a 49 per cent stake in n-tv (Germany). It is a subscriber to APTN, the Associated Press Television News, the result of a merger of APTV and WTN in 1998, Reuters TV, and a participant in news pools covering the Far East, Europe, North America, and the Middle East.

CNN is therefore a news network, and also a network organisation. Its structure is unconventional and arises from the confluence of its core mission and its core capability, delivering breaking news:

> If you think of CNN as a wheel and the hub of the wheel is newsgathering, its thirty bureaux around the world, its units like the medical unit, the nutritional unit, the environmental unit, the entertainment news unit ... the hub's producing all that and the spokes of the wheel are the networks, CNN, CNNI, CNN Spanish, CNN All News Radio, CNN All News Spanish Radio, Headline News, the Airport Network, News Source Domestic (which is an affiliate feed service), News Source International (which is an international feed service). Every one of those spokes uses material that comes out of the hub but those spokes also feed back and are a revenue stream back in to feed the hub, so the hub stays healthy and it can continue to grow.
>
> (CNN interviewee)

CNN is also a lean organisation. This was necessary when it started, but it has maintained a leanness of staffing, even at senior levels, and a low budget approach (Peters, 1992). Through leanness it avoids bureaucracy, thereby increasing flexibility, improving the information flow, and, hopefully, both enriching and speeding up its decision-making:[14]

> Well it's not flat, it's circles more than anything else. Spheres of importance, and certain people in a certain circle are always there but you got other circles out here, of importance, promotions, Ted even out here. At

any moment this circle may move and engage this circle, hitting particular people in that particular circle of expertise to come and join in the
discussion or this circle, the main circle may broaden all of its ties and
speak to everybody ... That's one of CNN's strengths. That's how I see
it and no chart's gonna show you that.

(CNN interviewee)

Physical infrastructure plays a role too:

The facility is designed [in such a way that] control rooms are small so
that communications is enhanced rather than having to reach out to
people or spread out over great distances. It's rather compact. The
communications set-up for both internal and external communications
is excellent and instantaneous. The staff has worked here, many for
5,6,7,8 and more years – some have been here the whole fifteen years –
and they are all geared towards doing that – so we've learnt how to do it
... we have people who have done it and for whom it is not something
unusual ... and we have equipped ourselves technically with the essen-
tials to do it, we're able to do it.

(CNN interviewee)

DISTRIBUTION INFRASTRUCTURE

CNN has a unique delivery infrastructure. Domestically it benefits from
locked-in, 'must carry' agreements with most cable operating firms:

[We have had] a stranglehold on the means of distribution. So in an era
of limited network space, it owned the only 24-hour news trucking
service and nobody else could get a licence because the free market
didn't have any space to offer up.

(CNN interviewee)

Internationally, its signal, carried by eight satellites, covers most of the
populated earth. By blocking off an increasing number of satellite transpon-
ders to provide segmented delivery worldwide, it has created the largest and
most flexible footprint of any broadcast service in the world, and made it
harder for competitors to establish similar arrangements. (Increasingly,
global news arrives at CNN via satellite.) By splitting its signal up in so
many ways, CNN uniquely can offer both global advertising and regionally
targeted advertising.

NEWSGATHERING INFRASTRUCTURE

CNN's skills in the field of alliances have contributed greatly to its fast-paced growth into one of the world's leading news providers. In addition to its relationships with cable operators, it has reciprocity arrangements with local stations (network affiliates) all over the world to exchange their national and international news in return for significant national and local stories from other stations, the end result of which is a vast newsgathering system.

Moreover, it has made large and consistent strategic investments in developing its newsgathering infrastructure (by enlarging its affiliate base and opening more international bureaux) and in the technology (recently completing a digital upgrade). These investments provide an important strategic edge in an era when competitors are scaling back their news operations. CNN has a long history of investing in technology – it pioneered the use of collapsible satellite dishes that can be carried on board commercial aircraft, and it can cover breaking stories live, anywhere in the world, in the time required to get a reporter on site.

CNN's infrastructure benefits again because it is a financially sound organisation, ensuring it has the capital for continuing investment in further expansion of its newsgathering activities. Collectively, CNN, Headline News, CNNI, CNNfn, and CNN Interactive made profits in 1995 of $265 million against revenues of $765 million (1994 figures were profits of $227 million on revenues of $667 million). In addition, it is a highly cost-conscious organisation.

This is supported by a network of high-level relationships. Like many commercial media moguls, Turner has made it his personal mission to cultivate world leaders and heads of state, which has enabled CNN both to extend its newsgathering network into parts of the world closed to other broadcasters and boosted its profile (Rosenstiel, 1994). This practice stems in part from Turner's idealism – he believes that the cause of world peace will be best advanced if world leaders are given a forum to communicate their ideas via global television – but it also brings pragmatic benefits. For example, CNN was the only news organisation to receive permission to open a bureau in Havana (possibly the result of Turner's duck-hunting expedition with Fidel Castro), and was of course uniquely permitted to leave its journalists in Baghdad during the Gulf War. As a result, CNN became *de rigueur* viewing for world leaders, opening whole new communications systems between governments (Whittemore, 1990).

Together, CNN's organisational, distribution and newsgathering infrastructures create a unique business 'ecosystem', a network of internal and external relationships that creates significant competitive advantage.

TOTAL CONTROL OF AIRTIME

Guaranteed immediate airtime is an important element of CNN's news capability:

> What we have that the broadcast networks domestically don't have is 100% control of our own airtime. We can blow out anything on air without any consequences save moving advertisers around which is sometimes a problem, and do whatever we want. Broadcast networks can't do that because it's not just the news division, its the entertainment division and the daytime division, and it's expensive for them to blow out a soap opera to show OJ, as they found the first few weeks of the trial. They lost millions of dollars pre-empting their soap operas to show OJ and they finally gave up.
>
> (CNN interviewee)

REAL-TIME DECISION-MAKING SKILLS

Unsurprisingly, the journalistic emphasis on speed has infused the entire organisation. Even staff in non-broadcast areas are skilled at making fast decisions:

> It's a 10-minutes horizon, we live in real time, this is a real-time company, everything we do is in real time, that's a very complicated way of operating ... you can make split-second decisions that look like they're capricious, that's what people don't understand about real-time businesses, people making capricious decisions have so much information the decisions actually aren't capricious ... it looks like nobody talked to anybody, the reason nobody talked to anybody was ... you've already gone over this 20 times in your mind.
>
> (CNN interviewee)

TRACK RECORD OF SUCCESS/NEWS COUPS

CNN's track record of news coups has helped create a powerful brand with worldwide associations of immediacy and drama (US research has found CNN to be 'the most believable' of any television network and ranked second only to the *Wall Street Journal* in terms of overall public confidence (Bibb, 1993)). In 1986, when the Challenger Space Shuttle exploded, CNN was the only television channel to cover it live. It then sold its footage to broadcasters all over the word, creating an awareness of CNN, particularly in Europe, which would have been hard and expensive to achieve through marketing campaigns. As a result, a few months later CNN was available in over 150,000 households. In subsequent years, CNN's consistent investment in its international newsgathering infrastructure meant it could repeatedly score against its competitors by being the only news service to broadcast exclusive live coverage of events such as Tiananmen Square Massacre (1989), the US invasion of Panama (1989), the release of Nelson Mandela (1990) and the 1991 Gulf War bombing of Baghdad.

Secondary competence – repurposing

> Mr Turner ... knows how to make a little television go a long way.
> (*Economist*, 22 March 1997, p.96)

Associated with the core competence in the area of breaking news is a secondary capability, repurposing. Simply put, this means that central to the CNN way of business is to re-use, or repurpose, as much of its copyright material in as many ways as possible to spread costs and maximise income. This does not in itself create fundamental customer benefit, but it is a vital supporting element of the core capability of covering breaking news. Hamel and Prahalad (1994) remark that 'CNN managed to provide 24 hours of news a day with a budget estimated at one-fifth that required by CBS to turn out an hour of evening news', and Peters (1992) notes that 'everyone at CNN knows what things cost. ... People have a "feel" for budgets, for what's excessive, for what's not'. The value of this approach, and the company-wide commitment to it, is illustrated in the following quote:

> ABC goes to Kuwait, does three follow-up stories on the war how many years after, puts one on the air, the other two sit on the shelf until they are dated and are not used. We go over, spend a little bit less money doing those same three stories, those three packages get used, they don't get used just on one network, they get used potentially on eight networks, so we amortise that expense and find so many other ways to make money off of it that that's why by the end the hub keeps growing. That's why we're growing bureaux while the networks are shrinking bureaux, and we continue to be profitable.
>
> (CNN interviewee)

In 1994, around 36 per cent of CNN's revenue derived from such activities (Turner Broadcasting Systems, 1995). This policy of 'leveraging' content derives from its parent:

> Every part of our Company strategically enhances another part ... All of the parts fit together and are fulfilling our basic business premise: to

create and own programming, to develop as many different ways as possible to generate profits and enhance shareholder value.

(Turner Broadcasting Systems, 1995)

This competence rests on the combination of three elements: conduit, culture and the content generated by its significant newsgathering infrastructure (described above):

CONDUIT – MULTIPLE OUTLETS

In an era of ever increasing competition for 'conduit', one of CNN's core assets is the wide range of channels it owns, ranging from domestic and international networks to its online sites, all of which serve as outlets for original programming.

> For us to do offshoots of CNN ... we'll be launching next year CNN SI which is CNN Sports Illustrated ... for us to launch a new network, it doesn't cost. We have the infrastructure, we have the sales force already intact, we have the traffic departments already intact, we own the copyright on the programming, we have the producers, we have the bureaux, we have the information. All it is is repackaging. Repackaging, re-doing, re-launching with our copyrights, with our ownership, and using our infrastructures.
>
> (CNN interviewee)

CULTURE – ORGANISATION-WIDE COMMITMENT TO CONCEPT

Repurposing contradicts the media assumption that messages must be tailored for their intended audience, and a certain snobbery about such low-budget approaches. It is interesting therefore that there is such universal buy-in to the concept:

> I think the genius behind a company like Turner Broadcasting is that you take base products and you market them and market them and market them again, and the question is how do you repackage this product.
>
> (CNN interviewee)

CONTENT

CNN's newsgathering infrastructure provides a constant stream of copyright material it can use and re-use over its extensive distribution architecture.

Uneven ratings and weak scheduled programming

Paradoxically, CNN's unique strength in news creates strategic limitations. News events of world interest may be its 'elixir of life' (*Frankfurter Allgemeine Zeitung*, 14 February 1994), but they also make for very uneven ratings. Major stories bring surges in viewers (the so-called 'news junkies') which fall off dramatically once the event is over – during the Gulf War average ratings were five times pre-war levels. This, coupled with the fact that international news stories are often intrinsically disturbing, decreases the attractiveness of CNN's channels to advertisers.

A related problem is that a single-minded concentration on news precluded the development of the regular programming that might bring consistency to its viewing figures. The challenge for CNN therefore is to find a means of solidifying its ratings 'binges' into steady gains of viewership in 'normal' times, that is, of 'hooking' news junkies into regular viewing patterns.

CNN's strategy explicitly addressed this issue, but resolution is not without conflict. It is not simply an issue of resources, but of mindset. CNN's successful business model rests on the organisation having found a unique niche and having exploited it as creatively as possible. The entirety of its structures and processes are dedicated to that single goal. Appointment-based programming will require new skills and the blocking-off of time slots in dedicated news channels, thus reducing the organisation's ability to cover breaking stories.

Perceived low-browism

A knee-jerk reaction to CNN, often on the part of those who seldom watch its output, is to criticise it for superficiality: 'a mile wide and an inch deep' (Bibb, 1993) or 'visual wallpaper' (Auletta, 1996). Indeed, CNN appears to have become a whipping boy for the oft-deplored 'dumbing down' of US society. Such criticism no doubt stems from its early days when its espoused editorial policy was 'if it bleeds, it leads', but the organisation rightly claims that such days are long gone. Critics, though, are slower to revise their judgements, despite the fact that the organisation's prime international competitor, BBC World, itself admits that the old stereotype of CNN dominating breaking news situations as a result of technology and resources rather than of analysis, is no longer true.[15]

Commentators' criticism of CNN's approach could be due in part to CNN's editorial strategy of covering rather than analysing events:

> We offer breaking news live, as it happens; we don't comment on it. Judgements are up to the viewers themselves.
>
> (CNN interviewee)

CNN is also accused of parochialism, of displaying an 'Atlanta perspective':

> Though CNN has a global reach, its heart is in Atlanta, Georgia. Its programming tends to be stamped with a particular editorial standpoint and a certain way of exploring issues, events, and the actors involved in them.
>
> (Blumler, 1992: 213)

This criticism is hard to support. The editors that staff the international desk include German, Croatian, Irish, Tajik, Chinese, Scottish and Danish nationals.

Concerns about CNN's editorial standards were revived in 1998 when the organisation had to apologise for and retract a high-profile piece which claimed that the US used nerve gas on its own troops during the Vietnam War. As a counterweight, however, came the network's critically acclaimed documentary series 'The Cold War' which was viewed in many quarters as representing a renaissance of high-quality current events coverage in the US.

Strong business in a strong segment

Ironically, while CNN might have started life in what was considered an inferior corner of the television universe, through its concentration on cable it now finds itself in one of the most prosperous areas of the media sector. The Turner cable networks, to which CNN belongs, are now regarded as one of the most promising businesses within the Time Warner group, which now controls one of the largest concentrations of cable channels in the US. CNN is therefore one of Time Warner's growth-drivers.

Cable businesses are prized by media businesses because they combine growth with defensive potential. In terms of growth, cable and satellite are already in over 70 per cent of US households and that number is anticipated to grow to around 85 per cent, driving growth in pay and basic networks. Ratings for the major cable networks are increasing, leading to an increase in advertising and the ability to get rate increases. On the defensive side, a significant revenue stream comes from subscriptions from cable operators. Unlike advertising revenue, this income is not dependent on the economy and is therefore highly predictable.

The CNN brand

> CNN is the premier news brand in the world. We intend to do what it takes to keep this brand on top.
>
> (Tom Johnson, Chairman, President and CEO, CNN News Group)

One of the consequences of convergence is to increase the strategic importance of brands, which are viewed as one of the most important weapons in maintaining customer loyalty as channels fragment and competition intensifies. In this respect, CNN, like the BBC, is in the enviable position of owning one of the world's best-known media brands, a source of great strategic strength. However, CNN does not see its brand as simply the key to the future. The organisation believes its brand has played an important role in establishing the organisation in its current position:

> The CNN brand for us is everything – much larger than the sum of all our parts ... a single, uncluttered brand is the way ahead ... Our brand – and our reputation built up in those short seventeen years since 1980 – is, I believe one of the reasons we managed to secure access to people and places where others fail.
>
> (Cramer, 1998)

CNN may well be an unorthodox organisation which has reinvented the news. From a management point of view, though, it is a classic example of a successful business in harmony with its competitive environment. CNN has a clearly defined mission and a straightforward, if initially heretical, business concept. As a strong business in a strong segment with a strong brand it is excellently positioned to thrive strategically. Chapter 9 explores CNN's organisation culture and the role it plays in sustaining CNN as one of the world's most innovative broadcasting organisations.

Chapter 8

'Part of the British way of life'
The BBC's culture in its own words

At the heart of the culture of any organisation lies, according to Schein, an interrelated set, a paradigm, of deeply held beliefs. These beliefs, so ingrained that they are unconscious, are the hidden determinants of actions and the ultimate source of beliefs and attitudes. They govern, amongst other things, what that organisation feels its fundamental mission to be, how it perceives its environment, and the strategies it judges as appropriate responses to that environment.

This chapter and the one following it present the findings of the cultural research conducted at the BBC and CNN in the form of a 'Scheinian' paradigm of interrelated assumptions. To avoid repetition, the following text will serve as an introduction to both chapters.

In each case, the chapter format is to present each paradigm in its entirety, followed by discussion of the various individual assumptions[1] which together make up the paradigm. Relevant comments are closely analysed,[2] highlighting the latent values and attitudes arising from the assumptions and discussing their organisational implications. In selecting particular values and attitudes the aim was not to interpret the data, but rather to pinpoint concepts and variables that provide coherence to a large quantity of material.

Extensive use is made of quotes[3] from the different interviewees and, to a lesser extent, of company documentation. Direct quotes from interviewees (uncredited), as well as indirect quotes from secondary sources (credited), appear as indented text. The purpose is to elaborate and deepen understanding in three ways: first, to present the actual data on which the analysis is based, so that readers can make their own analysis and interpretations; second, to allow them to assess for themselves whether the analysis here is correct; and, third and most important, to allow the data to tell their own story (all quotes are from the interviews, unless otherwise indicated). Where appropriate, data from field notes (evidence of artefacts) and staff surveys are also included.

Schein emphasises that assumptions are interlinked. This research indicates that this is indeed the case, so much so that it is common for two or more assumptions to be evident in one comment: the BBC's commitment to professionalism expressed in terms of commitment to the Reithian heritage or motivation arising from the licence-fee funding, CNN's cost-consciousness expressed in terms of a pioneer spirit, or its bottom-line commitment to viewers as a distinguishing feature of an organisation on the sidelines of the US television industry.

The BBC's cultural paradigm

Assumption I

'Public funding makes us different'

- The BBC is special, different and important because of its public service status.
- It's in the public good that we exist; it's good for the nation.
- This means that we are not 'just' broadcasters, and our public service goals must be viewed as superior to financial or commercial priorities.
- This marks us out from our commercial peers, and makes us a special case.

This assumption derives from the public service ethos which has been present in the organisation since its earliest days (Burns, 1977). It concerns a definition of broadcasting conceived in terms of the public good, of public betterment:

> It is the commitment to an organisation that is different in character from other organisations, it is the public service commitment, it is the commitment to quality ... that drives people.

Sense of higher purpose

As the quote above suggests, this belief encapsulated a profound conviction that the BBC makes an important contribution to the nation; that its programming does not just fill empty hours in the audiences' evening, but, to echo Reith's views, actually enriches the viewer's life:

> Our aim is to provide entertainment that is morally sound and has a bit of the Reithian extra about it. Television producers are like doctors, good producers make good moral judgements as well as good programmes, I think it's as important as in medicine.

Indeed, such a belief is not unjustified. In the course of its history, the BBC

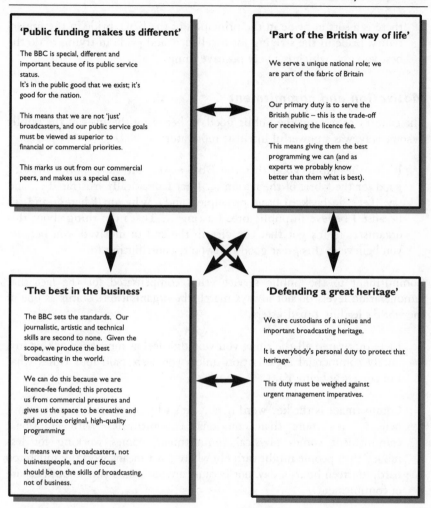

'Public funding makes us different'

The BBC is special, different and
important because of its public service
status.
It's in the public good that we exist; it's
good for the nation.

This means that we are not 'just'
broadcasters, and our public service goals
must be viewed as superior to
financial or commercial priorities.

This marks us out from our commercial
peers, and makes us a special case.

'Part of the British way of life'

We serve a unique national role; we
are part of the fabric of Britain

Our primary duty is to serve the
British public – this is the trade-off
for receiving the licence fee.

This means giving them the best
programming we can (and as
experts we probably know
better than them what is best).

'The best in the business'

The BBC sets the standards. Our
journalistic, artistic and technical
skills are second to none. Given the
scope, we produce the best
broadcasting in the world.

We can do this because we are
licence-fee funded; this protects
us from commercial pressures and
gives us the space to be creative and
and produce original, high-quality
programming

It means we are broadcasters, not
businesspeople, and our focus
should be on the skills of broadcasting,
not of business.

'Defending a great heritage'

We are custodians of a unique and
important broadcasting heritage.

It is everybody's personal duty to protect that
heritage.

This duty must be weighed against
urgent management imperatives.

Figure 8.1 The BBC's cultural paradigm

has made an unquantifiable contribution to the cultural development of the
UK. For the price of a licence fee it provides every member of the nation
with full access to an enormous cultural heritage, previously available only
to a privileged minority. It helped Britain develop into one of the musical
capitals of the world and sponsored the development of new forms of
dramatic writing.

There's a deeply ingrained integrity in most of the people who work in
the BBC; there are always some exceptions to these rules but I think

there is a sort of pride in the principles of the BBC, pride in the impartiality, pride in the striving for excellence, and pride in trying to do the best you can, which is a very positive thing.

Motivation and commitment

The concept of serving the public good, of bettering the lives of the public in some way, was a powerful intrinsic motivator:

> It's in the public good that the BBC exists culturally, politically; it's good for the fabric of the nation ... I get fantastically frustrated ... and say, 'Let's go back to basic principles' and, 'Why am I here?', and it's because I believe in public broadcasting ... That's the thing about this organisation; it's got that capacity in the end to motivate you because you believe in this great good that you're contributing to.

Commitment to the public service ethos compensated for the fact that remuneration levels do not always match the organisation's status as one of the world's leading broadcasters:

> I feel motivated all the time; you wouldn't feel as motivated as this in a purely commercial organisation unless you were paid four times what I'm currently being paid.

> Commitment is the key word here ... it's why people still want to work here ... it's more than emotional commitment. With emotional commitment comes physical commitment, comes working for less money than people might earn elsewhere ... it means working much too hard, fourteen hours a day, not because anyone asked you to but because of commitment.

Again, this is recognised by official publications:

> All who work at the BBC feel a pride in what we do and a belief in public service broadcasting. This – not financial reward – is why many of the most talented people in broadcasting are already at the BBC or want to work here.
>
> (BBC, 1994a)

Anti-commercialism

A corollary of the concept that the organisation is serving a 'higher purpose' is that it can become estranged from the commercial world. Placing the organisation's task above the standard broadcasting mission of providing entertainment, education and information militated against attempts to introduce a greater understanding of the business problems faced by the organisation, and, it could be argued, engendered an almost anti-commercial ethic:

> People get very ashamed of talking about working in the public interest and working for broadcasting purposes which are greater than their commercial returns. The BBC shouldn't be ashamed talking like that. There's been far too much concentration on talking about it as a very big broadcasting business; it's not.

Such sentiments reflect a widely held belief, shared by many in the UK, not just BBC employees, that the BBC was never meant to be a business,[4] but rather a centre of broadcasting excellence which existed to serve the public (indeed between 1933 and 1963 there was an established tradition of 'protecting "creative workers" from the responsibilities and preoccupations of administration' (Burns, 1977: 217)).[5] But these sentiments also place management and programme-makers in conflict, and foster a discernible prejudice against anything that could be construed as the encroachment of commercial principles on public service activities, thereby inhibiting change:

> People get a lot of things mixed up. 'We're not a business', you hear that a lot. And no, we're not a business, because we don't exist to create shareholder wealth. But they use that as a kind of mantra to cover 'Leave off efficiency', 'Stop squeezing me on costs' ... No one would argue that we are a business, and yet one of the things that Birt has introduced to squeeze efficiencies in resources is to introduce an artificial return on capital ... and people see that as utter madness and say 'We're not a business, we're not a business', so they're confusing the business argument with the efficiency argument.

Assumption 2

'The best in the business'

- The BBC sets the standards. Our journalistic, artistic and technical skills are second to none. Given the scope, we produce the best broadcasting in the world.
- We can do this because we are licence-fee funded; this protects us from commercial pressures and gives us the space to be creative and produce original, high-quality programming.   *continued*

> • It means we are broadcasters, not businesspeople, and our focus should be on the skills of broadcasting, not of business.

This assumption relates to the ethos of professionalism, a concern to offer broadcasting of the highest possible quality. This strand of BBC culture appeared to serve as the 'motor' behind the organisation's unparalleled excellence in programme-making:

> We've been a Rolls-Royce organisation, everything has been done very well. I would argue, if you were looking for best practice in broadcasting around the world, you'd probably find quite a lot of it here, in terms of product, in terms of the level of service that has sustained that product.

> Essentially, the BBC is an organisation in which people care passionately about output and genuinely debate and think through in a very rigorous way how to make that output the best it can possibly be.

It features prominently in official statements:

> It has had a dedication to programme excellence; to innovation and originality. Reaching for the highest quality in all we do; a commitment to large programme departments which recruit and train people of ability.
>
> (Birt, 1993b)

Commitment to licence fee funding

It is part of the BBC's mythology, and extremely plausible, that its programme-making excellence is inextricably linked to the fact that it is licence-fee funded. The two elements have combined to create a 'virtuous circle', whereby guaranteed funding from the licence fee has enabled creativity and professionalism to flourish, and a critical creative mass to develop, which has enabled the BBC to raise public service broadcasting to the highest standards possible, which in turn has created a discerning and demanding viewing public, which is then prepared to finance the organisation on an ongoing basis. Threats to the licence fee, or proposals to alter the organisation's financial basis, were construed therefore as threats to the organisation's fundamental activities and as such highly emotive:

> I think ... in a way the corporate culture is driven by the guarantee of income, because in terms of taking risk and thinking for tomorrow

rather than just for today, you create a kind of creative culture, in which people thrive, and have energy and so forth, and that is the corporate culture if you like, the two things sort of come together. And I think it is crucially this issue of funding.

That relationship with the public being reinforced by the fact that people are still prepared to hand over their money by way of licence ... that gives them a very strong commitment.

A 'virtuous micro-circle' helped to explain why licence-fee funding helps to produce high-quality broadcasting:

The key argument for the licence fee is that you must take risks, you have a duty to take risks. If you have a commercial imperative you probably can't afford to.

Pride

The organisation displayed great belief in its creative and professional skills. Some people, however, were concerned that this brought the risk that pride in its achievements, taken to an extreme, can turn into arrogance and complacency:

Certainly it's one of great self-belief, enormous pride ... the downside of that is smugness and arrogance, but the upside is a real self-driven belief, even when you might be irritated, cross, angry you're still doing everything possible to produce the best possible programme ... but you'll also not like anyone else to disagree ... That's an important part of the culture. It's also one of great independence, that's partly a journalistic thing, to do with 'I'm an objective reporter', but it's also found in with programme-making areas away from the news where 'My job is to be creatively free, and I must be free to express what I want to express.'

But whatever difficulties this means for management, the BBC sees its deeply rooted self-belief as a vital contributory factor in the quality of its programme-making:

This argument (that quality and popularity are inversely related) is predicated on the belief that quality and popularity are fundamentally opposed: that you cannot be serious about quality if you are also going for a big audience. Lurking behind it is the prejudice which says that viewers and listeners do not really want quality, but that they want pap.

(BBC, 1992)

Insularity

Just as employees worried that pride could turn to arrogance, so too were some concerned that élitism could cause insularity: that because the BBC has set the standards for worldwide television for so long, its employees would see little reason to look outside and consider what others in the field may be doing:

> I believe the organisation is at almost all levels deeply introspective, and I think there's a certain culture of, and attitude 'We're just better than the other guys, always have been and always will be'.

This was viewed as a by-product of its protected history:

> The BBC historically was an organisation run by and for itself. It did what it did in a non-competitive environment ... its position was unshakeable, and in a pretty benign way it did what it thought should be done and ran itself with some appropriately high-flown ideals, but also with the idea that it knew what was best and got on with it.

It was also buttressed by a belief that the BBC must be protected:

> I think essentially the culture is one of 'We're different, we're the best, leave us alone, protect us'.

The organisation was aware of the risks of élitism and of the limitations this can create:

> Without a strong bond of understanding with our audience we run the risk of self-indulgence, élitism and in the age of broadcasting choice, irrelevance ... BBC news is trusted and respected. The challenge is not authority but accessibility.
>
> (BBC, 1992)

The 1994/5 (BBC, 1995c) staff survey (which coincided with the research for this book) provides further evidence of insularity (again, the top possible rating was 5.0):

- the BBC is outward looking (2.8)
- to what extent do you believe that leaders in the BBC think about future events and possibilities when making decisions? (2.8)

Since then steps have been taken to address the issue of the organisation's insularity:

We are also (now) an organisation which is much more outward looking. The BBC that I joined didn't look out of the window. It was utterly obsessed with itself and its own ethic.

(John Birt in 1998[6])

Disdain for management

Ironically, the organisation's profound commitment to excellence in broadcasting was perceived as a block on attempts to improve how the organisation itself functioned. BBC employees pride themselves on their broadcasting, not their business skills. Status accrues with creativity, with programme-making prowess. Senior management positions tend to go to those who have won their spurs in creative areas, from production to scheduling; as is the case in many media businesses, from newspapers to films, it is felt that someone who has the talent to master creative functions can of course master the more mundane ones associated with managing the organisation, that broadcasting is special but anyone can manage.[7] Quality comes from creative staff, and management exists to make this happen.

Interest in the organisation *per se* therefore was related to its ability to enable employees to produce the best product possible, thereby fulfilling the core mission:

> People are not interested in hearing a corporate view, and that's another key part of the culture.

> Essentially, the BBC is an organisation in which people care passionately about output and genuinely debate and think through in a very rigorous way how to make that output the best it can possibly be ... Where they are poor is in using traditional management tools to increase the effectiveness of their activity.

Interestingly, although the culture was not interested in management, it was critical of management within the organisation. These were the responses in the staff survey (BBC, 1995c) to the following statements (5.0 is the highest score):

- to what extent does the BBC operate with the full involvement of all staff? (2.3)
- to what extent does the BBC manage itself well? (2.4)
- to what extent do you believe leaders in the BBC inspire others? (2.4)
- to what extent is communication – open (2.4), timely (2.4), responsive (2.2), engaging (2.3), consistent? (2.1)
- to what extent are the views and concerns of staff listened to and taken seriously by the senior managers in your directorate? (2.3)

Artefacts provided visible evidence of these attitudes. Offices display the paraphernalia of journalism, of intellectual activity, rather than of executive prowess. Offices at both CNN and the BBC tend to be rather cramped, but there similarities stop. At CNN available surfaces were crammed with technology and most offices had at least one television on; offices at the BBC were strewn with paper and books, sometimes punctuated with the odd industry award. Televisions were seen less frequently and were seldom switched on.

Culture of questioning

It could be argued that a journalistic mindset will inevitably militate against a management culture. The BBC is an organisation that prizes itself on the ability to think independently, to question, to challenge. For journalists, immediacy is all ('stories are written in the snow', that is, impermanent, transitory). Thus management and strategy, analytical activities which require a long-term perspective, are things towards which successful journalists are perhaps professionally indisposed:

> Journalism is in the blood of the organisation, whether people are formally working as journalists or not ... they're trained to trip people up, ask cynical questions and be difficult, but on the other side of the coin people are very creative and very full of ideas and if it's done in the right way and if they feel that they are genuinely being listened to and have a say and are motivated and they are discussing a subject which they are interested in, it can be very stimulating indeed and very interesting and exciting.

The picture emerged of a culture that respects broadcasting rather than management skills, that seeks to distance itself from commercial activities. This made managing difficult:

> More important, though, is the issue of questioning, scepticism, all of which is a good thing, which is one of the things that makes good journalism, and one of the attitudes that we've tried to sell that has been very hard amongst the top is to say that we can't on one hand say it's a very good thing that we are questioning and investigative and independent as journalists, but that it must stop in terms of internal attitudes.

> There are in the BBC, as there are in many broadcasting organisations, a whole range of extremely clever people who have a view on everything, and often their views will be extremely informed, well informed, very articulate. That makes working in broadcasting a pleasure, because those people are around ... but I can't help but think that sometimes our culture of questioning not only whether we're right to make a deci-

sion, but we end up with a decision having been made and still the questioning will continue whether the right decision was made. You expect this in a large organisation, but at times it becomes very difficult for people who want to move things on.

It is clear that in broadcasting organisations, where the communication of ideas is a core skill, the way in which management initiatives are communicated, and the language used is vital:

> Television journalists are communicators. Clarity ... is paramount ... That the use of language is particularly important to journalists has a special relevance to managing them ... like the language of any specialised field, [management jargon] does, more or less, make sense when you learn the rules, but it is rarely elegant, often ineffective, and sometimes barely English.
>
> (Georgiou, 1998)

That consultants had often failed to grasp this point was a frequently mentioned source of exasperation:

> On the whole you are dealing with a workforce, and certainly at the production end, the sharp end of the business, which takes language very seriously indeed, it's our job, so it would have been bad enough anyway because jargon ... builds barriers. It's even worse if you are dealing with an articulate workforce who prides itself on its use of language. It's very very counterproductive ... When I see consultants I tell them that ... one of the major risk areas is not learning our language, because we pride ourselves that our language is the language of the public at large ... so we don't think that there's anything arrogant in saying learn our language because it's the language everybody speaks ... but we've had a lot of information technology development over the past few years and we've had the same problem, IT jargon, and again it's taken a lot of us turning around and saying 'No, no, no, you learn my language, in my language a programme has two "mm"s and an "e" and goes out on air.'

Assumption 3

'Part of the British way of life'

- We serve a unique national role; we are part of the fabric of Britain.

Continued

> - Our primary duty is to serve the British public – this is the trade-off for receiving the licence fee.
> - This means giving them the best programming we can (and as experts we probably know better than them what is best).

The third assumption concerned the BBC's view of its national role. Research indicated that the BBC conceived of its role as being far, far, more than merely supplying television and radio programmes. It was not simply in the service of the nation but a fundamental part of the nation, and its programming should both reflect and help define the national identity:

> As everything else fragments around you and becomes multinational, international, satellite and all the rest of it, the BBC remains a sort of touchstone for the identity of the nation.

This deeply internalised remit has its roots in the licence-fee funding. 'Everyone' pays for the BBC, and therefore everyone should receive 'something' (i.e. programming that appeals to their specific and individual interests):

> We are committed to reflecting national and local identities in every aspect of our programming, not solely in regional programmes but also in those made for the whole network audience.
>
> (BBC, 1994a)

Because of its long and august history, because of its wartime role, because of its decades spent dominating the national airwaves, the BBC occupies a unique national position – neatly summed up by a CNN interviewee as 'somewhere between The Beatles and the Queen'. The reference to the Queen is apposite. The BBC is certainly not part of the official machinery of government, but it is definitely a semi-official adjunct to it:

> I'm not even sure it's unofficial, I think it's as near official as makes no matter … we're set up by Royal Charter, that's quasi-constitutional; I'm appointed by the Queen and Privy Council and can only be sacked by her … and the licence fee is a hypothecated tax which we're given by Act of Parliament … it's not quite right to call it unofficial, it's quasi-official, somewhere between the two.

It is also the unofficial official 'information carrier' about national events – from royal weddings to elections:[8]

It's a noticeable, quantifiable phenomenon that when there's a really big news story, Gulf War or whatever, people turn to the BBC, and the audiences for ITN and commercial radio slump accordingly ... Equally the quid pro quo is that we're perceived as being aloof, stuffy, boring, establishment, conservative, etc.

Responsibility to UK licence-fee payers

The cultural conviction about the importance of the national role played by the BBC had deep roots, extending back to Reith's view that public service broadcasting should be:

a dependable keeper of the nation's conscience ... standing as an arbiter above the clamour of social and political factions ... the paragon of impartiality, honesty and respectability.

(Cited in Burns, 1977: 155)

Nowadays, a sense of fulfilling a unique national role generates feelings of motivation and responsibility:

This is the great thing with the BBC ... the sense of acting on behalf of the nation, the BBC as a unifying culture – I'm sorry these are grandiose words but these are really what, if you talk to people in some areas of the BBC ... they believe in.

Such sentiments underline how intimately the BBC is tied to Britain, and how dedicated it is to serving the needs of its many communities:

I think our responsibility is fairly clear. It is to the licence-fee payer. That's a grandiose statement. That's 98 per cent of the people in Great Britain who pay the licence fee ... My responsibility is not to serve the Queen, it's not to the Prime Minister ... it is to serve the interests that make up, the very very diverse interests that make up this country ... this differing assembly of needs.

They are echoed in its official statements:

Together with my colleagues in the BBC, we will do our utmost to provide a BBC that will inspire, that will bring people together in good times and in bad, and a BBC that will continue to make Britain a better place for us all to live.

(Birt, 1993b)

Indeed, the BBC could also be said to conceive of its role as somehow 'defining Britishness'. In Reith's day this meant creating a common culture that transcended the distinctions of class. Today, it appears to see this task as overcoming the boundaries of ethnicity.

Evidence of the BBC's strong innate sense of 'civic' duty was apparent at artefact level in the access it offered to researchers, the low-key friendliness of many support staff, and its exhaustive list of public services (fact sheets, information lines etc.). It is conveyed also in the bright functionality of its newer office buildings ('We don't waste the public's money') and the chirpy style of its official communications, which seem to suggest that 'everyone in Britain pays for us and must therefore feel able to approach us and understand what we do'.

Self-importance

The BBC's sense of fulfilling a unique national role had both positive and negative connotations. Like the pride associated with Assumption 2, there was concern that the sense of responsibility engendered by Assumption 3 could easily mutate into self-importance, and thence into arrogance:

> There's a sort of Auntie knows best, condescending, patriarchal, matriarchal 'We'll look after you' old-fashioned welfare-state public service and a more sophisticated 'We're aware of your needs', 'We're in tune with the nation', 'We're part of the nation and we can enrich it.'

> It cuts both ways; there is a negative, it can be perceived as imperialistic, boring, colonial, dull, old-fashioned if you like, but the other side of that is trustworthy, authoritative, high quality, second to none, impartial, those sorts of values which people actually do value, and which can place an organisation in a position where they remain incredibly competitive despite being less well funded or despite … a lower audience share, because they have a special place. It's an emotional thing and a psychological thing rather than a straight bottom line results thing … And an organisation like the BBC has terrific roots in order to do that.

Assumption 4

'Defending a great heritage'

- We are custodians of a unique and important broadcasting heritage.
- It is everybody's personal duty to protect that heritage.
- This obligation must be weighed against urgent management imperatives.

Just as children of famous parents have difficulty shrugging off the expectations of their heritage, so too, it can be argued, is the current-day BBC to some extent weighed down by the organisation's extraordinary track record of power, influence and broadcasting success. For many, the BBC represents the pinnacle of televisual achievement, and that achievement was made possible by the rigorous values instilled by Lord Reith.

> I think that one of the tensions of the BBC is that the staff see themselves in a way as the custodians of the Reithian ethos ... I think the tension arises not that the people at the very top don't see that, but that they see changes are necessary ... whatever else people feel about the BBC they feel a very strong sense of identity with the BBC. They may dislike a huge number of things about the changes, but they feel extremely strongly, and therefore extremely possessively, about this thing called the BBC. They are very proud of it and defensive of it. And defensive of what they see as being the true ethos of it ... and so if you're there making television programmes and making radio programmes you feel extremely strongly that ... the way you do it and your views about why you do it lie at the heart of what the BBC's about ... It's an enormously conceived commitment and it's an area of enormous strength, but it can also be an area of great tension, if the BBC, in the shape of its Chief Executives ... or the senior team around those entities wish to do something different, or something which the staff feel runs against the true interest which they feel they represent.

The BBC's official statements make frequent references to defending this tradition, upholding Reith's values in a modern world:

> The ideals and quality which fashioned that BBC are more relevant than ever. They stood like beacons in the old broadcasting world. They will shine as brightly in the new.
>
> (BBC, 1995a)

In its publications the organisation has a strong predilection for 'historicising' itself and its situation:

> Let me argue tonight for one of the twentieth century's greatest institutions, in this or any other country.
>
> (Birt, 1993b)

Motivation and pride

For BBC staff, this heritage was part of what made the organisation, and by extension, its employees, special. It was a great source of motivation:

It is a great privilege to me to work for an organisation that has such a heritage, that has made the greatest radio and television programming in the world for so long ... and still produces world-beating output. Even though competitors have come along and they are increasingly well funded we can still beat the rest of the world.

This motivation clearly counteracted the sense of frustration some felt about the deep-seated changes taking place in the organisation. This combination of feelings – frustration and motivation – resulted at times in highly emotional statements:

That idea is the only thing that keeps producers working here rather than anywhere else; the place is so fucking painful to live in.

The motivation appeared to be intimately connected with perceptions of Reith's unique contribution to the history of broadcasting, and could explain the latter's curious longevity and appeal. Reith left the organisation over sixty years ago in 1938, having disengaged mentally two years earlier after having been forced to found a staff association (McIntyre, 1994), but nonetheless his name is still regularly invoked in national discussions about broadcasting (Blumler, 1992: 9). The impression given was that for many inside the organisation and outside it Reith and Reithianism have become shorthand terms which encompass emotionally bounded concepts of what the BBC once was, still is (just), but may, unless everyone takes care, soon cease to be. Others, however, viewed the concept with a certain pragmatism, if not cynicism:

It's certainly symbolic – heaven knows of what, but it has a symbolic importance.

Reithianism died thirty years ago; it's curiously more alive in television than in radio. The basic principal was leading public taste ... Reith was a boring old fart actually, he thought he could give people a bit of variety to keep them quiet, and then get the good journalism and the opera. What people mean when they talk about Reithianism goes back to the late 1950s ... which was the sense that you could lead people from one thing to another and stretch them gently, but also the BBC in the '50s started to tap into a rich vein of entertainment, of drama, so I think when people talk about Reithianism they are talking about that. A lot of people talking about Reithianism have never read John Reith, but it's become a phrase. ... He's a useful fiction for the BBC.

Resistance to change

Problems arise when the exigencies of the environment dictate a strategy which threatens to compromise the organisation's heritage, to force it off the Reithian path. There was concern that employees see themselves in the role of impoverished scions of a once-wealthy family, battling to save the family treasures from the auction houses. Indeed its 1996 restructuring initiative was described in the press as 'throwing away the crown jewels' (*Financial Times*, 26 June 1996).

> This is a deeply conservative organisation that hates change of any kind and fights it in every possible way ... I think that view of the heritage is ... part of an excuse or weapon used in the argument to stop change ... heritage is used as a kind of emotional argument.

> There is huge resistance. Part of the problem is that people have got used to living in comfortable environments. They don't like change, and we've been living in perpetual change for five years.

There was worry too that the organisation's Reithian inheritance was turning aspects of the organisation into museum exhibits which must be preserved:

> Take the decision to abolish, effectively, network radio. We've had a network radio directorate ... since 1927, and there's probably no other organisation in the world that's had effectively the same structure for the best part of three-quarters of a century, but this was established by Lord Reith, and there's a momentum about that.

Retrospection

The BBC's commitment to its heritage – so evident in its public pronouncements, in the architecture of Broadcasting House with its Latin inscriptions and busts of previous Director Generals – like so many aspects of its culture, had positive and negative implications. It engendered extraordinary levels of commitment, pride and motivation, but also inflexibility and a backward-looking focus. It meant that quality was often conceived of in terms of what went before, of old values and standards:

> The BBC is sodden with history and does nothing to try and get beyond that. If you walk around Broadcasting House, the corridors are endless framed pictures of *The Radio Times* back to the 1930s, the place just echoes with history, there's lots of portraits of old Director Generals and

things around, which is very comforting in a way and very special, but just heightens the introspection.

The interrelationships between the assumptions at the heart of the BBC culture, and the attitudes and values arising from them are summarised in Figure 8.2.

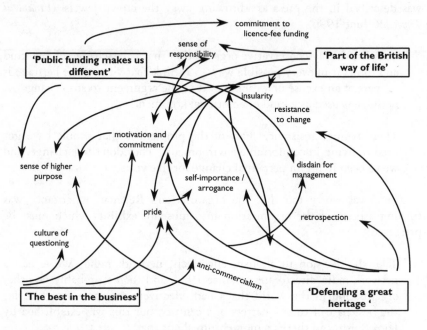

Figure 8.2 The BBC's assumption and attitude 'map'[9]

Conclusion

This chapter has explored the four governing beliefs that drive the BBC's culture and the attitudes that arise from them: a deep commitment to the UK; an equally strong conviction that the organisation is special, different and important because it has public service status; a belief that it is special not just because it is publicly funded, but because it is simply 'the best in the business'; and finally a conviction that those that work at the BBC are custodians of a unique broadcasting heritage and have a personal duty to defend this.

The chapter also considers the intriguing paradoxes arising from these beliefs, namely that while they generate intrinsic motivation and a set of exemplary attitudes (responsibility, a sense of higher purpose, commitment, a passion for broadcasting quality), they bring with them a set of 'shadow' attitudes, including insularity, resistance to change and an anti-commercialism.

How these strong cultural values have assimilated the BBC's new strategic directions is the subject of Chapter 10.

Chapter 9

'Underdogs and outsiders'

CNN's culture in its own words

The four dominant beliefs that drive CNN's corporate culture and the attitudes arising from them are the subject of this chapter. As with the BBC in the previous chapter, the organisation culture of CNN is presented in terms of a Scheinian paradigm of interrelated assumptions. Full discussion of how this analysis was reached and how the paradigms should be 'read' can be found in the introduction to Chapter 8.

CNN's cultural paradigm

Assumption 1

'News lies at the heart of CNN – CNN is the news'

- Our news makes a difference to the course of world history.
- Our news is a force for the good.
- Our news connects the world with the world.
- Our news is unique.
- A global product for a global market.
- We have reinvented news.

At the heart of CNN's culture lay a commitment to breaking news which is as fundamental as the BBC's commitment to public service broadcasting:

> Breaking news is the head of the comet.

> We're just the world leader in news.

> What we do that's really special that nobody else does like we do is

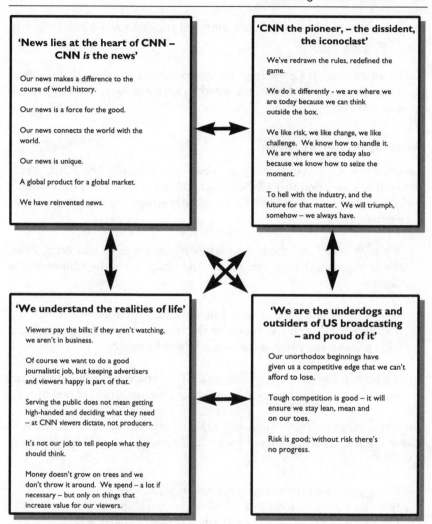

'News lies at the heart of CNN – CNN *is* the news'

Our news makes a difference to the course of world history.

Our news is a force for the good.

Our news connects the world with the world.

Our news is unique.

A global product for a global market.

We have reinvented news.

'CNN the pioneer, – the dissident, the iconoclast'

We've redrawn the rules, redefined the game.

We do it differently - we are where we are today because we can think outside the box.

We like risk, we like change, we like challenge. We know how to handle it. We are where we are today also because we know how to seize the moment.

To hell with the industry, and the future for that matter. We will triumph, somehow – we always have.

'We understand the realities of life'

Viewers pay the bills; if they aren't watching, we aren't in business.

Of course we want to do a good journalistic job, but keeping advertisers and viewers happy is part of that.

Serving the public does not mean getting high-handed and deciding what they need – at CNN *viewers* dictate, not producers.

It's not our job to tell people what they should think.

Money doesn't grow on trees and we don't throw it around. We spend – a lot if necessary – but only on things that increase value for our viewers.

'We are the underdogs and outsiders of US broadcasting – and proud of it'

Our unorthodox beginnings have given us a competitive edge that we can't afford to lose.

Tough competition is good – it will ensure we stay lean, mean and on our toes.

Risk is good; without risk there's no progress.

Figure 9.1 CNN's cultural paradigm

bring you the live breaking story of the day. There's nobody quicker and more competent at bringing the breaking event than CNN.

If there's a worldwide crisis, contemporaneous news events going on in six continents, we know how to switch. What CNN does well is live breaking news, better than anybody else.

News is the engine, it's the end-all and the be-all of this channel. We hope that our competitors and our would-be competitors like ABC and NBC cannot understand as clearly as we do that the engine is news.

> We cover the news in an interesting and engaging and compelling way.
> That is the mission.

> In fifteen years it's gone from being the caboose to being the engine of
> American news broadcasting, whether anybody likes it or not ... all
> over the world ...

Sense of higher purpose

Underlying CNN's commitment to news was a deeply held, and deeply
motivating, conviction that CNN's news makes a difference to the course of
world events and can be a force for the good, perhaps even one that unites a
fragmented planet:

> We want [that] everybody who wants to can get news, can bring down
> the news, should have the news. And that's been the philosophy of
> CNN.

> Where CNN is unique ... and where its obligation has got to be ... is
> that at any point in the course of the day ... if something significant
> takes place in any place in the world, it will be on CNN.

> It's utterly brilliant at moving quickly to cover real-time events and
> organise those real-time events into some coherent strand of oral history.

This sense of historical mission and higher purpose can be traced back to
Turner himself, as demonstrated by his 'dedication' at the official launch of
CNN:

> To act upon one's conviction while others wait,
> To create a positive force in a world where cynics abound,
> To provide information to people when it wasn't available before,
> To offer those who want it a choice,
> For the American people, whose thirst for understanding and a better
> life has made this venture possible,
> For the cable industry, whose pioneering spirit caused this great step
> forward in communication,
> And for those employees of Turner Broadcasting, whose total commit-
> ment to their company has brought us together today,
> I dedicate the News Channel for America,
> The Cable News Network.

Such attitudes can develop into a kind of frenzied grandiosity:

We're gonna go on the air on June 1, and we're gonna stay on until the end of the world. When that time comes, we'll play 'Nearer my God to Thee' and sign off.

(Turner, cited in Whittemore, 1990: 143)

CNN's news style – fast, immediate, with an emphasis on action rather than analysis – is replayed in its cultural artefacts. Speech patterns are quick, communication is fast and informal and ideas are followed up fast.[1] These values, and the associated ones of urgency, curiosity and accessibility, were also evident in the built environment. Doors were kept open, offices close together and most had at least one television tuned to CNN, while some had additional sets tuned to competitors.

Global outlook

CNN saw itself as a 'news missionary', bringing news to and from far-flung reaches of the globe. Its global outlook was a critical constituent of its unique formula:

The mission of CNN is to cover the news ... That is the same, nationally and internationally.

The overall mission of CNN is to produce live news coverage ... the quickest and the best ... and to broadcast it to the world.

CNN is determined to create the first truly 'global information company'; to be the 'global network of record' seen in every nation on the planet, to broadcast in most major languages, to focus on non-US journalists, to become world citizens who just happen to be based in the US.

(Tiven, 1993)

If you take a look at us now, 85 per cent of our programming is produced for the international feeds, so there really is a very, very little domestically produced programming and the ones that are domestically produced are of interest internationally – 'Larry King', 'Money Line' – things of that nature.

The global outlook contributed to making the organisation unique:

We've redefined the borders ... we're as relevant to a sheikh in Saudi Arabia as we are to somebody in Detroit.

In seeing its news as a global product for a global market, and by concentrating on the similarities between customers in those markets rather than on the differences, CNN was a perhaps unwitting adherent of Levitt's (1983) theory of global markets and contravenes classic approaches to broadcasting, which stress the unique characteristics of national markets. CNN's philosophy, regarded as eccentric by domestic peers, has been reinforced by the organisation's newsgathering coups (the Gulf War, Tiananmen Square) which have resulted from it.

The organisation also made a deliberate effort to avoid ethnocentrism and to diminish an 'Atlanta perspective' that could inhibit consumer acceptance:

> To a very large extent we've tried to make CNN International place and country of origin neutral. We never tell you that it's coming from Atlanta ... and we've hired – you could be an anchorwoman here because you speak a very nice British English – there's a fixation on ... well, on not sounding like an American. We've tried to make it place-neutral and we've tried to take a kind of androgynous perspective on what constitutes news.

At the same time, it sought to capitalise on its unique position by producing something for those populations that domestic producers might not be able to match:

> When we created Business Asia ... the perspective we wanted to achieve was to be a show about Asian markets for people who were doing business in Asia, be they native to the region or from outside of the region doing business in that part of the world ... one of the things we learned early on is that there's an interest in us getting Administration people on and saying, 'What is your policy on China? What do you think about this?' People say they want to hear more of that, because they want to know what Washington's saying.

CNN's emphasis on a global outlook has been deliberately cultivated by Turner:

> None of my bureau people here and none of my people in Atlanta are allowed to use the word foreign ... 'foreign' means alien, like ET ... We have small fines at CNN to eliminate the word 'foreign' when talking about other nations and other individuals on this planet ... I think we're all neighbours. Instead of foreign affairs, 'international' affairs. The word 'foreign' has bad connotations because it says 'somewhere else'.

> (Turner, cited in Bibb, 1993: 230)

The global outlook is of course both reflected in and reinforced by CNN's international structure. Through its many affiliates worldwide, staff are exposed daily to different approaches to news and to television. Informed references to differences in national television systems cropped up frequently in interviews.

Assumption 2

'We understand the realities of life'

- Viewers pay the bills; if they aren't watching, we aren't in business.
- Of course we want to do a good journalistic job, but keeping advertisers and viewers happy is part of that.
- Serving the public does not mean getting high-handed and deciding what they need – at CNN *viewers* dictate, not producers.
- It's not our job to tell people what they should think.
- Money doesn't grow on trees and we don't throw it around. We spend – a lot if necessary – but only on things that increase value for our viewers.

CNN held a deeply pragmatic attitude towards its broadcasting activities. Statements about mission invariably included a qualifier stressing that viewers have the ultimate say over what gets broadcast:

> Our mission is to cover the biggest stories in the globe, in a way that people want to watch them.

CNN exists, like the BBC, to serve its public, but the balance of power is different. At CNN, viewers have the upper hand, they dictate, they know best – even if programme-makers personally hold different views:

> You are in the business of providing news and information to people, the theory being that if you are doing it well you will have lots of people watching. If you don't have lots of people watching maybe you should examine how you are providing it.

On a macro level CNN felt that its programming can make and has made a difference to the world. On a micro level its assumptions were less grandiose, and far more prosaic than those that underpin public service broadcasting. CNN does not seek to 'improve' viewers; its view is that it cannot afford to alienate them by adopting a lofty tone or screening 'stretching' material:

We deliver information. We do not necessarily deliver wisdom. What people do with the information is outside of our control.

(Tiven, 1993)

We want to educate them, but if you can't get them to watch you can't educate them, and that's where a lot of people get lost. If they aren't watching it doesn't matter how good what you're doing is.

Pragmatic understanding of role as a broadcaster

CNN's perception of its duties as a broadcaster was hard-nosed and businesslike:

There is a general awareness ... that we are a business, and the business to one degree or another exists to attain revenues from a variety of sources ... without those revenues, which are indirectly but tightly linked to the consumer, we're out of business, no one to pay for journalists to trot around the world and interview world leaders. So there is a reality-based perspective ... The degree to which people believe in that and use that as a primary sort of mission varies depending on who you're talking to, but it's at least generally recognised that that's a fact of life.

CNN attributed its financial realism to the wider industry culture:

There's a perspective, it's a cynical perspective but it's true, which says that the purpose of television is to deliver advertising ... And the less cynical extrapolation of that is that in order to get viewers ... you must attract viewers and you must appeal to viewers. And in order to do that in a competitive environment it is not only important that you must be providing them with information that they want or need, but you have to present it in a way they find attractive to get.

Its financial realism was even attributable to national culture:

That's what you think about, this is a consumer society, welcome to America! ... viewers are what pays all the bills.

From a clear understanding about financial realities of life came clarity over stakeholder priorities (note the associated references to the underdog mentality):

Our concern is how do we do a good job of journalism and have all sides presented and not piss off the advertisers. I'm not supposed to say that, but the fact is we do do that.

The content creators at CNN understand that they don't have a job unless we sell advertising, so they have to make programming that is more than just plain interesting [but] that people watch, and a certain type of people watch, and they have to worry about targeting certain demographics and we help them worry about that.

Commentators? We could save ourselves grief if that was what we thought about, they would write nicer things about us, we could put our nose in the air and act like they act, but where does our acceptance come from, it comes from the public. Who are we ultimately serving, the public ... it seems to me our job is to serve the public – that's low-brow-ism.

We do [consider employees] but, let's be honest. We're a business, we're here to make a buck as everybody else.

CNN watches environmental developments closely, and an important element of this is looking for business opportunities that may emerge. The BBC, CNN and many of the consultants interviewed produced during interviews very similar diagrammatic representations of the impact of dis-aggregation. Intriguingly, CNN's diagram had one unique feature, an indication of where in the disaggregated processes revenue can be made. This was pointed out by an interviewee:

The big piece that's missing from those others is the exploitation of all this ... it's exploitation of the copyrights ... it's licensing and merchandising, it's home video, it's syndication, it's all those things ... that's where the genius is ... it's multi-dimensional.

CNN's formula was therefore an intriguing combination of the altruistic with the commercial, and would appear to be part of the unique Turner 'signature':

This company is about making money while doing something that needs to be done, like the pioneers.

(Ted Turner[2])

Cost-awareness

Financial pragmatism translated into extreme cost-consciousness:

I think that no company watches money the way that we watch money – they account for everything – and what is interesting is that the journalists do. In other news organisations it is a problem for accountants, we go out and we do the story and the accountants will take care of it, but we will pour in the resources that we need to do it. I believe that Turner looks at the resources and says 'These are the resources. What can we do with those resources? And in doing that, what will give us the cutting edge?' And that's why you've got people who are willing to work all hours and will continue, because there is also something about being on air and progressing a story, and you keep going with it.

Interestingly such cost-awareness was not demotivating. It simply served to underline CNN's unique and special character:

> You could even be unflattering about it. It's very money-conscious. Which can get very wearing sometimes. On your less flattering days you call it a cheap environment ... I've never gotten a bonus, which is one thing in this culture which won't change – but I get all these cheesy stupid Christmas gifts, you know, a really ugly bad clock, a Goofy ... by corporate American standards these little things are ... a joke. But I make fun of it and make a joke of it. I can connect this all back to Ted and I know I work for Ted, and ultimately Ted is the driving identity.

Associated with this was a disdain for the corporate trappings so beloved of the US television industry:

> We spend money where it creates added value for the consumer.

The unorthodoxy of this approach for the US media industry was underlined at post-merger meetings between CNN and Time Warner:

> You know, when the meetings first started, when we'd fly up to meet them, we'd fly into Newark, because it was two hundred dollars cheaper to Newark than it was to La Guardia, the New York City airport. They would fly down to meet us on the corporate jet.

CNN's physical office buildings provided evidence of its conviction that it must stay close and accessible to its viewers, and of the organisation's thriftiness. The offices are basic, but more importantly, they are located in the CNN building, a standard development built on spec, comprising offices, a hotel and a food court, acquired at a bargain price by Turner during a recession. Offices are modest in size and utilitarian. The only evidence of investment in fixtures and fittings was technology (every office has a television plus at least one computer terminal; many have several of each).

Access to the building is via an indoor food court, thronged with tourists, who can take a tour of the CNN studios (more repurposing). Staff 'lunched' with the public downstairs in the food court. In the centre of this is a studio where *Talkback Live*, an afternoon chat show, is broadcast live every afternoon. Passers-by sipping Diet Coke stand metres away from cameras, watching the recording – they can be part of the studio audience too if they wish.

Assumption 3

'CNN the pioneer, the dissident, the iconoclast'

- We've redrawn the rules, redefined the game.
- We do it differently – we are where we are today because we can think outside the box.
- We like risk, we like change, we like challenge. We know how to handle it. We are where we are today also because we know how to seize the moment.
- To hell with the industry, and the future for that matter. We will triumph, somehow – we always have.

CNN saw itself as a crusading pioneer, its success rooted in taking risks, doing things differently, ignoring received industry wisdom. In part this has been driven by necessity: for many years CNN could not afford to follow standard industry practices. But now it has made a virtue out of necessity, and ironically many of its practices – the VJ system, its affiliate network – have been adopted by its detractors and have become standard industry practice.

Over the years CNN's iconoclasm has transmuted into an 'official' policy of disregarding convention:

> ... an edge that we have because we started off as nothing fifteen years ago and people made fun of us, and nobody thought Ted knew anything about the news, so why was he starting a news network ... and that's an important edge to keep, whether you call it underdog or whether you call it the lean and mean machine.

> It's institutionalised lateral thinking, because you are allowed imagination ... it goes back to you don't have 'No' in the vocabulary, you have people who find solutions.

For CNN success rests on breaking moulds, disregarding received wisdom:

> I'd say we question what the industry says: we have proved that it pays to question what the industry does.

Opportunistic style of decision-making

CNN's history is one of first finding success through unexpected areas or approaches to broadcasting – satellite technology, repurposing – then of being ridiculed for such activities, and finally of being copied by detractors. This has generated an opportunistic approach to decision-making. For CNN, the challenge is not the new developments themselves, but ensuring they keep an open mind:

> When you think your way is the only way, what a trap. In fact our mothers and our fathers told us that when you think you know it all, that's when you stop learning, you're not listening any more, you don't know when the change happened, but you're still fighting it. You have no clue the winds have changed, that it's a new day, a new order, a new way of looking at things, people are marching to a different drum ... but you don't even know that's a drum playing, it's noise to you.

> So you have to be able to let go of what's not working, and you have to be able to let go of it fast, so I think the organisations that get in the most trouble, and I think it's true personally in life, are the ones that stay the most attached to being right.

This 'official' opportunism is rooted in Turner's founding of the business:

> The Ted Turner genius is to see an odd view of the utilisation or impact of a technology without necessarily understanding or giving a damn about the technology itself in the short run. Ted's genius was to comprehend that the arrival in 1975 of satellites that could transmit television signals meant one guy could get his signal out to lots of places in the country without the extraordinary cost of individual wires connecting them all together ... But Ted didn't go 'Wow' and say, 'That's fabulous technology'. He said, 'I got this little itty bitty TV station in Atlanta that doesn't have an audience and I've bought a bunch of programmes for it; if I put those programmes on a satellite and gave them to cable systems all over the US I'd get a ton of viewers I don't have and I could raise my ad rates!' He said, 'I need an audience to pay my bills, we're broke, we don't have any money!'

Confidence

When discussing environmental trends, it was noticeable that for CNN the future is not a threat but a challenge, one they are sanguine they will master. For example:

We're not worried about digitalisation, we're trying to engage in the age of digitalisation.

Assumption 4

'We are the underdogs and outsiders of US broadcasting – and proud of it'

- Our unorthodox beginnings have given us a competitive edge that we can't afford to lose.
- Tough competition is good – it will ensure we stay lean, mean and on our toes.
- Risk is good; without risk there's no progress.

The concept that CNN is an underdog, a battling outsider in a hostile industry, was central to its cultural paradigm and linked many of its beliefs:

This place grew up with a cultural inferiority by being in Atlanta and with a total underdog mentality by virtue of being on cable when cable wasn't chi-chi. As a result it has been driven by a desire to get as big as its competitors. At the same time it's a cash-poor, capital-poor, betting-the-farm-on-the-next-acquisition kind of place ... the corporate goal was never high through-put in productivity, the corporate goal was to be bigger than we were because we were too small.

We always feel like we're the underdogs to the big three [networks]. They carry greater clout simply because they have a 100 per cent penetration nationally ... domestically we are the little guy ... we may not act like it but we think like it; we think like the step-child.

Interestingly, CNN is also a physical outsider:

We're the outsiders ... we're still outsiders ... because we're not in New York ... we're just not in the same ball game, we're not in that little New York–Washington power corridor.

In its underdog role, CNN is tapping into a seam in its national culture:

I think the key word here is outsiders, which is pioneers, which is mavericks, which is not in the mainstream. Americans love underdogs ... We tend to root for that.

'Can do' mentality

CNN's pioneering culture led to a bias for action, for hands-on activity:

> This is the 'do it' school of business here. You have an idea, you get it approved by the hierarchy, and then you do it and nobody tells you how to do it.

> One of the things I learned here very early on is that 'No' is not a word, the word becomes challenge, you don't say 'No', you look for a solution and you look and you say, 'That is a challenge and how do we solve it?'

CNN looks for such attitudes in new recruits:

> I want people who have a 'can do' attitude, who are extremely competitive with the other news organisations and competitive with each other. I think competition is extremely healthy. I want producers who are anxious to do better than the producer before them, anchors who are anxious to do better than the anchor before them.

> At CNN it meant that you were going to be more entrepreneurial, faster, you had to work harder ... it meant a different kind of individual coming to CNN than to the Beeb.

Fighting spirit

For the underdog, the pioneer, survival is a battle, and CNN's view of the outside world was highly combative and spiked with military terminology:

> We used to say, 'You want to be an overdog, then you wanna to behave like an underdog.' No matter how good you are you want to wake up every morning figuring there's somebody smarter, crazier, luckier than you are out there who's gonna reinvent something and then you're in trouble.

> Because we feel we're the underdogs we have to fight so much harder for recognition, we have to hold on so much firmer to our grip ... we have the fear of becoming less.

> You lead ... what is the phrase? 'Lead, follow or get out of the way.' You do certain things because it's easier to compete if you're in the lead, it's easier to maintain your lead and whip up on competition if you're out in front of the mess as opposed to being in the back trying to catch up. So the idea is that you stay out front ... you are able to recognise and seize

a problem or recognise and see an opportunity and grab it ... as opposed to 'Oh fuck, everybody's doing that but me ... I'm back in the back of the line aren't I?'

These are exciting and challenging times. We face new competitive challenges around the world. CNN is gearing up for war. We will strengthen our brand and preserve it, but it is war, no illusions. NBC, Murdoch, and CBS want to kill us.

(Eason Jordan, President of CNN International[3])

Now the organisation is established, the battle is one against complacency:

We cannot believe our press cuttings. We cannot. If we start to believe them, we're gonna start to lose the battle.

Again, there was ample evidence to show that these assumptions can be traced straight back to Turner himself:

I never quit. I've got a bunch of flags on my boat, but there ain't no white flags. I don't surrender. That's the story of my life.

(Cited in Whittemore, 1990: 5)

Tolerance for risk

Unsurprisingly, pugnacity was partnered with a strong stomach for risk:

We wouldn't be here if we were afraid of risk. In young companies ... you have to be risk-takers ... if you're not willing to take a risk, you'll be gone. Because there's always somebody smart. Nobody owns these ideas.

But there was also an allowance for the occasional associated failure:

If you foster the notion that it's better to make fifty decisions and fuck up a few than make three and never make a mistake ... we're not gonna penalise you for making a mistake, we're gonna penalise you for not making an effort to do something terrific.

The 'network' of assumptions at the heart of CNN's culture, and the attitudes and values arising from them, is summarised in Figure 9.2.

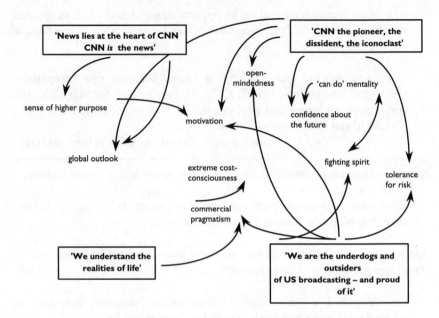

Figure 9.2 CNN's assumption and attitude 'map'

Conclusion

This chapter explored the four unconscious shared beliefs that lie at the heart of CNN's culture: a commitment to breaking news as fundamental as the BBC's commitment to public service broadcasting and rooted in the firmly held belief that CNN's news makes a difference to the course of world events; a conviction that CNN understands the realities of life – the organisation is proud of its pragmatic view of the role of broadcasting and hard-nosed about its business priorities; a belief that CNN is successful because it takes risks and does things differently – the organisation's unorthodox beginnings have given rise to an institutionalised iconoclasm which in turn leads to an 'official' policy of disregarding convention; and, fourth, the ingrained feeling that the organisation is an underdog, a battling outsider in a hostile industry, something that creates a combative attitude to the world outside. The impact of these beliefs on the organisation's performance, processes and strategic options is the subject of Chapter 11.

Chapter 10

Reithianism versus Birtism

New strategic directions versus old cultural values at the BBC

How did the BBC's culture, with its distinctly Reithian overtones, respond to a set of strategic priorities designed to ensure the organisation's success in a highly competitive multimedia era? This chapter explores the relationship between the shared hidden assumptions at the heart of the BBC's culture and the ambitious programme of organisational and strategic change initiated during the Director Generalship of John Birt.

As a starting point for this analysis, it must be observed that the emphasis placed on strategy and best managerial practice by John Birt was new for the BBC. The latent cultural attitudes towards strategy within the BBC which were uncovered during research were inevitably affected by the fact that overt strategy-making of a positivist, rational type was a relatively new activity for the organisation. Because for decades its environment was basically benign, its income generous and secure, and its mission clearly bounded, the BBC needed classic 'corporate strategy' far less than other organisations of similar stature in different sectors:[1]

> I think particularly in the BBC you had a culture where because the income had been growing by and large ... there was usually a bedrock of sustainable income growth and even though the licence was not being upgraded, then your income was growing. Because of that ... there wasn't a huge amount of long-term planning in the BBC. The strategy wasn't there.

> The BBC has not had this kind of planning process because it's been in a relatively protected market, and therefore you are seeing a lot of convulsions in the past few years.

The organisation's intellectual tendencies also militate against strategic action:

> We make them [strategic issues] very complicated. We spend ages debating the various subtle nuances, there are a lot of them, but I'm not

sure they're really that complicated ... one of the things the culture here is very good at is, to go back to Tom Burns ... is to discuss and debate, in an intellectual common room sort of way, but very little is set into action. There is a danger we do that, we become fantastic at analysing the competition, so we know that Microsoft, Disney and Time Warner and Berlusconi and BT are all different types of competitors – we don't do a lot about it because we can't quite work out what to do.

Cultural assumptions are credited with determining how an organisation perceives its environment and governing the strategies judged appropriate to respond to it. How then does the BBC's culture influence its response to its wider context?

This research suggested that those at the 'strategic apex' of the organisation, that is the top management, do feel themselves to be fully conversant with the dramatic environmental change taking place, and with the drastic measures that may be required to counter it (despite the 'restraining' influence of many cultural assumptions). They were, however, concerned that their understanding of the challenges facing the organisation might not yet have permeated throughout the entire organisation:

> For many of the strategic objectives that have emerged over the last three to five years ... one of the real difficulties of those objectives has been the absence of shared understanding as to why the BBC is going down those paths, and so if you talk about *Extending Choice*, the conferences, seminars and workshops that were held, people didn't understand what *Extending Choice* was, they didn't know what it was supposed to convey, they didn't appreciate the values the BBC was trying to develop, and it was this sort of mismatch between where the strategic intent of the BBC was and is, at its most senior level and what the vast mass of people in the BBC thought was the right thing to happen, perhaps this is inevitable in large organisations, it's just disconcerting in an organisation that is the premier broadcaster, or perhaps one of the premier broadcasters in the world.

> And yet, though this [digitisation] sits right at the edge of our future ... about to be part of us, and our strategy is built on it, we have a culture ... that enables us virtually to ignore that and for significant individuals in significant positions of authority, who should be fully versed in this sort of difficulty or opportunity ... actually see it as something distant, and I find that sort of thing troubling about the BBC; very interesting but troubling.

The 'balancing act' of reconciling environmental pressures, strategic demands and the organisation's core values may well be the core competence required of senior managers. For some, this was relatively effortless:

> The BBC news brand is respected worldwide, and in commercial terms it's exploitable worldwide, and we have a responsibility to the licence-fee payers in the UK to make sure that the UK division, the UK broadcasting division, is well funded, and one of the things we're going to have to do is make sure that we exploit our commercial assets, to move that money back to support the licence-fee funded services.

Others lower down in the organisation, whose roles were more creative than strategic, were demonstrably less traumatised by environmental developments, and dismissive of the organisation's emphasis on strategy. This gives rise to the suspicion that such individuals had chosen to handle environmental complexity by, effectively, ignoring it, by holding on to a mental picture of the world as it has always been:

Strategic initiatives. How do they impact the culture?

As far as I'm concerned not an awful lot. They impact on the producer very little, but the culture of lots of resource people who work in the BBC and have always worked in the BBC very much ... fine we've got cable and satellite as competition and we can think about going worldwide, but I actually think it doesn't make as big a difference as people think it makes ... All that's changed is that competition has grown and the means of dissemination, but ultimately it doesn't make a lot of difference whether you spew it out through an aerial or a satellite; the difference is how you pay for it, and as long as it goes on being paid for by the licence fee it won't change, and when it stops being paid for by the licence fee then it will change.

What's your scenario for that?

Not imminently likely to collapse, but ultimately possible ... I really don't know.

What do you think are the most important external influences?

Competition, purely that there's going to be a lot of channels. The technology will change things a bit, but I don't think a lot. Producers may do more things themselves, so what?

So you're pretty unconcerned?

Very unconcerned.

Alienation from strategy

When this phenomenon was discussed during feedback interviews, two possible grounds for such lack of interest were mooted. First, some within the organisation felt that strategic goals have not been well explained:

> Management generally are perceived as the harbingers of doom and gloom. Another problem is that a lot of this is communicated poorly. The message is communicated without the rationale.

Second, some expert interviewees suggested that the organisation's use of management consultants could be to blame, in that staff felt little ownership of, or commitment to, strategies described in terms of management jargon and developed by specialists who didn't really understand the industry or the unique characteristics of the organisation and its history:

> For thirty years McKinsey and other management consultants have been marching in and out of the BBC and ... they behave as if the company is just like any other company. All you have to do is install the correct processes, the correct systems, and by and large they tend to be insensitive, not only to corporate culture ... but extremely insensitive to non-economic issues.

It could certainly be argued that the assumptions underlying management consultancy are unlikely to gel with those at the heart of the BBC's culture. There was evidence of a certain hostility to consultants (and of an organisational 'habit' of walking out of their presentations):

> *How has that been received {i.e. a theoretical model used as a basis for climate surveys}:*

Oh, terribly.

> *Why?*

People become incandescent with rage at the mention. There's one famous occasion recently when the whole senior group rebelled, and refused to listen any more to any further talk about it.

> *What was the root of the rage?*

The root of the rage is that it is psycho-babble, and that bloody diagram is farcically complicated.

You bring in the efficiency experts for example ... I was invited to a meeting about efficiency that was scheduled for four hours. Well, I walked out after one hour. I said, 'This is not an efficient use of my time. If you were having a fifteen-minute meeting on efficiency then I'd be most impressed.'

Such hostility is not surprising, considering the differences in the respective industries' value orientations. Consultants measure the success of institutions in economic terms and are generally insensitive to soft unquantifiable issues. The BBC has only relatively recently, and with some difficulty, come to accept economic viability as one of the standards by which it should be judged. However, it is also possible to speculate that this hostility could result from the underlying cultural similarities between the two groups, from a clash arising when two élite professional groups, both highly educated, articulate, confident and accustomed to assuming a dominant position, are brought together to discuss issues concerning the fundamental activities of the organisation.

However, those responsible for the complex task of strategy development within the BBC felt that the use of consultants was unavoidable:

We've got currently working for us ... three or four sets of different management consultants, all doing different bits of the business. Why do we have them? Well, we have them because we are all doing full-time jobs, so you don't really have time to take the step back or the four steps back that are necessary to get the level of distance required to change the way you think.

Does the BBC's culture support its strategic goals?

The BBC's strategy was developed in response to three specific environmental 'triggers':

- the squeeze on the organisation's financial resources, arising from 'flat' income and rising costs
- increasing and ever better-funded competition
- instability and uncertainty – the combined implications of convergence, digitisation and unclear intentions on the part of the UK government towards the organisation.

In response to these factors, and the government's requirement that it become a global player in the media field, the BBC developed a five-pronged strategy: innovative high-quality programming (including new non-commercial services such as BBC Online), efficiency, commercial activities, world development, and alliances and partnerships. These represent an entirely logical response to the organisation's strategic environment.[2] Greater financial efficiency will relieve pressure on the organisation's finances and free up resources to invest in its non-commercial programmes and services, so that the organisation can maintain its market position in the UK better and compete with its commercial peers. The strength of the BBC brand provides an ideal platform for expansion into international markets and the growth of its commercial activities. The fact that the organisation's permitted sphere of activities in the UK, especially commercial activities, is limited, means it makes sense to concentrate commercial growth on world markets. Continued domestic funding, and its ability to fight off domestic competition and expand overseas, obviously depends on the organisation continuing to produce innovative high-quality programmes. Finally, since it cannot raise risk capital, and since its own funds are stretched, it can only expand commercial activities via joint ventures and alliances.

The strategy therefore was an appropriate response to the organisation's environment: there was a strong logic and coherence between these strategic goals and environmental pressures. The critical question asked by this study is how did the culture perceive the strategy? How well were the organisation's strategic goals accepted by its culture?

Innovative quality programming

There was no evident tension between the organisation's culture and its prime strategic goal, the production of innovative high-quality programming. Indeed, this was so integral to the culture that some staff did not even perceive this as a distinct strategic priority:

> I've stuffed the BBC strategic priorities. My priority is to make the widest possible range of high-quality drama in the knowledge that if we don't get drama right on BBC 1, we are the defining factor on BBC 1, then BBC 1 will be sunk; if BBC 1 is sunk, then that in the public perception probably means the BBC. BBC 2 is irrelevant, the radio stations, the symphony orchestras also in that context, only in that context, are also irrelevant, so it's the survival of BBC 1 with a substantial audience loyalty, and an audience out there that believes they get things they don't get anywhere else that is important, and if you then focus down, well what can you do about this? You can't mend the BBC, you can mend bits of it, and in mending bits of it you might mend the BBC.

Efficiency

The second strategic goal is greater efficiency. This too appeared to pose no conflict for the culture:

The audience is who we serve, programming is how we serve it, and efficiency is how we fund it.

Efficiency was perceived as a logical response to a tough environment:

It has to be cost cutting, there's no alternative to cost cutting, because there's nowhere else to go, so it has to be the most imaginative ways of cutting costs.

(Interviewee 1)

And trying to find ways of cutting costs that don't impact what appears on the screen.

(Interviewee 2)

Everything at the moment is going back to that dilemma, range diversity, serving different people in different ways as against fixed income – it's like working with an old-age pension really.

Nonetheless, the introversion and élitism latent in the culture militated in some ways against efficiency:

We are incredibly bad at understanding how others operate; there's virtually no understanding at all, for example, how Channel 1 produces programmes for £2,000 an hour.

Commercial activities, joint ventures and world development

The third, fourth and fifth strategic priorities can be considered together. All concern commercial activities, focusing on world development to be achieved via joint ventures and alliances. Here the BBC's public service ethos, its commitment to serving the British public, traits of anti-commercialism and insularity, and the low priority given to business activities generated tension between strategy and culture:

[We are] involved in trying to get a couple of hundred million pounds in through commercial activities, via enterprises and via world satellite services and all the rest of it, and it scares the pants off me, because actually it's diverting probably management attention and time from what is absolutely essential and what the UK viewer will only see as important, which is the services in this country. I don't know if the BBC can compete as bloody Heseltine and the others want it to as an international broadcaster, I'm not even sure that it's necessary for the BBC to compete as a major international broadcaster and channel operator, but it's in an economic bind that it can't deliver its home services unless we get more funding directly from the public purse, without becoming a major international operator and broadcaster.

> There's a lot of cynicism within the publicly funded part of the BBC about our commercial activities. I think there's a natural snobbery about anything to do with business generally ... in some areas people are rather cynical about the calibre of the personalities and the projects involved. It's very much a sense that Worldwide has to prove itself, demonstrate ... it's a first-class commercial media organisation.

Where there was acceptance of such activities, it was on the understanding that they are secondary to the core UK ones. No concessions were to be made for the needs of the other markets:

> [The BBC should] keep making the best programmes that it possibly could make in the most efficient way it could possibly make, and try to get it onto an international satellite and be a world-class player, and all that's funded by the British licence-fee payer, and presumably what you'd try to do is get some money back from the people you sold it to without reneging editorial control ... so the licence-fee payer has to pay less towards making the product with your primary market always being here.

In relation to joint ventures, cultural tendencies towards élitism and ethno-centrism, coupled with anti-commercial sympathies put the organisation at a disadvantage:

> Joint ventures and alliances – I think there is a certain élitism or cultural snobbery amongst some ... [but] in reality the BBC is very poor at having joint ventures and alliances in many areas, not least because we lack the business skills to do them well.

Culture's influence on competencies, strengths and weaknesses

Core competence: broadcasting creativity

The BBC's core competence, its broadcasting creativity, rests on an amalgam of creative, professional, technical, technological and behavioural compo-nents. While some of these are 'structural', arising out of the organisation's unique history and position – its protected environment, the creative mass provided by the scope and range of its activities, its tradition of recruiting the best and the brightest, and the length of time in which it has been able to experiment and learn – the majority of such elements could, albeit at

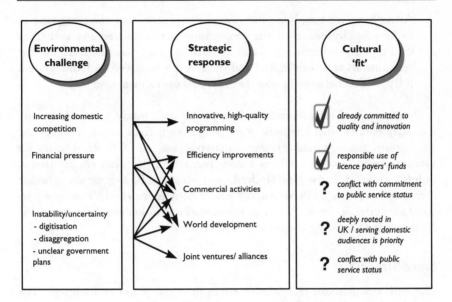

Figure 10.1 The 'fit' between the BBC's environment, strategy and culture

great expense, and with varying degrees of difficulty, be replicated by a competitor. What is not reproducible is the spirit that mobilises them, that catalyses them into a world-beating capability, and that is the emotional investment underlying the capability.

The BBC's commitment to excellence in programme-making runs deep and lies at the heart of its culture. It represents the sum total of multiple commitments: to improve life in Britain, to provide entertaining, stretching or stimulating programming for all audience groups, to preserve what is seen to be a great broadcasting heritage and to raise the craft of television to the highest form possible.

> I think there is a genuine commitment to fulfilling the mission ... I think that for all the change and all the catharsis and the restructuring and the redundancies and everything else, I think running through the organisation like a really strong cord is that commitment. If you do look at staff attitude surveys the one thing they say, throughout it all, [is that] they are deeply, deeply committed to the BBC.

And indeed, it was striking that while much discussion at the BBC was couched in abstract terms, laden with conflict, controversy and uncertainty, comments about programme-making were typically confident, straightforward and non-controversial.

> At its heart it's simply a collection of craft teams that come together to make programmes, then the programme is transmitted and then they disintegrate and reform ... and the BBC in its bones understands that relationship very well indeed and those teams were vertically integrated, fully unified between production staff and operational staff.

Programme-making represents the organisation's area of true mastery, and is fundamentally what the bulk of its people want to be doing. Perhaps the antagonism towards management initiatives and the lack of support for some strategic priorities reflects a deep frustration that staff are not free to indulge their true passion. (Indeed, it is hard not to question whether directing the organisational energy and resources currently consumed by strategic activities back into programme-making might not be a more efficient means of securing the organisation's future.)

Brand strength

The BBC's paramount competitive strength is the power of its brand. The organisation's culture contributes directly to this, via the support it channels into the core competence of programme-making. Simply put, the assumptions in the BBC's culture appeared to mobilise and motivate staff to excel at programme-making. The BBC's brand is so strong because it is backed by the organisational learning acquired through many decades of producing top-quality programmes.

> Somewhere at the back of all that there is still a sense of, with all the uncertainties and difficult changes and so on, [the BBC is] still maintaining its audience share in an incredibly competitive environment, still winning prizes all over the world, still genuinely respected as one of the best broadcasters in the world, and that sense of the name being known, the strength of the brand name.

Stakeholder complexity

Stakeholder complexity has clear links to the multifarious allegiances present in the culture, which is itself committed to many different parties at once: to the British public and to all the various minority and special interest groups within it; to its staff, because they are the source of its programme-making excellence; to the government, because it controls the licence-fee funding without which the BBC, it feels, would not be the BBC; and to the organisation's past, to the principles of operation, of strategy and purpose enshrined by Lord Reith:

The whole combination of those things means the BBC is not a nimble or dynamic organisation, it can't be, arising from all those things, the history built on the brand, the funding, the relationship with government, or the contract with government, and that is a major problem going forward, because if, as seems inevitable, the broadcasting market in the UK is becoming ever more dynamic, it is changing more quickly, new things are happening, new competitors etc. etc. The BBC must become more nimble, more reactive, more proactive, but I'm not sure the organisation really can because there are so many constituencies, it is so big, and there are so many complicated spins on any theme, most of which to varying degrees the ITV companies, Channel Four and certainly Murdoch, are not constrained by.

This meant that many strategic aspects of planning, such as scheduling, were far more complex for the BBC than for its competitors:

I tell you I've got to get a schedule together eighteen months before the budget stage which has 33 per cent regions, on the nose, 27 per cent hours of independents ... within the regional spend I've got to make sure that the national regions have 20 per cent of the money, and that's got to be split between the three national regions; you've got to do this within a cash framework, with all the complexities attached to that, and then you've got to get great shows on the air that are very competitive, that's the complexity. So if we were a commercial broadcaster we start from let's get great shows on air which are very competitive, but for us we got to start with our regional policy, this policy, that policy, and we can't borrow from the banks, and it's a very very complex task.

It's a hideously complicated organisation sitting in the middle of a complicated sector that is also changing very rapidly, so all these factors are multiplying on top of one another and on top of that I do get the impression, and I'm speaking still as an outsider, that the BBC is particularly hamstrung by a number of powerful constraints, both internal and external.

The requirement to be all things to all men (or all audiences) in an era of fragmenting markets and increasingly sophisticated consumer segments is a marketing requirement indeed. This is a concern to the organisation:

There's a risk of mediocrity. One thing I learned from my marketing background is that you cannot serve all markets all of the time, and that's precisely what the BBC's mission is, if you like, to offer every licence-fee payer something from one of the services, but it may be that in the end no organisation can function with that kind of mission, to serve everyone.

Bureaucracy

Just as the multiple relationships implied by the organisation's complex mandate and multiple commitments make its stakeholder picture inevitably complex, so too do they make a certain level of bureaucracy inescapable. The BBC's stakeholders are many and they pose incompatible claims. Conflict with such groups is only avoidable if these relationships are 'managed', which requires careful monitoring and analysis, regular briefings and skilled communication, which in turn requires specialist staff (in 1992/3 over 1,000 people were employed by the 'corporate centre'):

> An awful lot of things which people label as bureaucracy are the necessary things you have to have to manage the relationships.

It is difficult to be lean and mean while receiving public funds in return for fulfilling a complex mandate from the state. The organisation must account formally for how these funds are spent, and for the extent to which it fulfils the various criteria demanded of it by the government (e.g. independent production quotas). It must document these activities so that they can be formally audited:

> What we're all struggling with is to make sure that the sinews of the place, the bureaucratic sinews of the place, which are necessary, are much simpler; they're much too complex now, but they're complex for the reasons I've just outlined, you've got to hit all these targets ... the negative side which is bureaucracy, the civil service element ... I've been trying to strangle it by the throat in telly but it's still here, it reinvents itself, the capacity for baroque labyrinthine processes is still inside the place, because it's so big, partly because of all the responsibilities I was talking to you about.

An important part of the BBC's culture relates to its pride in its heritage, and its desire to keep this alive. Yet a heritage brings with it historic relationships and allegiances which add to those arising from its current strategic activities. Maintaining a heritage means contributing to stakeholder complexity:

> There are real traditional civil service type aspects of the culture which were very focused on process, on hierarchy, on the way we've always done things around here, on very traditional aspects of management, very command and control, the fact that until recently if you were a

programme-maker and you wanted to make a programme, you couldn't go and buy a studio as you could outside, you had to persuade someone to allocate one to you in Soviet kind of style and there was no mechanism, no concept of customer service, but a lot of aspects that you might find in a traditional university, say, of 'I'm essential, I have a right to exist. The country needs to support what I'm doing, and I'm going to sit here in an ivory tower and do what I like, because that's the way it should work.'

Weak marketing

The BBC was well aware of the growing importance of marketing. Increased competition, the need to fight for audiences and build its brand nationally and internationally, were together prodding many levels of the organisation to address the issue spontaneously:

> One of the biggest skills we've identified is marketing ... that is a very fundamental need for us. We've got a lot of good strategic planning and research skills, but the actual marketing skill has to be developed much more strongly.

> An underlying weakness is that we are short of really skilled marketing people, because we've not really been in the marketing business. The second weakness is the amount of money we have to spend. So however sophisticated and imaginative some of our campaigns are, they can't be sustained because of the cost.

To an extent this was seen as a natural extension of the need to serve the UK licence-fee payer, and therefore non-contentious:

> Marketing is definitely taken much more seriously than it was before when it was called Press and PR and wasn't really marketing. So there's that on a structural level. But there is also the fact that any producer has to be in touch with the audience otherwise he would make programmes that nobody would want to listen to, and I think there is a much greater awareness of that.

In discussions about marketing one metaphor cropped up frequently, that of 'blowing one's own trumpet' – an intrinsically negative idiom with connotations of self-publicising, of 'bad form':

We've never had to have that sort of markety [sic], jostling, we're not very good at trumpeting our successes actually.

Our problem is that people don't like us blowing our own trumpet, and viewers don't like it on their screens, they'd rather watch programmes than watch ads about us.

It is possible to conjecture that the BBC's culture would militate in many ways against a strong marketing function. If the organisation believed its fundamental purpose was to put its programme-making skills to the service of the UK public, anything that directed scarce funds away from such activities, especially into a 'purely' commercial activity such as marketing, would probably be resented. Further, the BBC is already intimately enmeshed in the fabric of Britain, so why waste resources advertising something with which the UK public is already familiar?

The figure below provides a graphic summary of the relationship between the BBC's cultural paradigm and key dimensions of its strategic profile.

Two dilemmas[3] in particular arise from the confluence of the BBC's culture and strategic priorities.

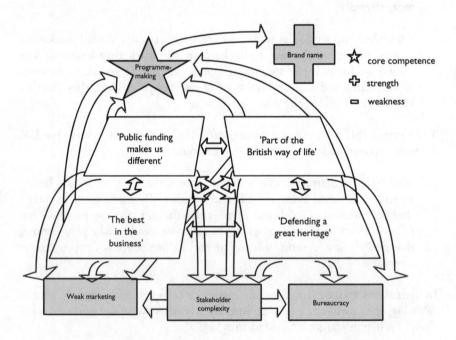

Figure 10.2 The influence of its culture on the strategic dimensions of the BBC

Dilemma: commercial activities undermine public service commitment

In view of the BBC's culture, it is unsurprising that the organisation's strategic aims in the area of commercial activities were contentious. The goal of increasing commercial activities raised conflict in many areas. These are shown in Figure 10.3.

Cultural objections

First, the BBC's culture had difficulty reconciling itself to commercial activities, which contravened many assumptions in its cultural paradigm – the public service ethos, the commitment to broadcasting 'for broadcasting's sake', the commitment to serving the UK public, and the commitment to the Reithian heritage. For many, commercial activities represented an inversion of the priorities the organisation had hitherto embraced. Organisational discomfort centred on a suspicion that acceding to commercial pressures would threaten quality, and was frequently expressed in terms of another metaphor,[4] that of 'the commercial tail wagging the public service dog':

> Again, it's a balancing act, because on the one hand the BBC has to try to exploit its assets to the fullest extent to supplement the licence fee

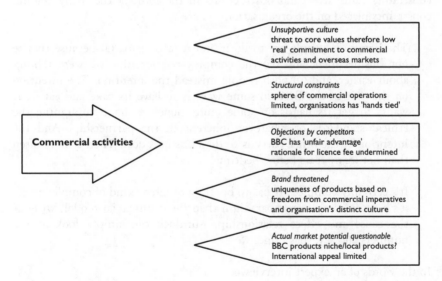

Figure 10.3 Tension between commercial activities and public service remit

with commercial revenue; on the other hand, you can't have the tail wagging the dog. We're not making programmes primarily for an American audience, and I think that any notion that we should concentrate our energies on programmes that are sellable, where the primary focus is 'would this sell overseas', would be quite wrong.

We are not in the business ... of finding a segment of the market which they will then provide a product to and make some money in the process ... we are in a different world.

There is a deep unease because I have described to you a culture of programme-making and an audience as centre of our activity. There is a concern that the commercial tail will begin to wag the public service dog.

There isn't a global culture within the domestic BBC. People think domestic programming for domestic audiences. We are funded by the UK for the UK and that's that. Parochial.

Structural constraints

An unsympathetic culture was one aspect of the tension arising from the organisation's commercial plans. But in addition to the attitudinal constraints came structural obstructions in the form of the many trading constraints placed on the organisation:

The danger is people try to do it and it falls apart, (a) because they're not businessmen, and (b) the complex relationships we were talking about earlier, and (c) both people misread the intention. The intention on the part of the BBC in some ways is to have its cake and eat it. It wants to get its hands on some more money without impugning the ethical standards or whatever inherent in the partnership. And the intention of the other party is to do a business deal. There's more often than not many tears before bedtime.

It's certainly complex. It has to be. It's a different kind of complexity ... it's a more complicated paradigm than the commercial model, without the cause and effect relationship. Murdoch can simply look at the numbers and say, that's fine.

In the words of an expert interviewee:

They can't really fight with both fists because they have to look for a set of values and ethics which inhibit them from cutting costs or making deals.

Objections from competitors

Further 'structural' objections came from competitors:

> If its job is to compete in the new media arena then [the BBC] has to change out of all recognition and must lose the licence fee, because if it's competing aggressively with everyone else, there's no reason why it should get a licence fee and we shouldn't.
>
> (Competitor)

> The extent to which we are successful {at using the BBC's own networks and channels for cross-marketing] is the extent to which our competitors cry 'Foul!' so that anybody thinking about the amount of money spent by the BBC on marketing will always pitch in the fact that your channels make a substantial contribution, and if we say too firmly 'You're right', then they say 'Well, that's not right.'

Brand undermined

A further aspect of the dilemma concerned the tension between the BBC culture and brand on the one hand and commercial strategic priorities on the other. The BBC's culture has traditionally reinforced its brand, whereby the deep commitment to broadcasting as a public good available to all, to serving the UK public, and to excellence in broadcasting combined to create a unique style of broadcasting, firmly anchored in national needs. The new strategy was perceived as threatening three key aspects of the BBC's culture, and some saw a direct conflict between building the brand and commercial activities:

> The brand that we are selling [commercially] is a brand that has become what it is because it hasn't had a commercial imperative ... what you are selling is the brand, and the brand is based on all those cultural attributes ... independence and non-commercial and so on. If you distort that then what you have to sell changes because it becomes more like other products, the more like other products it becomes, the less distinctive, and the less distinctive the brand the less attractive to buy, so the virtuous circle becomes a vicious circle.

Doubts about feasibility and potential

Doubts also existed about whether the organisation could become a profitable competitor in global media markets:

> People ... particularly politicians, but [also] some people who ought to
> be more thoughtful, think that there's this great bonanza that somehow
> English, British television companies are not tapping, and that's just
> complete bollocks.

Some felt that the BBC's expectations in this area were optimistic:

> My own private view is that it has to be very careful about making the
> mistake of assuming that the universality of the English language in
> some ways is equivalent to a desire in the world for everything in
> Britain ... There may be an interest in the world purchasing, if it can
> afford to do it, a version of the world different to the CNN version of
> the world, but that's separate from the world wanting to buy
> programmes that are intended for the UK market.

> Just appearing in a BBC uniform doesn't work any more.
>   (US expert commentator)

This point was also raised by CNN, which is finding it a challenge to
generate revenue from overseas markets (to date no pan-European television
channel is profitable):

> It's a niche market at the best of times, ... a niche market with niche
> advertisers which are not that easy to get at.

Reconciling the dilemma

The organisation's route to reconciling tension between commercial and
public service activities was to set organisational priorities by which the new
commercial activities were secondary to the public service domestic ones. In
this way it hoped to win internal acceptance for its commercial plans:

> I think the understanding that our commercial activities will derive
> from our public service objectives is a critical part of getting acceptance
> for the commercial activities. The public service ethos drives the
> commercial activities in terms of ... the products that are produced
> must have some relationship with the programmes from which they are
> derived, the public service purpose underlies those programmes.

Underlying this was a realistic attitude (perhaps more so than that of UK
government policy-makers) about the potential offered in overseas markets:

> Commercial activities, world development, joint ventures and alliances
> are only a means. It's not our job to compete with Murdoch and Time

Warner on the international stage, nor are we going to. Anyone who says that doesn't understand the world market for television, doesn't understand the risks we take, we are not going to do that ... So why do we do it? We do it because it generates income for the licence-fee payer. But we're not doing it to bring better programming for the PBS audiences in the US or bring a breadth of British culture to the Australians. That's not our job. We do it because we get money selling the ancillary rights to our programming and that reduces the costs and enables us incidentally to fund better and more programmes ... they are secondary [markets] in both senses. They are a secondary objective and they are secondary because they are run off the back of our UK domestic broadcasting production.

It should also be stressed that since the BBC identified commercial activities as a key growth area it has achieved notable successes, particularly in the areas of consumer magazines nad video.

Dilemma: licence fee – doomed source of revenue and motivation?

The second major dilemma was posed by the licence fee. This not only provides over £2 billion in revenue each year, but also acts as a powerful source of intrinsic motivation. The fact that the BBC is publicly financed and operates in the public interest led to high involvement and performance at all levels in return for moderate financial compensation. It engendered creative energy, high levels of professionalism, and an innovative, award-winning standard of programming.

What we are about is providing a classic public good, we are a protection against market failures, in the provision of education, entertainment of a superior kind, news of the highest quality, drama of the widest range.

Equally, though, licence-fee funding is, as bankers would put it, no free lunch. In return for this revenue the BBC must effectively be all things to all men. It must explain itself constantly (as evidenced by the plethora of strategy, policy and other publications). It must cater for all needs, and maintain an extraordinarily wide span of output to the highest possible creative standards. It keeps the organisation's focus squarely on domestic markets, while committing it to the delivery of top-quality programmes across an enormous range and simultaneously developing into a global media entity – all against a backdrop of falling revenues.

The opportunity cost of such funding is therefore significant. This is a cost that competitors do not have to bear, and can, if they are clever, with judicious lobbying and a few well-judged press reports, even increase.

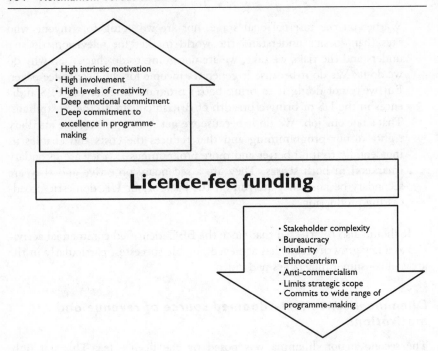

- High intrinsic motivation
- High involvement
- High levels of creativity
- Deep emotional commitment
- Deep commitment to
  excellence in programme-
  making

Licence-fee funding

- Stakeholder complexity
- Bureaucracy
- Insularity
- Ethnocentrism
- Anti-commercialism
- Limits strategic scope
- Commits to wide range of
  programme-making

Figure 10.4 The licence fee – source of cultural strength and organisational
weakness

The more closely the BBC is analysed, the larger looms the conundrum of its funding – and the strong feelings associated with it. This issue will become ever more pressing. In an era of pay television and digitisation, the licence fee is increasingly anachronistic.

If the licence fee is abolished, and if at the same time the BBC's unique role of serving the entirety of the UK public is diluted with a requirement to provide niche channels for domestic and international audiences, two assumptions of its cultural paradigm are effectively negated. Important components of the internal justification which pushes people to perform at the levels they do will disappear, and there is a risk that much of the organisation's uniqueness will evaporate. Elements of the psychological contract[5] between employees and organisation will have been breached. The threat this poses was referred to frequently by senior-level interviewees:

> I think there's a great deal of unease, and nobody would deny that it's a difficult thing to do; critics would argue that there are two possible problems. One of them is that the public service organisation stops being public service when it starts to become aggressively commercial, and the other one is that the public service organisation is by its very

nature ill-equipped to be successful commercially because it has hired people who reject those principles.

Public service status has been one of the things that enabled employees to ride out the radical changes within the organisation. Its removal could have a detrimental effect on motivation at all levels. The question then becomes whether an alternative organisation concept can be found which motivates employees to perform at the same level as before. This is not a straightforward task, since there appears to exist an inverse relationship between financial rewards and motivation:

> By paying them more you would lose the motivation. Once you say, 'We can buy your commitment' then you would lose it, because people want to believe their commitment is above pearls.

Development of an 'apex' culture?

The BBC has always been an organisation primarily focused on the art of broadcasting, and the individuals who rose to the top of the organisation were drawn from the 'charmed' and élite circle of successful producers. Management skills were not highly valued, and those occupying purely administrative or managerial roles were generally rather low in the organisational hierarchy. However, research indicates that in recent years the complexity of the strategic task within the organisation has led to the development of an executive 'élite' at the top of the organisation, in which expertise in strategic issues is concentrated.

What is interesting about this new 'apex' group is their sophisticated understanding of the management task and emphasis on improving management practices within the organisation, not because they believe in management *per se*, but primarily because they see this as a means of improving its creative output. This group therefore appears to have achieved a 'counter-cultural' shift in its attitudes towards management, and added a managerial and executive expertise to its creative skillbase.[6]

This makes them a formidable group, and also exclusive. Membership is 'invitational', normally through involvement in task forces assembled to develop and drive through strategic initiatives, such as ensuring the renewal of the Royal Charter, or co-ordinating a response to the challenges posed by digital technology:

> *Programme Strategy Review* was all the best programme-makers in the BBC coming together in a kind of parliament of programme-makers.

This 'élite' group is therefore exposed to environmental challenges and dilemmas very different from those which face the rest of the organisation. It could be argued that in the course of resolving these, a subculture is developing which contains a set of tacit assumptions about issues of mission and strategy which differ from those shared by the rest of the organisation.

Conclusion

This chapter looked at how the BBC's resolutely Reithian culture responded to the strategic priorities of the Birt era and the dilemmas and contradictions that surrounded the organisation's programme of strategic change. It explored tensions between the organisation's intellectual tendencies and management initiatives, between public service and commercial activities, and between the deep commitment to licence-fee funding and the ever more prevalent norm of commercial funding in the UK broadcasting sector.

Chapter 11

Adrenaline

Culture's impact on performance, process and strategic options at CNN

How does CNN's culture influence its ability to respond to its environment? How does it affect business practices and priorities? This chapter explores the degree of synergy between CNN's cultural values and strategic goals, and the extent to which its culture predisposes it to cope with the current broadcasting environment.

The starting point for analysis was the observation that CNN and its culture are products of environmental change (albeit less dramatic developments than those currently under way). Consequently, and unsurprisingly, there was little evidence of cultural 'tension' about environmental upheaval. Culture and environment seemed broadly in alignment, and there appeared to be a widespread understanding of the environmental pressures shaping its strategic direction:

> Those companies, those leaders, those executives, who look at all of these developments as opportunities to shape the information flow, to control the ideas in circulation within their spheres of influence – well, those people will be leaders tomorrow. Those among us who remember the past – and even the present – with more fondness than it deserves, will be left behind.
>
> (Tiven, 1993)

This is not to say that the organisation was not aware of the velocity and breadth of impact of the changes under way:

> ... the speed of change, the technologies are changing, the content, the nature of the players because the regulatory agencies have shifted the field ... So everything's changing at once. It's like being stuck in an earthquake.

But there was a latent confidence that the organisation was equipped to deal with them:

It's a bit of a race right now. Fortunately we're already out there. Distribution is going to be very difficult for our competitors. As we say, the price of poker has just gone up.

Deliberate 'ad hocism'

An interesting facet of the impact of CNN's culture on the strategic aspects of the organisation was that it predisposed the organisation to disregard formal strategic planning (an activity which it happily left to its parent). This could have stemmed from its desire to break moulds and do things differently, from its immersion in the world of news, which means a concurrent focus on real time, on action rather than analysis and on short time horizons. Whatever the root, it promoted flexibility in the organisation. Unblinkered by complex menus of strategic priorities, staff were more exposed to the environment and better able to respond to environmental uncertainty – and opportunity:

> There is a certain impermanence that comes [when] the environment keeps changing, you've no guarantee that whatever you've built yesterday is workable tomorrow. That's been a part of our thinking and our attitude.

Perhaps because of its self-styled outsider position and maverick nature, CNN felt no need to create a façade of strategic rationality. This freed it to respond vigorously and laterally should the need occur. Such an opportunistic approach has a long heritage within the organisation:

> Consider if you will the brilliance of Turner, which was to go into cable television as a programmer in 1976 and then in 1980 with CNN, at a time when there were about 18 million cable homes in the United States. Today there are about 63 million. The sheer growth of subscribers was likely to throw off lots of revenue. Consider the brilliance of a rapidly expanding business ... a 400 per cent increase in size in a fifteen-year period, not too shabby. At the same time the universe of channels, while it went up significantly from twelve to thirty-six or from twenty to forty, didn't go from twenty to two hundred. So while the cable universe is exploding, the number of people who could compete with you by creating new channels, and the distribution problem of getting global distribution, is a significant inhibition on competition.

Culture's support for espoused strategic goals

During the research period, CNN's strategy sought to address two environmental threats. The first was increased domestic competition, for at least four organisations announced plans to challenge CNN's supremacy in news. The second was industry instability – convergence between media, telephony and computing was at a more advanced stage in the US than in Europe. In response, CNN developed three strategic priorities:

Continued global expansion

Further global expansion offered a way of consolidating existing strengths, and was in some ways a wider application of existing competencies – newsgathering on a global basis and repurposing. Unsurprisingly, there was little conflict with cultural assumptions.

> Programmes like *World Report* establish the value of our connections with the World Report contributors, from whom we get news, which helps fill our airtime and supplies us with pieces of the world in terms of newsgathering capabilities.

Expansion globally requires corporate readjustment. In line with its functionality, the organisation approached such tasks from a practical perspective:

> If you want to have an international agenda you really have to look at how you localise your themes, how regionalised you are going to be, what kind of people are you going to hire to be on air ... correct means regionalisation of the signal. How do we create a really internationalised, sectionalised news agenda? If we are going to regionalise our news programming, what does that mean in staffing, in personality, in osmosis into the culture?

Development of new businesses

Equally, this strategic goal posed little conflict. CNN's achievements had long been rooted in exploiting new developments. Its associations with new technology are positive. Like its host nation, CNN's culture embraces the new, and the organisation tackles challenges with the customary underdog mentality and fighting spirit:

> They're talking about in this country in five or ten years' time there'll be five hundred channels ... So if we as a company say, 'Okay, we've got our five networks right now, we're ready, we're in a good position', that would be naive, because even if these other channels get only a few people to watch, they're still going to break down our total numbers of viewers. So we will make a conscious decision that ... we need as many

networks or stations as we can ... In other words, if somebody is going to take away viewers from CNN, it might as well be us.

Questions about new business areas yielded further evidence of how deeply inculcated the concept of repurposing is at CNN:

What is your scenario for the future? What should CNN be thinking about?

How to remarket the products in new ways.

Indeed, three key assets – brand, infrastructure and a commitment to repurposing – provide a powerful basis for expansion:

We create new networks very cost-effectively because we are able to utilize not only the CNN brand, but also the infrastructure that was put in place for CNN, CNN International and CNN Headline News. We create new networks at very low incremental costs.
(Tom Johnson, Chief Executive Officer of CNN, in Time Warner, 1997)

Strengthened domestic programming

However, CNN's objective of shifting more emphasis towards scheduled programming certainly offered the potential for tension. The cultural commitment to news militates in many ways against the development of strong programme schedules:

CNN networks are all news 24 hours a day. We may have some commitment to running circus shows like 'Larry King Live' which we don't easily push out, but by and large we are news.

Indeed, underlining the organisation's commitment to, and identity with, news, open-ended questions tended to be answered in terms of news:

How do you see this industry developing?

Again, we have to be careful we don't ever lose track of what it is we do, and that is cover the news, that's our responsibility.

If you wanted to make this organisation ideal, what would you do?

I mean we cover the news. All the goals and all the money should be focused to cover the news the best way we can.

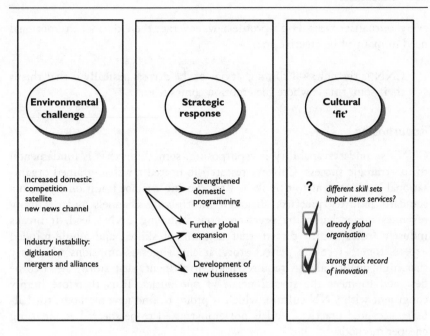

Figure 11.1 Assessment of the 'fit' between CNN's environment, strategy and culture

Culture's influence on capabilities, strengths and weaknesses

CNN's chief capability is its skill at covering breaking news. An analogy given for this was the following:

> To discern and gather on a global basis, video and information about major stories of interest. It's not unlike a wholesale greengrocer whose skill is getting the right vegetables and keeping them fresh and selling them while they're fresh.

Chapter 7 discussed the physical aspects of the organisation (distribution and news infrastructure etc.) and professional skills (real-time decision-making) that are important components of this. Analysis of CNN's cultural paradigm demonstrates how the unconscious beliefs at the heart of the culture supported and reinforced this competence as strongly as did the more tangible aspects of the organisation. For CNN staff news delivered adrenaline, fame, and the chance to make a difference to the world. In its commitment to the news CNN tapped into the main artery of the journalistic culture, allowing its employees to achieve the goals that lie close to every journalist's heart. High-profile news coverage therefore met an emotional need in many of its creative staff.

> CNN is the news – I think that one of the drivers basically is that this is their soul, this is where the emotion comes from.

Repurposing

CNN's secondary capability is repurposing, something that is fundamental to its strategic success. Cultural research indicated a well-ingrained organisational commitment to this skill. Repurposing has not traditionally been a standard industry practice, although multiplying channels and declining revenues mean that many peers are now following CNN's lead. It breaks industry 'rules' which dictate that a group of skilled and single-minded experts together craft a perfect story; it challenges assumptions which say that high quality always requires high investment, that stories need to be designed to meet the special needs of one outlet. It is therefore highly congruent with CNN culture, which is proud to find new methods, to challenge accepted practices, and is not embarrassed to be sneered at for using cheaper methods:

> It's part of this culture, it's part of the CNN culture, because CNN is driven by this theory of leverage and synergy between its companies and its products, because of the way that you take a product. If you take a basic CNN product, all that news that's coming in, all the raw footage, the sound, and you think 'How are we gonna take it, how are we gonna make a pie?', so you're cutting one cost of bringing it in, and you are basically cutting a pie which lessens the original cost. And it's how you make more money out of the original costs. So you do radio, you do videos, you do airport channels, you do CNNI, you do schools, you do text, all the things that can leverage it, and give it more financial value.

CNN's commitment to repurposing appears to have infected its new parent, Time Warner:

> Don't look to us to take our cash and stock and make a big acquisition. Our philosophy is to leverage our infrastructure.
>
> (Gerald Levin[1])

Brand strength

The relationship between CNN's culture and the strength of its brand is self-evident. Its brand strength rests on its capability at breaking news. Its dedication to breaking news is firmly embedded in the deepest aspects of its culture.

> It's a news network. It's expensive to cover Bosnia. It's expensive to cover presidential campaigns when they're flying all over the place, but we do it to maintain our credibility, because all that we have is our brand.

> It's all we have, our integrity and our credibility, that's all we have and it's what the name implies. That's it. Lose that and we've lost a lot ... And it's supported by the quality of our information. And quantity in our case because we're seven days a week, 24 hours a day.

> Because what do you own but your brand? In essence what does CNN own but its brand name?

Weak scheduled programming

CNN's difficulties with regular scheduled programmes also proved to be closely linked to its culture. Again, it is self-evident that a business system geared to news, which is by definition unpredictable, is not conducive to the long-term development of scheduled or 'appointment-based' programming:

> CNN has to find ways to make our product watchable ... we're very cyclical, when there's news that affects a lot of people, people tend to watch ... somehow we have got to find a way to get people to watch all the time ... Somehow we have to fight to maintain the eyeballs.

Seeking to move into a more conventional style of programming, something which has always been the province of 'traditional' television organisations, raised many different conflicts. CNN's cultural energy comes in part from its view of itself as a pioneering outsider; but is it pioneering to do exactly what the networks have done for decades? Second, it requires a very different editorial approach. CNN's news programming is characterised by its attempt to create an adrenaline-rush with attention-grabbing news drama. Scheduled programming, by contrast, is more directed towards entertaining, relaxing and distracting viewers (Bosshart, 1990: 53).

A further problem is associated with the fact that scheduled programming is focused around 'stars' – high-profile individuals whose personalities draw audiences. CNN has always chosen to give star billing to breaking news.

Ratings 'binges'

Uneven ratings can also be seen as an indirect outcome of its culture. The culture is dedicated to news, and to a television formula fundamentally different from that of the conventional networks, which are entirely focused on maximising advertising revenue. By being different, by 'majoring' in news, CNN is bound to jeopardise its advertising revenue, although its alternative revenue streams, from subscriptions and repurposing, help to cushion it from extreme 'binges'. This is a concern, but not a primary one:

> But what we've done is ignore the advertisers, advertisers who find our content unattractive don't need us and we don't need them. We're perfectly willing to just pre-emptively not deal with certain people.

Low-browism

This again could be seen as stemming directly from aspects of CNN's culture, for it is an organisation which places viewer attractiveness at the top of its list of priorities. This inevitably means presenting material in a way that achieves maximum impact, which in turn means concentrating on action rather than analysis, on the moving or the shocking at the cost of the important (but perhaps worthy and boring). Further, if all material is prepared with an eye on repurposing, there will be an inevitable urge to keep it general and multi-purpose.

Figure 11.2 provides a graphic summary of the relationship between CNN's cultural paradigm and key dimensions of its strategic profile.

Research indicated one key area of tension between CNN's espoused strategy and its underlying cultural assumptions.

Dilemma: news versus scheduled programming

In many ways, CNN's cultural commitment to news and its strategic ambition of improving its scheduled programming could be viewed as mutually exclusive. If you are an organisation dedicated to, and whose audiences expect, round-the-clock coverage of big breaking stories, you cannot afford to 'clutter' channels with fixed, immovable scheduled programmes. By concentrating completely on news, by building a newsgathering infrastructure unparalleled worldwide, CNN has created a multi-billion dollar business. It has also virtually committed itself to uneven ratings, problems with fixed schedules, accusations of sensationalism and unattractiveness to advertisers:

> There is a sub-problem here, which is that we want to strengthen our domestic programme schedule. Everything tells us that outside of this

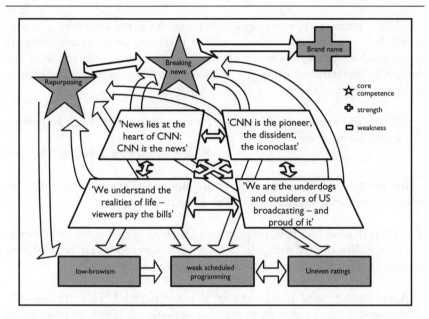

Figure 11.2 The influence of culture on the strategic dimensions of CNN

breaking, just-in news, you need appointment-based programmes that have a special shape and content. How can you do that and make it important if every time the shit hits the fan, as we say in English, you throw out these programmes? 'The programme XYZ won't be seen today because we've got this continuing coverage of a bomb threat in Abu Dhabi', or wherever we are. How can you reconcile being a 24-hour news channel with the need to put in programming posts, mileage markers, that tells people where they are in the day and when they can watch?

News and scheduled programming are fundamentally incompatible. Until now, CNN has stayed firmly with the news, understanding that this is intrinsic to its success formula:

> There was a story a couple of weeks ago when we went wall to wall, we covered everything that could possibly happen on this story, and the BBC covered it, and then said, 'And now World Service brings you the fashion show', and they went off and did a half-hour fashion show because that's what was in the schedule. They did not for whatever reason think that the story was big enough to stay with it, and we did ... But we understand that we're in the news business ... when you see breaking news you get on it and you go with it for as long as possible.

CNN's strategy to move into scheduled programming (the category 'scheduled programming' includes within it drama, documentary, comedy) represented a significant change of direction, one that conflicted with the culture by inevitably diluting the organisation's focus on news. The organisation was aware of this:

> These are appointment-viewing programs, but our most important appointment is with breaking news.
>
> (Rick Kaplan, President of CNN/US[2])

Its solution was to try and create appointment-programming that upholds the culture and keeps the news focus intact:

> What'll limit the new programmes [is that] they'll have to be news-driven. We created a couple of pilots that never made air because they didn't feel right, they didn't fit within a news environment.

Appointment-based programming also threatened CNN's traditionally modest cost structure, and its position as underdog outsider. Appointment-based scheduled programming is high-budget, and the mainstay of the US networks. It also requires conventional broadcasting skills outside CNN's then sphere of capability:

> What we used to do was cheap and cheerful and we knew how to do it. To get appointment viewing you've got to have resources and you've got to spend money ... it's a different kind of marketing, different kinds of people. A person who does news, a minute and a half, is not necessarily a person who can produce and do an hour.

> The new skill sets require, for instance you need a big studio, which we're building a $2 million building, you need sets ... different kinds of talent, instead of news deliverers news readers, you've got people who are hosts ... who drive a programme rather than the content driving a programme – fewer of them and they're higher dollar – and it takes a different kind of producer.

Onset of cultural ossification?

Analysis suggested that CNN was in the fortunate position of experiencing little tension between culture, strategy and environment. Cultural perceptions of the environment were fundamentally empowering, and, apart from the area of scheduled programming, deep-seated cultural assumptions were broadly in support of its strategic intent.

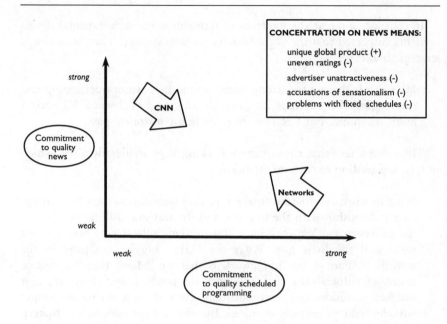

CONCENTRATION ON NEWS MEANS:

unique global product (+)
uneven ratings (-)

advertiser unattractiveness (-)

accusations of sensationalism (-)
problems with fixed schedules (-)

Figure 11.3 Tension between news and scheduled programming at CNN

CNN's strong culture developed in response to a particular set of circumstances – internal and external. Many of these circumstances have now changed: it is established, profitable even, has merged with a media giant with deep pockets, and the organisation's founder is less involved with the business. As has been demonstrated, CNN's culture predisposed it towards action, towards aggressive responses to environmental developments. Some feared, however, that the culture could also be failing to keep in step with the changing organisation:

> I think that one of the places where CNN might be stuck today is that I'm not sure we all share exactly the same mission ... I think that we've probably got to the stage where we need to redefine our mission.

There is some tension, rooted in a certain nostalgia for the 'Chicken Noodle Network' day, that if CNN becomes a more traditional-style major league player its unique culture might ebb away:

> As we get bigger, as we become more established – I've been here since 1981 – I can see less and less of this. From the early days, where you just shot from the hip, you just did it, we're becoming more corporate.

In contrast, some at the forefront of responding to environmental developments suspected that the organisation's cultural strength risks becoming a strategic brake:

> My sense is that a very strong norm around here is not questioning and challenging the way it is ... that's the dilemma of 'I was a VJ once. I know it's dumb, but I don't want to do in my historical past.'

There was a fear that the culture was being kept artificially alive, which in turn was leading to cultural ossification:

> We still work very hard to make sure that we position ourselves, in our own relationship with the universe and the way our colleagues relate to the universe, as, 'We may be a 700-million-dollar-a-year business but we're still the little guy. We're the littlest biggest company in the world!' ... Part of our framework is that we believe there's a certain degree of vulnerability that goes with the product, and therefore ... it surfaces in underdogs and outsiders even though we're no longer outsiders and we're really overdogs. But that is a convenient way to keep everybody's focus, to in effect pretend that we are underdogs and we are little guys.

CNN's continued use of the underdog term was curious. Even before its merger with Time Warner, which made it part of the largest media organisation in the world, CNN had established itself as a leader in news broadcasting, and one of the best-known media brands worldwide. The fact that it continued to describe itself as an underdog, despite ample evidence that it was fast becoming the overdog, gives rise to the suspicion that the underdog concept was functioning in the same way as that of Reith does at the BBC, as a useful fiction that motivates and unifies.

Conclusion

The influence of CNN's culture on its strategic activities was the subject of this chapter. It explored the synergy between CNN's cultural values and strategic goals, and the way in which these beliefs predispose the broadcaster to ride out the environmental turbulence arising from convergence and underpin key aspects of its competence profile, particularly its core competencies such as repurposing. It discussed how the organisation's self-styled 'outsider' status and maverick approach deter it from too heavy an involvement in classical strategic activities, and help free the organisation to respond vigorously, laterally and opportunistically to environmental developments. It also looked at the close connection between its mindset and uneven ratings performance and explored the tension generated by its goal of increasing the amount of fixed scheduling programming. The conclusions to be drawn from this and the previous chapter about the specific challenges of managing media organisations can be found in the next, and concluding, chapter.

Chapter 12

A special case?

Why media organisations need managing differently

What, if any, lessons can be drawn from this study for those managing media organisations? What can be learnt about corporate culture's potent influence on strategic activities in broadcasting organisations? Why do many management prescriptions not translate into a media context?

This book has explored the special challenges associated with managing media organisations. In particular, it has sought to reveal how the unconscious beliefs shared by managers at the BBC and CNN – their underlying convictions about the meaning, function and purpose of their professional activities – shape those organisations' strategic developments, and affect responses to their strategic environment. As a conclusion this chapter presents a number of general insights arising from the investigation into these two organisations.

Precision required in conceptualising culture

The first point concerns theoretical understanding of the relationship between strategy and culture. This research suggests that theoretical approaches are imprecise from a number of different perspectives. First, they approach the subject from the wrong vantage point. The tendency is to overemphasise the potential 'up-side' or benefits that accrue when the two elements are in harmony, when the real point at issue, the area where the strategy-maker's concern should centre, is on the negative aspects of the relationship, on the 'dis-' benefits that result if they are not aligned.

Culture is first and foremost a potential constraint on strategy, and it appears that an organisation's strategic processes and priorities can only extend as far as culture 'permits', unless action is taken to resolve the tensions that result when strategic activities push outside the 'boundaries of action' pre-ordained by the culture.

This can perhaps be best understood by using Schein's analogy of organisation culture as equivalent to the personality, or even the psyche. Forcing a 'culturally unacceptable' strategy on an organisation is equivalent to asking an individual to do something that is against his or her deepest ethical principles. A politically astute individual might seek to ignore or circumvent the requirement. If co-operation is forced, resentment will ensue, and the individual may well, consciously or subconsciously, subvert the activity. The only option is to encourage the individual to change the mindset, alter his or her principles, but this cannot be done by force. It can only be done by persuasion, by explaining the necessity of the action in terms of the rationale behind it. In organisational contexts, exactly the same process applies.

(Incidentally, this conclusion has particular relevance for policy arguments[1] about what should be 'done with' the BBC, particularly for proposals that it should be split up and privatised. This study would indicate that these proposals are simply not an option. Such a step would negate many of the deep-seated cultural assumptions which underpin the quality of its output. This would in all probability have a negative effect on the quality of its output, which in turn would depress or even destroy the 'value' owned by shareholders.)

Culture need not be a 'hidden' force

The second area of imprecision relates to the understanding of the fundamental nature of culture itself. Lurking behind virtually all writing on organisation culture, whether popular or scholarly, is a suggestion that culture is an almost mythical entity, indisputably powerful but essentially 'unknowable'. Thus for best-selling business books, culture is a magical ingredient that can turbo-charge strategic initiatives, but which only charismatic leaders know how to harness – indeed, this ability counts as a qualifying criterion for such descriptions (see, for example, Peters, 1992). Theoreticians rightly dismiss such simplistic functionality, stressing in contrast the complexity, subtlety and pervasiveness of the phenomenon, but they still tend to describe culture in terms of an 'invisible force', a mysterious and all-powerful hidden element of organisations (Morgan, 1986; Tichy and Sherman, 1993).

A conclusion to be drawn from this study is that while the culture of an organisation probably can never be revealed in its entirety, charting an organisation's underlying cultural assumptions pertinent to a specific issue is both entirely feasible and surprisingly straightforward, provided access and co-operation are forthcoming, and resources (financial, temporal and analytic) are adequate. In this study, the ease with which underlying cultural assumptions were accessed, and the quality of organisational insights they yield, surprised both the researcher and researched. Culture need not remain a mystical hidden force.

However, while this study provides empirical evidence that culture is accessible, it also demonstrates the essential irrationality of culture, and by extension, of the strategic decisions it influences. On the basis of this study it can be argued that the actual processes of environmental analysis and strategic evaluation are highly irrational and very different indeed from the rational approaches promoted in classical management theory and used by classical management consultants. This fact may go some way to explaining both why only a fraction of formally developed 'rational' strategies are ever implemented (less than 10 per cent according to Mintzberg, 1994), and the poor uptake of strategies produced by external consultants who do not share the organisation members' underlying cultural assumptions.

Culture is context-dependent and non-predictive

A further conclusion to be drawn is that great subtlety is required in identifying the innate characteristics of a culture and in extrapolating from these prognoses for the future – whether for a particular organisation, or for organisations in general. Indeed, it could be argued that an organisation's culture is unique and so complex that it is simply not possible to issue the type of generalised portmanteau 'culture recipes' frequently found in management literature.

For example, Moss Kanter (1984: 149–51) describes the benefits that accrue from a:

> culture of pride ... based on high performance in the past, [where organisation members] feel they belong to a meaningful entity ... can realise cherished values by their contributions ... and pride creates a self-reinforcing upward cycle – performance stimulating pride stimulating performance.

In the organisations studied by Moss Kanter, these traits were wholly positive. By coincidence, all feature prominently in the BBC's culture. However, translated to a different context, they are less than positive, contributing, amongst other things to insularity and inflexibility. Ironically, Moss Kanter contrasts such 'cultures of pride' favourably with 'cultures of inferiority', which are characterised by looking outside the company for innovation rather than inside it. It is interesting that one of the most powerful and constructive elements identified in CNN's culture is its sense of inferiority, its 'underdog' mentality which spurs it towards extremes of competitiveness, creativity and risk-taking.

It can be argued therefore that not only is every culture unique, with unique strengths and unique weaknesses, but that what constitutes a strength or weakness in a particular culture is context-dependent. Pride is a somewhat negative characteristic at the BBC, inferiority a positive one at CNN. Attempts to draw out general rules from specific cases must be made with care.

Culture and learning

CNN's culture exhibits a high tolerance for uncertainty, and as Schein points out (1993a, b), cultures that embrace uncertainty are inherently more adaptive. This raises the issue of culture's relationship to organisational learning.[2] It can be argued that one of the strengths of CNN's culture is that it predisposes the organisation towards a style of learning that is not simply adaptive, but 'generative' (Schein, 1995), which is characterised by learning new ways of perceiving and thinking about problems.

Indeed, it can be asserted that unless the assumptions direct organisation members to work, look, and reflect in a 'generative' way, the presence or lack of any other skills or resources which might normally be expected to promote such approaches are strategically irrelevant. Consider the BBC, and the sense of alienation from strategic matters and environmental issues that was highlighted by this study. To anyone unaware of its cultural paradigm such findings are surprising. This is an organisation inculcated with a journalistic ethic of open-minded investigation, with a staff of high intellectual calibre. Why does the spirit of investigation and innovation not permeate through from programme-making to strategic activities? Why is its outstanding innovation and creativity applied primarily to programme-making rather than to organisational issues as well? The answer, of course, lies in the culture, its tendency to look inwards and backwards and to belittle management-led imperatives.[3] Equally, how can CNN realistically persist in seeing itself as an underdog outsider on a permanent battle footing, when it has long been one of the world's most well-known and successful news organisations?

Table 12.1 defines and contrasts culture's impact on environmental adaptability at the BBC and CNN.

Table 12.1 The impact of culture on environmental adaptability

	CNN	BBC
Learning orientation	Generative	Adaptive
Attitude to change	Opportunistic	Questioning
Temporal orientation	Future	Past
Geographic orientation	Global	Domestic
Strategic approach	Empiricist	Rationalist
Starting point	Action	Analysis
Self-appointed industry position	Underdog, outsider, anti-establishment	Dominant player, élite, establishment
Assessment of output	'Cheap and cheerful', but the best news programming there is	When on form, 'the best' there is
Attitude to financial matters	Financially pragmatic	Money matters, but quality of programming matters more

Environment is key to resolving strategy–culture conflicts

There is thus a high cost to be borne when an organisation's culture is unsympathetic to its strategy. The critical question then becomes, how can a culture be reconciled to a 'counter-cultural' strategy?

While recognising that developing practical recommendations for the resolution of strategy culture conflicts is outside this study's remit, it is possible to speculate how this task could be approached. Two approaches in particular would seem to justify further exploration.

First, research indicates that a 'generative' approach towards organisational learning, coupled with strong environmental awareness, could be the key to successfully introducing counter-cultural change. An understanding of the environment is critical to ensuring that culture does not strangle strategy: if an organisation is seeking to improve coherence between strategy and culture, its starting point should be to improve awareness and understanding of general environmental developments, not of specific strategic responses to them. Energies should be directed to ensuring that members of an organisation understand the environmental rationale for strategy (and not the nuts and bolts of the strategy itself).[4]

The picture of CNN that emerges from the research is of an organisation which is highly sensitised to changes in its industry structure, and which consequently accepts the strategic priorities that emerge. By comparison, during the research period, BBC interviewees were acutely aware of changes in the existing structure of the UK's broadcasting ecology, but less informed about international developments, or about domestic developments actually outside its own sector but which would nevertheless have a serious impact on it.[5] As a result, the organisation's then strategic priorities were resented as the capricious whim of a management who 'don't understand what the organisation really represents', rather than an uncomfortable but necessary response to a potentially devastating set of external conditions. Some organisation members had difficulty separating strategy (an internal element) and environment (a combination of external forces) and so much energy and expertise was devoted to explaining and justifying proposals, the strategic logic of which was strong. For those involved in leading the organisation, in developing strategic priorities and in communicating them, the priority would therefore appear to be to develop understanding of the context, rather than the content, of strategies.

The second, and perhaps more controversial, proposal is that organisations seeking to limit tension between strategy and culture should limit their sphere of strategic activities to environments appropriate to their culture, or, to put it crudely, that organisations should seek markets that suit both their products and their cultures. In this sense, it can be argued that the nature of an organisation's culture delimits not only its general strategic scope, but also the territorial scope of that strategy.

CNN is an international organisation to its core. It exhibits little affiliation to its national broadcasting scene; its identity and activities are directed internationally. It has carved out a successful niche producing international news products for international markets (disregarding qualitative debates about the content of those programmes). It can do this with such panache and enthusiasm because its culture totally supports such activities. The BBC's core activities concern programming and other services for UK markets. It can do this to the standard it does because the organisation feels deeply committed to serving the UK licence-fee payers to the best of its ability.

Yet both companies are currently seeking to shift market focus: CNN wants to move into mainstream-style US programming, and the BBC is placing priority on international expansion. Neither of these moves is supported by the organisation's respective cultures. CNN defines itself as a news machine, whose practices, systems and technologies are outside the mainstream US television industry. How will these processes, and the unique values inherent in its culture, support traditional appointment-based programming? The BBC produces high-quality programmes with great editorial depth and a somewhat idiosyncratic British flavour for UK audiences. Its unique capabilities and organisational sensibilities predispose it for niche, high-quality markets. Viewers abroad are of course valuable, but chiefly as a means of generating extra revenue to improve domestic services (which overseas viewers will probably ultimately receive also). 'Abroad' therefore is primarily a market for material originally conceived for domestic audiences.

Founder as 'official interpreter' of environmental developments

Theorists such as Schein emphasise the role played by the founder of an organisation in laying the foundations of its subsequent culture. The cultural analyses conducted for this study support such assertions wholeheartedly – the personal beliefs of John Reith and Ted Turner are perpetuated to a surprising degree in the organisations they created.[6]

This study argues that one strategically critical aspect of culture is the environmental adaptability it bestows. In the case of these organisations, this characteristic can be traced directly back to their respective founders, whose beliefs still provide what is effectively the 'official interpretation' of environmental developments.

In both the BBC and CNN, the vision and foresight of their two extraordinary founders, Lord Reith and Ted Turner, created path-breaking organisations which have made a unique contribution to the development of broadcasting.[7] However, it can also be argued that, whereas the cultural values inherited from Turner are strategically enabling, those deriving from Lord Reith are, in the context of the organisation's current competitive environment, strategically disabling.

In strategic terms the BBC's Reithian legacy is a ball and chain of heroic proportions. Although a powerful motivator and a unifying myth, it narrows strategic thinking and commits the organisation to supplying something that it is increasingly unable to provide:

> You can't imagine that's the kind of thing that worries Rupert Murdoch when he gets out of the bathtub in the morning; he doesn't say 'Jesus, I can't throw the shop away, what will they say? I'll be the man who ruined Reith's ideal', which must go through the minds of successive Director Generals. Whereas Rupert Murdoch gets out and says 'Who am I going to eat today?' It's a very different view of the universe.
>
> (Expert commentator)

Commitment to John Reith's heritage is a big factor in organisational resistance to strategic change:

> One of the things that is most resented at the BBC is the rubbishing of the past by Birt, because we are but our past, and if we had enormous pride in the BBC, we have pride in the BBC because we thought what we were doing was good and proper and we believed our own propaganda to an extent, which I know is dangerous, but nevertheless, then when somebody comes along and says 'you know, nonsense, terrible, frightful, fix and fudge and Byzantine rules and so forth' and the programmes probably weren't much good either, then people, not unnaturally, get fed up.

Within this context, Reithianism and all it stands for becomes a barrier to change. Yet representing, as it does, a fundamental element of the culture, it cannot simply be discarded. This raises a fascinating strategic and communications challenge, that of 'remodelling' or updating a cultural myth. Can Reith, and the associated concept of public broadcasting, be 'reinvented' for the coming media age? Isn't the challenge for management to recreate Reithianism into something that will unify and motivate the organisation to excel in the new broadcasting world order, as surely as it did the last?

Just as many aspects of the BBC culture – commitment to public service, commitment to the UK – derive clearly from Reith, so too can many aspects of CNN's cultural paradigm be traced back to Ted Turner. These include its maverick, outsider, underdog philosophy, as well as its appetite for risk and opportunism:

> All of it ultimately goes back to Ted, who was sort of the ultimate underdog who came from behind and fought and scrapped and was made fun of for years, because he had this risky idea, initially, that turned out to be not nearly as risky as people thought it would be. I

think we take that mentality with us, that we are sort of still an outsider compared to, say, the three broadcast networks.

Within CNN, Turner appears to have taken on an almost mythical dimension:

Yeah, it's kind of omnipresent, I mean it's just Ted.

Ted Turner is a visionary, he is absolutely a visionary. And if you were in his presence and you were smart you would understand he's thinking at a level beyond where most of us will ever be.

From this comes an intensely personal – and emotional – commitment, unusual perhaps in a business context:

I mean, Ted's a whack job, he's a crazy man. But he's our crazy man, and we love him! He's our crazy mother-fucker, okay?

I love Ted. I think he's probably a bit off the wall in many respects, but he's certainly a great motivator, he takes care of his employees, the benefits that he gives his employees are better than most companies, he cares about his employees, and he gives us the freedom and flexibility to produce.

I can connect this all back to Ted and I know I work for Ted, and ultimately Ted is the driving identity, he's the one who drives this maverick pioneer image.

Both figures are men of their time: Turner, with his maverick mind, international focus, penchant for high-level networking and extreme competitiveness coupled with an almost naive idealism; and Reith with his deeply ethical devotion to the belief that broadcasting is a medium which should serve and improve the public. It is, however, hard not to conclude that in Turner CNN has a more appropriate figure to lead them into the new broadcasting age than does the BBC with their principles inherited from Reith. However, CNN's commitment to Turner and his vision of broadcasting could also become a potential barrier to future change. It is hard to conceive of CNN without Turner, yet he must inevitably weaken his links with CNN, either as a result of his larger role within Time Warner or even because of his political ambitions.

Culture as 'emotional capital'

So far discussion has concentrated on the power of culture, its potential to act as a negative influence, and its ability to constrain strategic activity, to place limits on organisations. But culture is, of course, not simply a negative entity. The cultural paradigms presented here demonstrate again and again that culture is also a motivator, an enabler, a liberator of organisational energy. For both the BBC and CNN, their core capabilities and competitive strengths are deeply rooted in their cultures, in some senses springing from their cultures. Their cultures are the emotional engines of their strategic successes. CNN would not be the world's best-known news organisation without a culture dedicated to producing the best news programming, nor would the BBC have maintained its exceptional programme quality during a decade of organisational turmoil were there not a deep cultural commitment to its professional standards and public service ethos, whatever disruption the environment (or management) might throw up.

In these cases cultures are also assets: they add value to the organisations. This raises an important issue. How can organisations be coaxed to take more consideration of something that contributes so directly to success? How can they be made to understand that an organisation's culture can represent an irreplaceable strategic asset, a real source of unique and irreproducible added value? How can they be made to understand that positive 'emotional capital' is as important strategically as 'intellectual capital' or straightforward financial capital? It is easy to speculate, but very difficult to prove, that careless damage inflicted to the positive aspects of the culture of an organisation will impair performance, and bring tangible, negative, financial repercussions.

Creativity, motivation and culture

The next question is, how does this cultural value work at an individual level? Equally, how does tension between culture and strategy surface in individual members of an organisation?

This book provides some clues about the way in which these elements interact. The mechanism appears to be connected, in some way, with intrinsic motivation. When a strategy is in harmony with the underlying commitments and priorities of the culture, then organisation members are motivated, mobilised to implement or realise that strategy. When a strategy conflicts with assumptions in the culture, the opposite occurs: intrinsic motivation is 'demobilised', and employees lose their motivation. Culture inhibits the organisation's response to the strategy.

Creativity and innovation are central to the future strategic development of both the BBC and CNN. Within this context, Amabile's (1988, 1990, 1993) work on the relationship between creativity and motivation raises a number of pertinent issues.

First, Amabile draws a distinction between creativity, the production of novel and useful ideas by an individual or small group, and innovation, the successful implementation of creative ideas within an organisation as a whole, stressing that the two are closely interlocked systems. This study's findings suggest that the BBC, with its pedigree of producing highly original broadcasting across all genres, excels at individual or small-group creativity. CNN, in contrast, manages to promote both individual or small-group creativity – as demonstrated by its unique approach to news – and organisational innovation, as shown by its ability to invent new organisational systems and structures (e.g., the VJ system and its co-operative network of affiliates). This raises the question of what is preventing the rampant creativity in programme-making areas of the BBC from translating into wider organisational innovation.

Second, according to Amabile, the most important, and most neglected, component of creativity – the critical component of motivation – is what she terms 'intrinsic task motivation'. It is critical because no amount of skill in other areas – factual, technical or creative – can compensate for lack of task motivation. Intrinsic task motivation is therefore essential for individual creativity. However, intrinsic task motivation is also dependent on environment (used here in the sense of the individual's work environment, rather than in the strategic sense of factors outside the organisation). In other words, specific features of an organisation determine an individual's intrinsic motivation to complete a task and therefore determine his or her creativity, and changes in environment can substantially affect individual motivation and creativity.

Factors that enhance or promote motivation and therefore creativity include the freedom to decide how the task or goal is to be accomplished, good project management (defined, amongst other things, as protection from unnecessary management distraction or interference), sufficient resources, encouragement and enthusiasm for new ideas, and various organisational characteristics, including a corporate climate marked by co-operation and collaboration across all levels and divisions. It is noticeable how many of these factors have been identified as being present at CNN: high levels of personal autonomy, lack of bureaucracy, organisational flexibility, a desire to do things differently, a track record of breaking received wisdom, a high tolerance for risk, and relatively high levels of funding.

Factors that inhibit motivation and therefore creativity include excessive red tape, a corporate climate marked by lack of co-operation between divisions, a lack of freedom in deciding what to do or how to accomplish the task, insufficient resources and an overemphasis on the status quo. It is equally striking that many of these features are present at the BBC, which suffers from bureaucracy, a highly complex government mandate and broadcasting remit, stretched financial resources, and an inability to shake itself free from the shackles of its heritage.

It can be surmised that high levels of intrinsic motivation, already present in BBC staff, coupled with their high levels of technical and creative skills, enable the organisation to maintain programme creativity – because programmes are the product of an individual or small team. However, the great number of environmental factors that inhibit creativity are preventing such individual and small-group creativity from being converted into organisational innovation.

Two conclusions can be drawn from this. First, reduced organisational creativity and innovation are, ironically, part of the opportunity cost the BBC is paying for being licence-fee funded, since, as has been established, complexity and bureaucracy are an inevitable outcome of its publicly funded status. If it wishes to become as innovative as an organisation as it undoubtedly is as a programme-maker, it must seek to restructure, reduce or eliminate these elements that inhibit creativity. Second, CNN has happily, through luck, good fortune or insight, created an organisation which naturally promotes many of the factors leading to high levels of organisational (if not programming) innovation and therefore creativity. However, many of these aspects are not shared by Time Warner – a complex organisation with a long and chequered history. CNN's continued creativity and innovation may rest on its ability to insulate itself from aspects of its new parent's nature.

If intrinsic motivation does provide part of the answer to the problem of mechanism, the next issue is one of 'therapy'. This study has underlined both the relationship between creativity and motivation, and the importance of creativity to the strategic success of these organisations. Can a better understanding of employees' intrinsic motivation be used to improve their acceptance of radical strategies and reconcile conflicts between strategy and culture? To what extent can motivation be 'manipulated', so that culturally unpalatable strategies can be made acceptable? Research findings from this study suggest that extrinsic motivators (greater creative exposure, bigger budgets, higher pay) would not be effective compensation for the absence of intrinsic motivators, but findings clearly do suggest that all strategies should be scrutinised in terms of their implications for intrinsic motivation, so that problems similar to those highlighted here can at least be anticipated.

Use culture to provide strategic leverage

If culture's influence on strategic processes is as powerful as this research suggests, then a clear implication for those involved in strategic processes is that they should base their activities, and their approaches to achieving change, on a 'knowledge' of their culture and the potential restrictions and leverage points inherent in it. The goal should be to 'work with' culture in matters of strategy, rather than develop the strategy and then confront the issue of how cultural acceptance is to be won. Organisations should actively seek to capitalise on the latent benefits of a culture, to use it to provide leverage to strategic performance. One analogy is to see culture as a garden with a specific type of soil. It will automatically nourish certain plants, (that is, certain strengths or competencies will thrive), but new 'plants' (capabilities, priorities, goals) need to be implanted with care, and the soil (culture) may require special 'preparation' before they can take root.

The first step in this process must be to know the organisation's culture, through the deliberate investigation and analysis of the unconscious assumptions that govern it (not simply of the surface attitudes making up the climate) and of the organisational implications of these assumptions.

Correlation between organisation and national culture

This study argues that those involved with strategy should take steps to 'know' their organisation's culture and use this knowledge to inform strategic processes. On the basis of the organisations studied here, an assessment of national cultural characteristics might serve as a helpful shortcut. The similarities which emerged during research between the cultures of the organisations and their host nations were striking. Corporate cultures appear to be fractals of their national parent. For postmodernists this will come as no surprise, for it is a typical example of subsystem-mirroring, which holds that there are a few basic structures and dynamics within any system that are replicated again and again in all subsystems as well as in the overall system (Bergquist, 1993).

Thus the BBC, like the UK, is struggling to come to terms with the end of an empire, the passing of a golden age, and seeking perhaps to play a larger role than its resources allow. The self-perception which developed during its days of glory is preventing it from coming to terms with the present and with future challenges. Similarly, CNN's culture is pure 'frontier spirit' and reflects the differentiated individualism, free speech and proactivity which are central values in US management (Lawrence, 1995). Its attitude to change echoes that of the US as a whole: change is normally associated with improvement and is therefore to be welcomed. CNN, it could be argued, is seeking to conquer new geographic frontiers and spread the gospel of independence, just as the American pioneers did centuries ago.

This has interesting organisational implications. Just as an organisation's sphere of strategic activity is constrained by its culture, so, it could be argued, is an organisation's culture bounded to an extent by the culture of the host nation, unless the issue is explicitly addressed. It is, for example, questionable whether CNN and the BBC could have developed in any other nation than their host country. Disregarding the fact that a dominant publicly funded television organisation would be anathema to American sensibilities, the US's commitment to the free market, to letting the customer dictate, and the belief that everyone's views, regardless of education level, ostensibly at least, carry equal weight, mean it could never have played host to the development of a broadcasting organisation which uses income from the masses to subsidise minority tastes, which felt for many years empowered to steer and direct public taste, which takes risks in the name of broadcasting art, even if it means alienating the audiences who have paid for the programmes. And the BBC's unquestioned skill at programme-making mirrors the national aptitude for creating highly original cultural products from advertising to pop music (one of the UK's major exports since the 1960s).

This has implications for companies seeking to 'import' strategies and working practices from organisations in other lands. For example, in an era of convergence, no media company can be ignorant of the benefits of 'repurposing', an activity CNN has raised virtually to an art form. It could be argued that the components of repurposing can be broken down into two categories: tangible aspects (such as distribution and organisational infrastructure, multiple outlets) and intangible aspects (such as organisational acceptance of the concept, expertise in creating 'repurposable' material, skills in cross-function communication). The first category of components are relatively easy (if expensive) to assemble by a media organisation anywhere in the world. The second, the intangible elements, are perhaps less easily created. Successful repurposing requires a specific set of attitudes and interpersonal skills. It requires flexible, easy, direct and fast interpersonal communication. Staff must feel empowered to ignore existing boundaries, overturn traditional work practices, and ignore industry divisions between different types of media. They must also, since different nations have different sensibilities, accept the concept of media as a 'window', not as an 'interpreter'. The attitudes and behaviours that support repurposing are, it could be argued, to a great extent already embedded in the US culture, which stresses approachability, casualness, and the necessity of remaining open to new ideas (Lawrence, 1995). US journalists do not share their German peers' belief that a central element of good journalism is lengthy in-depth analysis. It is difficult to envisage how countries favouring a hierarchical and formal work culture would be comfortable with the behavioural approaches required to implement repurposing successfully.

Broadcasting policy dilemmas

Although the research was primarily concerned with the management of broadcasting organisations, rather than their output, in practice it is impossible to divorce 'business policy' from 'broadcasting policy'. In the world of broadcasting, organisation strategy is intimately related to programming strategy, and a broadcasting organisation's ability to develop a clear strategy for its programming activities is complicated by a number of policy dilemmas intrinsic to the industry's current environment.

Broadcasting organisations are struggling to set and hold a course in a maelstrom of environmental change. Deregulation, new technologies, changing social attitudes and increasing competition have combined to dismantle the existing dominant paradigm of broadcasting, and to undermine a broadcasting ecology that had existed for decades. The strategic task for broadcasters is to devise effective responses to a cocktail of complex environmental changes, including disaggregation, convergence, digitisation, gateway control and a massive increase in the number of channels and therefore in competition. However, as consumer choice has increased, and the public service paradigm has been overtaken by a vision of multi-channel national broadcasting systems, the uncertainty surrounding key assumptions that underlie the activity of broadcasting has increased. Is it an important and influential part of societal infrastructure, or simply a market commodity? Are viewers citizens in a democratic society or just consumers in markets? Should broadcasting be regarded, and regulated, as a public good which contributes to the health of society by strengthening democracy, building social fabric, stretching public minds, and shaping sensibilities, attitudes and outlooks, or simply considered as an ephemeral source of relaxation and entertainment, a commodity available according to one's ability to pay?

As market forces look set to establish themselves as the dominant influence on broadcasting systems, a dilemma arises in the suspected inverse relationship between competition and quality. Quality within the context of a broadcasting system is of course a subjective term, but few would dispute that diversity is an important component. While increased competition appears to have created a range of broadcasting choice that is greater in volume terms than at any time in the past, many are concerned that choice does not automatically equal true diversity. Ostensible choice has increased, but real choice has telescoped, as more channels broadcast an ever narrower range of identical material, aiming always for the biggest audiences. The fear is that competition drives players to do the same but better, rather than to experiment.

In addition to diversity, a more obvious component of quality concerns the editorial and creative approach to what is broadcast. There is clear evidence that increasing competition for audiences coupled with talent inflation (vast increases in the fees charged by leading creative individuals) have combined to encourage programme-makers to concentrate on the formulaic and sensational. Where broadcasting systems were once characterised by a small number of competitors interacting repeatedly with one another, and sharing the same public-service-derived values about the kind of material that could be shown, in today's competitive climates such restraints are impossible to sustain; there is 'too much at stake and too many loose canons on the periphery' (Frank and Cook, 1995: 199).

A drop in programming standards, coupled with television's undeniable ability to shape public attitudes and moral sensibilities raises larger concerns. Followers of the total quality movement would claim that quality is determined by the customer – that quality means 'delighting' (Deming, 1986) customers by giving them what they want. Wants, however, are to a large extent shaped by the culture. If culture is shaping consumer taste, and market forces are shaping culture, then the market is simply fulfilling the desires it has itself created (Frank and Cook, 1995: 6; Grade[8]). A vicious circle is created whereby what we watch influences our tastes, and our tastes in turn affect what we are offered. The concern is that the impoverishment of television programming, created by an increase in competition, will, ultimately contribute to an impoverished society.

Lead or feed? Increased choice and programming strategy

For broadcasters seeking to fill their schedules, such issues are encapsulated in a dilemma which could be described as 'lead or feed?' Both of the organisations investigated for this study claim the same mission: to serve the public. However, different organisation cultures, reflecting also different national cultures, mean that an identical mission is interpreted in different ways, and as a result gives rise to very different priorities, structures and processes.

For CNN, 'serving the public' means giving the public what they want, even if this doesn't quite reflect the tastes of broadcasting professionals – the public after all knows best and viewers are the ultimate arbiter. The

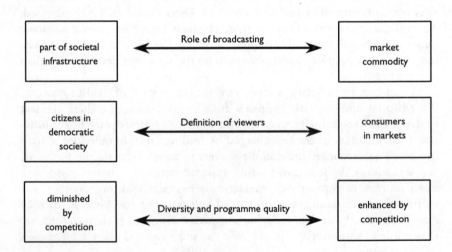

Figure 12.1 Broadcasting policy dilemmas

organisation sees its core task as catering for the existing public appetite for news, and in the process maximising audiences and thereby revenues. To do this it needs to 'seduce' viewers by making its news as attractive as possible – which in the context of CNN has traditionally meant more immediate, more global, more 'live'. In organisational terms this places a priority on the ability to react fast, on good audience feedback, on rapid production turnaround (even if production values are a bit rough and ready), and on quick communications, internal and external. For staff members it creates an atmosphere of action and excitement (an 'adrenaline buzz'); for viewers it means an emphasis on immediacy rather than on high production values, and a concentration on the mass market.

For the BBC, imbued with the Reithian ethos, 'serving the public' means giving viewers what the organisation's experts judge to be best, for how can the public be expected to demand beforehand a product that only specialist skills can develop? The BBC therefore has traditionally sought to stimulate an appetite for its programming, accepting that this means at times 'leading' public taste, since the public cannot be expected to evaluate output which is designed to stretch them, and people may need 'training' before they can truly value the BBC's products. Thus the reference group of broadcasting professionals is industry peers, not the audience. Such an approach is only feasible in an organisation with guaranteed resources and control of its own schedule, which brings with it the freedom to take creative risks, to place a premium on high production values, and to spend lavishly when necessary; it depends on the luxury of long time horizons and the freedom to build audiences slowly. It leads to high intrinsic motivation, a high-quality product, and a concentration on the mid-market.

Table 12.2 Organisational implications of programming policy

BBC: 'Leading public taste'	CNN: 'Feeding public appetite'
Needs: (emphasis on existing technologies)	*Needs: (emphasis on newer technologies)*
Long time horizons	Ability to react immediately to breaking news
High budgets	High investment in technology
High production values	Fast production turnaround
Maximum control of schedule	Maximum control of schedule
Freedom to take creative risks	Freedom to interrupt any programme
Freedom to build audiences slowly	Rapid audience feedback
Guaranteed resources	Good communications, inside and out
Creates:	*Creates:*
High intrinsic motivation	Adrenaline buzz
Greater value for audiences	Greater immediate interest for viewers
Concentration on the mid-market	Concentration on mass market

CNN's and the BBC's underlying programming missions have therefore traditionally occupied exactly opposite positions on the spectrum of 'serving the public', and over time these have come to be supported by appropriate organisation structures, processes and priorities. An intriguing aspect of the organisations' respective current programming strategies is that they are required to move along this spectrum towards each other. Both are seeking to adopt an element of the other's programming paradigm. However, a relatively straightforward shift in programming policy could, on the basis of the discussion here, require corresponding shifts not only in culture but also in core processes and priorities.

Enabling versus disabling cultures

While it may not be possible to derive generally applicable 'cultural recipes' from specific organisational examples, heavily influenced as they are by particular characteristics of an organisation's heritage and environment, it is perhaps possible to gauge from the culture the difficulty an organisation may have in terms of adapting effectively to its environment, especially when that environment is characterised by dynamic and discontinuous change.

What appears to be critical is not the presence or otherwise of particular attitudes or values, but the culture's overall orientation towards its environment, its predisposition towards the world outside. This study would argue

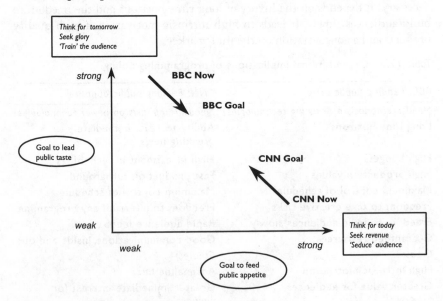

Figure 12.2 Lead or feed? The impact of increased choice on programme strategy

that, in terms of influencing strategic processes, the significant issue is whether the culture is environmentally 'adaptive' and therefore 'enabling', promoting an orientation towards learning and self-development, or 'unadaptive' and therefore 'disabling', causing an organisation to insulate itself from its environment. (In this sense, perhaps, the true weakness of approaches such as that of Moss Kanter lies in their inward focus, their preoccupation with culture's impact on internal activities, ignoring the equally important issue of how the culture causes the organisation to interact with the larger system in which it finds itself.)

It is clear that the cultures analysed in this study influenced the organisation's ability to respond strategically to environmental developments. For example, it is striking to see how CNN's culture promotes an open-minded hands-on 'give it a go' approach, while the BBC's mandates a long period of selling the concept and winning acceptance before new strategic initiatives can be introduced.

Culture, therefore, can be strategically enabling or disabling. It can predispose an organisation towards growth, or towards inertia and organisational decay; it can prime an organisation to flex, adapt and master its environment, or dismiss, ignore, underestimate developments and subvert the strategies developed to respond to them; it can direct an organisation to accept, promote and even enhance environmentally appropriate changes in strategic processes and priorities, or to subvert them.

Crudely expressed, culture can have a negative or positive influence on strategic processes. So what determines the nature of culture's influence? How can it be kept positive? Unsurprisingly, the critical issue appears to be the nature of assumptions at the root of the culture. The cornerstone of an organisation's ability to adapt is the paradigm of underlying assumptions that the organisation members carry with them, which determines how environment is perceived, and defines both the organisation's self-image in relation to that environment and the 'allowable sphere of operation' in terms of interacting with that environment. It is these underlying values that predispose an organisation to learn, to be open, to adapt, to perceive the environment without distortion. These values control whether existing assumptions are reassessed and modified and new assumptions allowed to develop as necessary.

Opportunity cost of dissonance between culture and strategy

It is axiomatic to suggest that if an organisation's culture offers unalloyed support for its strategic processes, and if those processes represent an optimal response to environmental demands, then a powerful foundation has been laid for exceptional organisational performance. This research does not claim to prove or disprove such claims but it does, however, provide evidence of

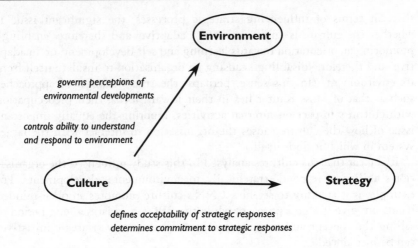

Figure 12.3 The influence of culture on strategic processes

the organisational implications when there is imbalance between such elements.

Somewhat inevitably, the example is the BBC. For decades it was in the fortunate position of enjoying a stable environment (characterised by protection from competition and high levels of guaranteed income). Its strategy was correspondingly fixed and focused, concentrating primarily on delivering high-quality programming to UK licence-fee payers. A stable environment, consistent strategy and market success, coupled with high national prestige and an élitist recruitment policy, gave rise to a powerful culture, driven by shared values of dedication to quality, innovative output, to public service ideals, to serving the UK and to preserving the organisation's unique heritage for future generations. A 'golden scenario', where environment, strategy and culture were in harmony, gave rise to what the organisation describes as its 'golden years', when it enjoyed unparalleled success as one of the world's leading broadcasting organisations.

However, the radical contextual change during the 1980s and 1990s destroyed the alignment between these factors. The BBC found itself for the first time both in a real marketplace, one that was commercial, global and multi-channel, and at a disadvantage *vis-à-vis* competitors. Changes in the environment forced a redefinition of its mission, goals and the means by which those goals were to be achieved.

Radical change required a radical strategic response. The BBC shifted gears, introduced an internal market (*Producer Choice*, 1991), forced producers to focus on a wider range of viewer needs (*Programme Strategy Review*, 1992), set up new divisions to reap the benefits of commercial exploitation of

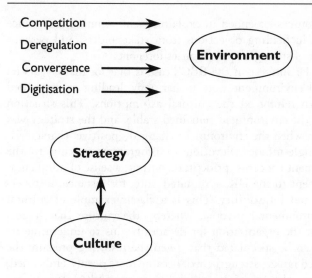

Figure 12.4 Radical environmental change destroys alignment between strategy and culture at the BBC

existing assets and to run international channels, and reorganised to cut administrative overheads and position the organisation for technological developments (*A Structure for the Digital Age*, 1996). Thus strategy and environment were 'realigned', and the assumption appears to have been that culture could be correspondingly brought into line, through the judicious application of management development interventions and internal communications initiatives.

However, despite such activities, the new strategic initiatives were poorly received by the prevailing culture. Not only did the new strategy countermand many of its intrinsic beliefs and values, but this was aggravated by the fact that many staff, because of the strength of the culture, had little understanding of the environmental developments which necessitated such radical responses. The fact that some of the strategy development task was 'outsourced' to consultants meant that many within the organisation were not privy to the underlying reasoning processes, and had limited exposure to the underlying environmental rationale for strategic change (indeed it is hard not to speculate that the 'cultural resistance' to consultants was in fact a 'transferred' resistance to the content of the strategic changes the consultants were explaining – suggesting that no amount of jargon avoidance or verbal sensitivity on the consultants' part would have reduced the organisation's hostility towards them).

As the diagram below shows, the result is that environment and strategy are in harmony with each other but in conflict with culture. The opportunity cost of such dissonance between culture and strategy is significant. It takes the form of resources expended in explaining and winning acceptance for strategic change, in fielding objections from stakeholders, and perhaps ultimately in the cost of strategic opportunities foregone.

A point of particular interest in the BBC's case is that for many years its culture, strategy and environment were in harmony, leading to continued success which in turn reinforced the cultural assumptions. This situation continued as long as the environment remained stable, and the strategy was unchanged. However, when the environment changed, 'positive' characteristics – such as a single-minded devotion to programme-making to the exclusion of management concerns, pride in its output, a sense of uniqueness and a deep commitment to the UK – 'mutated' into, for instance, introversion, ethnocentrism and inflexibility. This is a classic example of cultural success creating environmental myopia, whereby the culture that underpinned the success of the organisation for decades begins to undermine its survival. Indeed, it can be speculated that given the resulting pressure the culture actually 'closed ranks', strengthened, became more deeply embedded, thus further weakening the organisation's ability to respond to its environment.

Culture, strategy and the way forward

Perhaps the key general conclusion to be drawn from this research is that the culture of broadcasting organisations exerts a significant influence on their strategic priorities and processes, indeed that within broadcasters, culture's

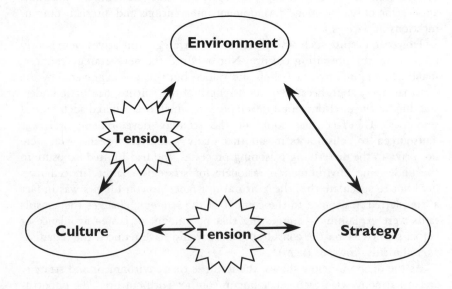

Figure 12.5 Dissonance between culture and strategy at the BBC

impact on strategy is pivotal. Culture does not preclude strategy, but it develops and shifts more slowly than strategic imperatives do; it is culture therefore that governs the rate of uptake of strategic imperatives. Culture not only governs how environmental developments are perceived, but also defines the acceptability of strategic responses to those developments, and, by extension, determines the level of commitment to achieving those responses.

Thus far, the research broadly conforms to the prevailing theoretical view, that culture has a potentially powerful impact on strategy. Where it diverges from prevailing academic understanding, however, is to suggest that theoretical assessments of culture's influence on matters of strategy greatly underestimate the potency of that influence. The 'latent power' epithets that are typically used to describe culture's potential impact on strategy do not adequately describe culture's power. Culture is far more than the 'starting point' for strategy. On the basis of the evidence presented here, it can be argued that culture effectively prescribes strategic activities, and that, in principle, the strategy of an organisation can only 'extend' as far as the culture will allow it.

Consider the organisational difficulties which have surfaced in relation to the BBC's attempts to move into international and commercial arenas, and CNN's intentions to develop 'appointment-based' scheduled programming. In both cases there are genuine 'stumbling blocks' in terms of tangible issues such as resources, expertise and such like. However, as the research demonstrates, underlying these are cultural constraints arising from a fundamental emotional acceptance of and commitment to certain spheres of operation, and a concomitant antipathy to others.

Conclusion – culture as 'emotional' engine of broadcasting success

This chapter concludes the study by underlining culture's often unacknowledged power to determine the strategic fate of media organisations such as the BBC and CNN. In media companies culture can exert a powerful restraining influence on strategic plans, and dissonance between cultural beliefs and strategic goals can carry a high opportunity cost. Even when the culture supports the strategy of an organisation, the resulting 'culture of success' can, ironically, cause that organisation to become insulated from its environment. In an era of rapid and radical environmental change an organisation dislocated from its environment is strategically disadvantaged.

However, although the culture of a media organisation has significant destructive potential, it is first and foremost a valuable strategic asset. Culture provides leverage to all strategic plans because the culture of a media organisation holds the key to intrinsic motivation and creativity, and creativity is, of course, the key to the task that lies at the heart of any media organisation – the development of creative content. Culture drives motivation, drives creativity, drives content.

For both the BBC and CNN, their cultures are the emotional engines of their success. CNN could not have achieved its track record of exclusive live coverage of key world events without its singular cultural obsession with live news, nor would the BBC have been able to maintain its exceptional programme quality during a decade of organisational turmoil without a deep cultural dedication to serving the UK public with programming of the highest professional and creative standards.

The distinct cultural beliefs held by CNN and the BBC – about broadcasting's fundamental purpose, about the nature of competition, about viewers, about the relationship between competition and quality – drive those organisations' products, performance and strategic options. Their cultural beliefs have laid the foundations for each organisation's striking current and past successes, and will also determine how each will respond to the coming media revolution, as well perhaps as their ability to survive it.

Appendix
Research methodology

This appendix provides a short description of the research methodology followed for this study.

Research design

The research adopted a qualitative and exploratory approach based on Schein's model of organisation culture, which blends elements of anthropological, constructivist, clinical and processual approaches. The methodology involved successive stages of data collection interspersed by data analysis and interpretation and incorporated feedback of findings to check validity and relevance. The methodology had seven stages, as shown in the Figure A overleaf.

The Schein model was selected for a number of reasons: it is a well-honed tool which has already been extensively applied and which therefore connects the study to previous work in the field (Krathwohl, 1985); it is comprehensive and uses a precisely defined vocabulary;[1] it already incorporates extensive consideration of the strategic aspects of an organisation; and its methodology provides a means of capitalising on available data and accommodates data-gathering constraints.

Accessing culture's layers

According to Schein, culture manifests itself at three layers: artefacts, espoused values and basic assumptions. Artefacts can be accessed by observation, espoused values by a review of 'official' literature containing an organisation's officially expressed goals, mission and philosophy, and basic assumptions via issue-focused long interviews.

Interviews

Selection of the Schein model makes the choice of issue-focused long interviews virtually automatic. As a research tool they offer many benefits. Logistically they make optimum use of time available, ensuring that all terrain is covered at each interview. From a methodological standpoint they facilitate the accessing of ingrained cultural assumptions, respect the perspective of those interviewed (Froschauer and Lüger, 1992) and provide access to subjects without violating their privacy or testing their patience (McCracken, 1988) – especially appropriate for busy senior managers handling commercially sensitive issues.

Interview themes were identified during desk research and expert interviews. These covered the key aspects of an organisation's strategic activities which are highlighted by Schein and include:

- *Environmental change*: how are structural changes in the industry perceived?
- *Stakeholders*: who are the most important stakeholders?

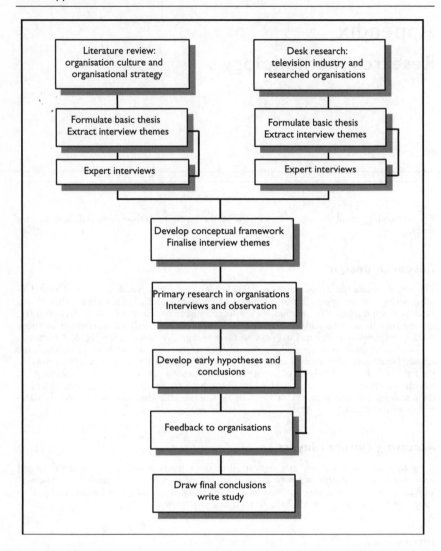

Figure A Research design

- *Mission*: what is the organisation's core mission – its basic function in the larger scheme of things?
- *Core capabilities*: what are the organisation's current core capabilities? Are these appropriate to environmental developments?

These topics were used loosely. Each theme was introduced at every interview, but questions were not followed slavishly if they failed to yield interesting discussion. Intriguing or puzzling comments, metaphors and terms were also followed up and used as triggers for discussion.

Expert interviews were carried out with prominent academics in the fields of management and media, leading practitioners in the television industry and industry analysts from the consultancy or financial communities. These served a number of functions. From a theoretical

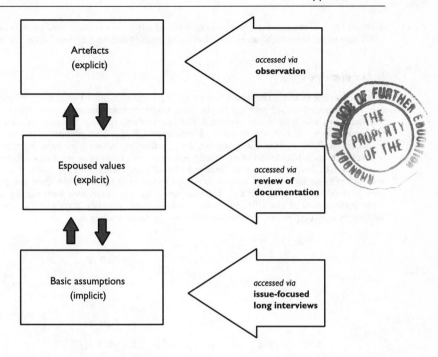

Figure B Accessing culture's successive 'levels'

perspective they provided a means of checking the validity and relevance of desk research, of generating new ideas and of checking the construct validity of the basic theses developed from the literature review. In practical terms they helped to refine the interview questions and provide practical advice on how to approach the in-company research, thus ensuring optimal use of time within the companies.

Feedback took place at two stages: after the basic theses and interview themes had been established, and after hypotheses and conclusions had been developed. This provided a further check on external validity, acted as a protection against false interpretation of primary and secondary data, allowed further relevant data to be gathered and functioned as a type of respondent validation (Bryman, 1988).

Sample

A characteristic of qualitative research is that it focuses in depth on relatively small samples. The sampling approach selected for this study was purposeful sampling (Patton, 1990) or criterion-based selection (LeCompte and Preissle, 1993). This involves the deliberate selection of a sample which provides information that cannot be accessed so well from other sources, and which is critical for the research question. The logic and power of this method of sampling lies in selecting information-rich cases for study in depth – that is, cases where a great deal can be learnt about issues of central importance to the research.

The sample comprised two organisations: the BBC, the UK's public service broadcaster, and CNN, a US commercial broadcaster.[2] The initial selection reflected the suspicion, subsequently confirmed by secondary and primary research, that the research topic would be highly pertinent to these organisations at present, since both had strong organisation cultures and were facing significant strategic challenges. An important point here is that the selection of organisations was not made on the basis of comparison, since they are involved in very different types of broadcasting activities (crudely, the BBC is a portmanteau broadcaster while CNN concentrates on niche areas) and operate in entirely different national contexts.

Interviewees

It is not feasible to study the whole culture of large organisations.[3] Further, not all parts of an organisation's culture are relevant to the issue under review. The sample for this study was restricted to those who would share cultural assumptions relating to issues of strategy (the 'structural apex' of the organisation (Mintzberg, 1983)). This amounted to senior-level managers involved in strategic processes. Face-to-face interviews were held in interviewees' offices (so that artefacts could be observed). All interviews except one were tape recorded.[4]

At the BBC twenty-one senior members of staff were interviewed, at CNN thirteen. The majority of these individuals[5] were interviewed twice, once for the initial data-gathering and once for feedback. In addition two 'information-gathering' interviews were carried out with other interviewees at the BBC to explore new areas of corporate activity. Nineteen expert interviews were carried out with senior industry figures or academics.

Notes

Introduction

1   Although both organisations are involved in radio as well as television broadcasting, this study concentrates exclusively on the latter.

2   Although analysis of each organisation has been approached in the same way, there is an inevitable imbalance. First, the BBC is an older and more complex organisation than CNN and is engaged in a wider range of broadcasting services. Second, published data on the two organisations vary widely. CNN is a favourite of management theorists and available material leans heavily towards business analyses. The BBC, as one of the world's pre-eminent broadcasters, has been and continues to be written about extensively, but primarily from historical, sociological or journalistic viewpoints.

1 What is organisation culture?

1   Tayeb (1994) reports the finding of Alder and Bartholomew (1992) that 70 per cent of all international organisational behaviour and human resource articles mention the concept of culture.

2   For discussion of the range and implications of anthropological approaches to culture see Sackmann (1991). For discussion of social psychologists' influence on the concept see Pettigrew (1985) and Bolman and Deal (1991).

3   Edward B. Tylor first introduced the term 'culture' to the field of anthropology in 1871, to denote 'that complex whole which includes knowledge, beliefs, art, morals, law, custom and any other capabilities and habits acquired by man as a member of society' (Brown, 1998: 4).

4   Schein also dismissed (1995) 'the glibness of those who [assume] culture could be ordered up like an item on a restaurant menu'.

5   Edgar H. Schein is Sloan Fellows Professor Emeritus of Management and Senior Lecturer at the Sloan School of the Massachusetts Institute of Technology. He holds a Ph.D. from Harvard's Department of Social Relations where he majored in social psychology but was heavily influenced by clinical psychology, sociology and anthropology.

6   Practitioners tend to use the term 'climate' interchangeably with that of 'culture', but academics tend to distinguish between the two terms. For example, Warner Burke (1994) defines climate as concerning the transactional level of human behaviour – the everyday interactions and exchanges that create a 'climate' – and culture as concerned with processes of human transformation, with sudden 'leaps' in behaviour.

7   Inconsistencies in the spelling of the term 'artefacts' arise from differences in British and American English. In the UK, it is spelt 'artefacts', in the US 'artifacts'.

8   This usage of the term 'paradigm' has roots in T.S. Kuhn's work on the history of science. Kuhn (1970) defined a paradigm as a way of looking at things, a shared assumption, which governs the outlook to an epoch and its approach to scientific problems. In social science contexts the term has come to mean 'a set of basic beliefs ... [that] represents a world view that defines for its holder, the nature of the "world", the individual's place in it, and the range of possible relationships to that world' (Guba and Lincoln, 1988: 107). In a management sense the word is now widely used to connote a metatheory that defines the basic problems and methods in a particular discipline and shapes the governing understanding of a particular time (Bleicher, 1992).

9   Schein (1996) highlights three subgroups in particular: the operator or 'line' culture (found in the subsystems responsible for delivering products or services); the 'engineering' culture (shared by the designers and technologists who drive the core technologies of the organisation); and the 'executive' culture (tacit assumptions held by CEOs and their immediate subordinates).

10 Research suggests for example that Swiss managers scan the environment less than their North American peers, and that the latter are less constrained by tradition and previous action and more pragmatic than European managers.
11 Schein points out that it is seldom possible to access a culture in its entirety, but that one can access enough to render significant phenomena comprehensible. What is critical is that one obtains access to the cultural grouping pertinent to the issues under review.
12 Schein 'bundles' together the terms 'strategy' and 'mission' and distinguishes them from goals: strategy concerns the evolution of the basic mission, while operational goals reflect the short-run tactical survival issues that the organisation identifies.
13 Indeed, during interviews, questions about mission frequently yielded responses mentioning vision.

2 'The status quo is not an option'

1 The title for this chapter comes from a maxim used by the BBC to introduce a strategic initiative. For full discussion see Wegg Prosser (1996).
2 Thus in the UK, the Thatcher administration's onslaught on the BBC arose as much out of a political conviction that such monolithic public service dinosaurs must be brought into line with the rigours of the twentieth-century world as out of dissatisfaction and distrust of the institution itself, although the latter was certainly present.
3 For discussion of the new 'anti-bureaucratic' approach to public sector management, see Pollitt (1990).
4 Examples include News International and Fininvest.
5 For example, Murdoch has, over more than three decades, developed celebrated friendships with heads of state in order to promote his ever expanding media interests – first in Australia, then in Britain and the US and later in Asia (Financial Times, 13 February 1995). Berlusconi used a friendship with Prime Minister Craxi to gain introductions into the French media system (and later, of course, used his media connections to become a politician himself).
6 Analysis is based on the Gomez/Probst (1991) network thinking methodology for analysing the interconnectivities between the economic, social, political and technological influences in an organisation's environment. In this network '+' denotes an influence of the same polarity, '−' an influence of the opposite polarity.
7 Cited in The Financial Times, 22 March 1995.
8 This is encapsulated in changing industry attitudes towards repeat broadcasts. These were once the symbol of low-quality television, almost synonymous with 'cheating the public'. In a market-driven multi-channel era, where content is the bottleneck in multi-channel systems, the connotations associated with the term have changed. Repeats are no more than 'alternative viewing opportunities' which bring benefits to the public by increasing choice for time-pressed viewers.
9 Indeed, in 1996 the BBC calculated that its main bidding rival for sporting rights, BSkyB, could afford to spend around four times as much as either itself or leading terrestrial commercial competitors for any event (Economist, 27 January 1996).
10 Chairman of the Board of Governors, Sir Christopher Bland, Daily Telegraph, 11 March 1999.
11 Lucent Technologies, 'Lucent's World', http://www.lucent.com/news/pubs/luworld/int.html, accessed on 5 June 1999.
12 Cited in The Financial Times, 28 May 1996.
13 Governments are anxious to ensure that domestic players are not 'locked out' of the developing global media marketplace and are amending national regulations as a consequence. For example, telecoms companies have been allowed to move into the provision of television services, cable television companies to provide telephone services, and newspapers to own television and radio channels. The 'fin/syn' rules in the US, which forced media companies to choose between content and distribution, are the starkest example of this trend, but similar legislative changes can be seen in the UK and Italy.
14 All figures from The Economist, 12 November 1997.

3 The mass paradigm fragments

1 For discussion of the special requirements such 'knowledge-workers' place on organisations see Handy (1989, 1994) and Nonaka and Takeuchi (1995).
2 The shift towards digital distribution, and associated increase in the use of encryption technologies to ensure 'one-time use' and therefore copyright production, represents a threat to the public good nature of the broadcasting commodity.
3 Two further means of funding, government grant and donation, are not discussed here. Australia's and Canada's public service broadcasting companies, CBC and ABC, are wholly funded by government grant. The US public service broadcasting networks, PBS, are funded 40 per cent by government grant and the remainder by audience donation.

For detailed discussion of developments in the funding of European broadcasting see Congdon (1992) and Blumler and Nossiter (1991).

4 For example, BSkyB has developed a monopoly in subscription management by investing heavily in a sophisticated service. Because it would be prohibitively expensive for would-be entrants to duplicate the standard of BSkyB's service, they find themselves in the position of seeking to outsource such services from BSkyB.

5 Commercial operators were tightly integrated into this paradigm. The original philosophy of public service broadcasting embraced an assumption that private broadcasters should share the public sector's principles and broadcasting philosophy. This was meant to prevent overtly commercial operators from impoverishing national culture and national creative ability, and whittling away public service audiences with imported mass-appeal programmes (Barnett and Docherty, in Blumler and Nossiter, 1991).

6 A typical figure for the US, where the sector is further developed, would be around 100,000 viewers.

7 Advertisers in the US tend to ignore outlets that reach fewer than 20 million households.

8 A study of the BBC showed that half the news and current affairs producers had gone straight from university to national television, and half of those had studied at Oxford (Tunstall, 1993).

9 An understanding of the culture of journalism is particularly relevant to this study, since CNN is predominantly a news broadcaster, and the BBC's 'News and Current Affairs' department is its largest programme-making division.

10 Multinational media organisations, such as News Corp., are proving hard for regulators to pin down because they are in some respects 'stateless' as well as being active in so many different geographic areas simultaneously. For example, in 1995, News International formed a $2 billion alliance with the American MCI, and attempted to use the cash acquired to purchase part of the Italian Berlusconi's television empire, while simultaneously negotiating a satellite television deal in Asia and holding discussions with the US regulators about its ownership of the Fox Network.

4 'Serving the nation'

1 The organisation's sense of propriety extended to the fact that radio newsreaders during the evening hours were expected to wear full evening dress.

2 *Marketing Week*, 28 January 1994.

5 The 'Mouth of the South' and his 'Chicken Noodle Network'

1 Cited in *Business Wire*, 24 August 1998.

2 After the interviews for this study had taken place.

3 Viewer/subscriber data from Time Warner Inc. Annual Report for 1997.

4 Figures from Paul Kagan Associates, cited in *Variety*, 5 January 1999: 50.

5 Cited in *Screen Digest*, October 1996.

6 *Financial Times*, 9 December 1996.

7 Perhaps connected to the bi-polar disorder, or manic depression, for which he was once treated, although a second doctor disagreed with this diagnosis.

8 Cited in *Reader's Digest*, 24 August 1998.

9 Cited in *Red Herring Online*, 3 February 1999.

10 Cited in *Time*, 15 March 1999.

11 Cited in *Time*, ibid.

12 Ci ted in *Fortune*, 15 March 1999.

13 Cited in *Knight Ridder/Tribune Business News*, 1997.

14 Marc Fowler, Head of the Federal Communications Commission, the body which oversees television, speaking in 1981 when loosening legislation controlling advertisements aimed at children.

15 Cited in *The Economist*, 11 March 1995.

6 Continuous revolution

1 This perspective was echoed, perhaps unwittingly, by Gerald Kaufmann MP, Chairman of the UK Government's Select Committee on Culture, Media and Sport, when he referred to the BBC as a 'hybrid' organisation.

2 Cited in *The Guardian*, 22 September 1997.

3 In 1990 public service broadcasters accounted for 65 per cent of Europe's television revenues, with the remainder going to commercial operators. In 1994, public service broadcasters took in only 54.4 per cent (*Economist*, 13 April 1996) including home banking and shopping.

4 An internal survey (BBC 1995c) provides insight into how BBC staff rank stakeholder priorities. The organisation was judged to be extremely responsive to parliament (ranking 3.9 out of 5.0), more so than to viewers, listeners and external customers (3.7). Responsiveness to competitors was 3.1.

5 A survey carried out by the organisation in 1995 indicated the threat posed by social fragmentation to the organisation's continued status as national broadcaster. Although it was still seen as the nation's 'official broadcaster', and widely respected for its authority and integrity, younger and less well-off audiences found it conservative, high-brow and part of the Establishment: 'It does not seem to be theirs at all, but to be part of "them" – London, the state and an exclusive educational class élite' (cited in *The Sunday Times*, 12 February 1995). Black and Asian viewers felt excluded and viewers in Scotland, Northern Ireland and Wales were angry about a perceived bias towards London and the south-east.

6 An indicator of the strength of regional interest pressure groups is the organisation's policy of shifting production where possible to the regions, even though this is not necessarily the most cost-effective way of producing programming.

7 The organisation divides its staff into three broad groups: managers (including creative staff such as producers, senior support staff such as policy advisors and accountants, and senior engineers), technical and craft staff, and administrative functions.

8 Cited in *The Sunday Times*, 16 April 1995.

9 The organisation's metaphor for this is 'managing in a goldfish bowl'.

10 Cited in *The Times*, 2 December 1996.

11 Competitors have founded a lobbying organisation, the British Media Industry Group, to campaign for more flexible media ownership rules. Its 1995 publication accused the BBC of being still fundamentally monopolistic and state-supported with a favoured position in domestic markets, judged on a basis of 'national share of voice' – the time people spend watching television or reading newspapers (*Financial Times*, 21 March 1995).

12 These include: Extending Choice (November, 1992), Turning Promises into Reality (January 1993), Producer Choice (April 1993), Programme Strategy Review (February 1995), Extending Choice in a Digital Age (May 1996), A Structure for the Digital Age (June 1996).

13 Cited in *The Guardian*, 19 February 1999.

14 Cited in *The Guardian*, 6 July 1998.

15 The BBC's own shorthand for this is 'to make the worthwhile popular and the popular worthwhile'.

16 The term is used here in the traditional marketing sense, to connote 'distinguishing name or symbol intended to identify the goods and services of either one seller or group of sellers, and to differentiate those goods or services from those of competitors' (Aaker, 1991: 7).

17 1994/5 staff survey results show that the suggestion 'Bureaucracy is kept to a minimum' elicited a response of 1.6, where total agreement is 5.0 and total disagreement 1.0 (BBC 1995c).

7 Reinventing the news

1 *Swiss Review of World Affairs*, November 1994.

2 These new US competitors are credited with denting audience figures for CNN Headline News, whose day average households declined 10 per cent in 1998 to 154,000 (*Daily Variety*, 5 January 1999). Ironically, Turner's merger with Time Warner further increased competition for CNN, since Federal approval of the deal was contingent on Time Warner companies agreeing to carry a rival to CNN. They agreed to carry MSNBC, angering News Corp., which had expected its Fox News Channel to be carried instead.

3 Time Warner Inc. Annual Report 1997.

4 *Financial Times*, 21 February 1996.

5 Cited in *Variety*, 19–25 June 1995.

6 *Advertising Age*, 24 February 1997, p.70.

7 Traditionalists, however, criticise CNN's reliance on affiliates, claiming it represents a shift from newsgathering to news packaging, and that it compromises editorial standards.

8 However, CNN is not automatically deferential to politicians – Peters (1992) tells of a senator left sitting in a studio, unused because he didn't fit into the producer's developing scheme of coverage.

9 Cited in *The Financial Times*, 7/8 December 1996.

10 When initially approached about access for primary research, CNN had no senior executive responsible for strategy.

11 According to CNNI's incoming president, Chris Cramer (recruited from the BBC), 'A few weeks after I arrived in Atlanta, Ted Turner described CNN International as rat droppings, although he didn't actually say "droppings" ' (*Times*, 5 June 1997, p.40).

12 Cited in *Communications Daily*, 19(14), 22 January 1999.

13 President of CNNI, cited in *Interspace*, issue 662.

14 These aspects of CNN became apparent when fixing interviews. Subjects often responded immediately by telephone (having received a written interview request) and fixed an interview directly, using first-name terms. Subsequent contact was via immediate communications tools (voice mail,

faxes) and informal. In contrast, meetings at the BBC were often arranged by letter, or by a secretary or assistant. Further, CNN appeared to have fewer individuals occupying 'pure' secretarial roles than the BBC.

15 Cited in *Brill's Content*, June 1999.

8 'Part of the British way of life'

1 Assumptions are, of course, unconscious, and those presented here therefore represent an amalgamation and synthesis of interviewees' *underlying sentiments*, not actual, overt comments.

2 The methodology used assumes an indirect relationship between individual language or rhetoric, group assumptions and the corporate unconscious. Coded assumptions were therefore derived directly from the language of the interviewees. Schein (1992) does not make this methodology explicit, but seems to follow it himself.

3 All quotes are verbatim. Grammar has not been corrected but to aid understanding excessive repetitions and non-sequiturs have been edited.

4 Alan Yentob, ex-Controller BBC 2, reported that employees have traditionally desisted from referring to broadcasting as an 'industry' (*Guardian*, 19 November 1996).

5 Tunstall (1993: 9) describes how until very recently, creative and commercial tasks were rigorously separated; indeed creative staff were not required to consider the business and financial aspects of their work:

> As late as the 1990s, BBC producers, those charged with spending the bulk of the BBC's significant revenues from the licence fee payers, lived in a world where cash and specific sums of money were not the effective currency. A producer worked within a budget, but not of money but of resources … Thus the producer had little idea of the real costs involved in programme-making. The concept of overspending was vague, since in an organisation with permanent facilities and staff there was no agreed cost that could be attached to one extra day with forty people and a studio. Thus producers might operate with a hazy idea of the intended audience, the real cost, or the real goal (from the company's viewpoint).

6 Cited in *The Times*, 17 August 1998.

7 The anti-managerial strains in the BBC's culture are long lived. Burns (1977) reported that senior managers were viewed as 'lepers' by the rest of the organisation. In 1996 its Personnel Director reported that 'some programme-makers would die if you used "manager" in their title, even if they're managing £200 million budgets and 160 people' (*Management Today*, November 1996).

8 The BBC is seeking to change the perception that it is an 'establishment institution'. One of the most noticeable ways is through the use of presenters who have regional accents (until recently, BBC pronunciation, an educated 'southern English' style of pronunciation, was used as a standard).

9 Approach based on the Gomez and Probst (1991) method of thinking in networks.

9 'Underdogs and outsiders'

1 This was experienced by the author. If an interview candidate had an idea for a further interview candidate, interviews were often interrupted while a meeting with that person was arranged on the spot.

2 Cited in *TV World*, June 1996.

3 Cited in *The Guardian*, 3 June 1996.

10 Reithianism versus Birtism

1 Even today, the majority of references to strategy in official publications deal in fact with programming strategy, rather than organisation strategy.

2 During the interval between the first and second round of interviews, the first goal, innovative high-quality programmes, seemed to have been in part replaced by, part combined with, a new one, namely that of 'achieving audience focus'. On probing, the new goal did not seem to be too different from the old one, simply ensuring in fact that the audience is served with innovative high-quality programming.

3 'Dilemma' comes from the Greek, and means 'two propositions'. In this context it relates to the tension arising from contrasting propositions, both of which have a claim on the organisation, and both of which are converging on an organisation simultaneously (Hampden-Turner, 1990). The need to 'manage' such paradoxes has been identified as a defining characteristic of dealing with complex environments (Handy, 1994; Gomez, 1995).

4 Metaphors can provide significant clues to deciphering culture, both encapsulating complex issues that cause organisational concern and highlighting cultural dilemmas experienced by the organisa-

tion (Pettigrew, 1985; Hampden-Turner, 1990). This particular metaphor can also be found in quotes cited in Macdonald's (1994) study of the BBC's then commercial arm, BBC Enterprises.

5 This term refers to the fact that each individual has a set of unwritten but mutually understood results that he or she expects from an organisation, that will satisfy certain of its needs and in return for which he or she will expend energies and talents. The end of publicly funded status could be viewed as a fundamental revision of the psychological contract. Many employee needs, including those relating to altruism, or the opportunity to address the entire population of the UK, will no longer be met.

6 This group was described by some interviewees as 'Birtist' (after the Director General, John Birt). Birtism, in turn, was defined as follows: 'A Birtist supports change, and does not mind the jargon that goes with it – anti-Birtists do the opposite'.

11 Adrenaline

1 Cited in *New York Daily News*, 4 February 1999.
2 Cited in *Multichannel News*, 19(22), 1 June 1998.

12 A special case?

1 See in particular Bracken and Fowler (1993), which argues that 'the natural self-interest of the [BBC] employees is not linked to the benefit of consumers', a conclusion which, on the basis of the cultural assumptions uncovered in this study, could be strongly disputed.

2 For discussion of culture's relationship to learning see Schein (1993a, 1993b), Argyris and Schön (1978), Senge (1990), Gomez and Probst (1995) and Nonaka (1995).

3 For detailed discussion of how closed and backward-focused cultures restrict organisational learning see Gomez and Probst (1995).

4 This has parallels to Lewin's (1951) step of 'unfreezing' as part of a process of planned organisational change. It also reflects Gomez and Probst's premise (1995: 205) that corporate transformations need to be 'culturally anchored' by creating a 'collective awareness' of the necessity and goals of the corporate changes.

5 It should however be stressed that since this analysis was carried out, senior managers at the BBC appear to have become sharply aware of international and global developments.

6 So much so, that someone about to undertake a similar research project could probably reduce the time involved significantly by first studying the beliefs of the organisation's founder and national cultural traits.

7 Both individuals were also charismatic communicators, a characteristic identified by Schein (1992) as critical to a founder's ability to impart his or her values to the embryonic organisation.

8 Cited in *The Financial Times*, 26 August 1996.

Appendix

1 Many culture definitions are hard to apply empirically because they tend to use a number of similar terms (beliefs, rituals, norms, theories, myths, climate etc.) interchangeably. Schein has been deliberately exact in his vocabulary, pointing out that terms such as beliefs, attitudes and values are fundamentally different psychological concepts.

2 For simplicity, 'Britain' or 'UK' is used in favour of 'Great Britain' or the 'United Kingdom', and the 'US' in preference to 'the United States of America' or 'the US of A'.

3 As Schein points out 'Attempts to study the entire culture in all of its facets is not only impractical … but also usually inappropriate' (1992: 148).

4 Although hard to judge, there appeared to be no evidence that interviewees were affected by the interviews being recorded. They did not apparently, for example, become more guarded about what they said.

5 A second interview was in some cases impossible because an individual was out of the office, or because new responsibilities meant his or her time was over-committed.

Bibliography

Aaker, D.A. (1991) *Managing Brand Equity: Capitalizing on the Value of a Brand Name*, New York: Free Press.

Alder, N.J. and Bartholomew, S. (1992) 'Academic and professional communities of discourse: generating knowledge on transnational human resource management', *Journal of International Business Studies*, 23(3): 551–70.

Amabile, T.M. (1988) 'A model of creativity and innovation in organizations', *Research in Organizational Behavior*, 10: 123–67.

——(1990) 'Within you, without you: the social psychology of creativity, and beyond', in M.A. Runco and R.S. Albert (eds), *Theories of Creativity*, Newbury Park: Sage.

——(1993) 'Motivational synergy: toward new conceptualizations of intrinsic and extrinsic motivation in the workplace', *Human Resource Management Review*, 3/3: 185–201.

Ansoff, H.I. (1965) *Corporate Strategy*, Harmondsworth: Penguin.

Argyris, C. (1977) 'Double loop learning in organizations', *Harvard Business Review*, September/October: 115–25.

——(1992) *On Organizational Learning*, Cambridge, Mass.: Blackwell Business.

——(1993) *Knowledge for Action: A Guide to Overcoming Barriers to Organizational Change*, San Francisco: Jossey-Bass.

——and Schön, D.A. (1978) *Organizational Learning: A Theory of Action Perspective*, Reading, Mass.: Addison Wesley.

Auletta, K. (1991) *Three Blind Mice: How the TV Networks Lost Their Way*, New York: Random House.

——(1996) 'The news rush: Why are the networks so eager to invade CNN's turf?', *New Yorker*, 3 March, pp.42–5.

Barnard, C. (1938) *The Functions of the Executive*, Cambridge, Mass.: Harvard University Press.

Barnett, S. and Curry, A. (1994) *The Battle for the BBC*, London: Aurum Press.

Barney, J.B. (1991) 'Integrating organisational behaviour and strategy formulation research: a resource-based analysis', *Advances in Strategic Management*, 8: 39–61.

Bartlett, C.A. and Ghoshal, S. (1989) *Managing Across Borders: The Transnational Solution*, London: Hutchinson Business Books.

BBC (1992) *Extending Choice: The BBC's Role in the New Broadcasting Age*, London: BBC.

——(1993a) *An Accountable BBC: The Role of the Governors, New Challenges, The Programme of Reforms*, London: BBC.

——(1993b) *The BBC – A Staff Guide to Life, the Universe and Extending Choice – The Workshop*, London: BBC.

——(1993c) *Public Service Broadcasters Around the World: A McKinsey Report for the BBC*, London: BBC.

——(1994a) *Report and Accounts 1993/4*, London: BBC.

——(1994b) *The BBC's Fair Trading Commitment*, London: BBC.

——(1995a) *Britain's Digital Opportunity: The BBC's Response to the Government's Proposals for Digital Terrestrial Broadcasting*, London: BBC.

——(1995b) *People and Programmes: BBC Radio and Television for an Age of Choice*, London: BBC.

——(1995c) 'BBC-wide staff survey results 1994/95', *Ariel*, 27 June, London: BBC.

——(1995d) 'Annual Report Special 1995', *Ariel*, London: BBC.

——(1996a) *Extending Choice in the Digital Age*, London: BBC.

——(1996b) 'Perfectionist in the powerhouse: feature on Alan Yentob', *Ariel*, 13 August, London: BBC.

——(1998) *The BBC Beyond 2000*, London: BBC.

——(undated) *The BBC's Commercial Policy: A Brief Guide*, London: BBC.

Bennet, P. and Carrot, S. (1995) *European Cable and Satellite*, II, *Competition and Companies*, London: Financial Times Telecoms and Media Publishing.

Bergquist, W. (1993) *The Postmodern Organization: Mastering the Art of Irreversible Change*, San Francisco: Jossey-Bass.
Bibb, P. (1993) *It Ain't as Easy as It Looks: Ted Turner's Amazing Story*, New York: Crown.
Birt, J. (1993a) *The BBC Present and Future*, speech to the Radio Academy.
——(1993b) *The BBC*, The 1993 Fleming Memorial Lecture.
Bleicher, K. (1992) *Das Konzept Integriertes Management*, Frankfurt: Campus.
Blumler, J.G. (1992) (ed.) *Television and the Public Interest: Vulnerable Values in West European Broadcasting*, Newbury Park: Sage.
——and Nossiter, T.J. (1991) *Broadcasting Finance in Transition*, Oxford: Oxford University Press.
Bolman, L.G. and Deal, T.E. (1991) *Reframing Organizations: Artistry, Choice and Leadership*, San Francisco: Jossey-Bass.
Bosshart, L. (1990) 'Fernsehunterhaltung aus der Sicht von Kommunikatoren', in M. Kunczik and U. Weber, *Fernsehen: Aspekte eines Mediums*, Köln: Böhlau.
Bracken, W. and Fowler, S. (1993) *What Price Public Service: The Future of the BBC*, London: Adam Smith Institute.
Briggs, A. (1961) *The History of Broadcasting in the United Kingdom: The Birth of Broadcasting*, 1, Oxford: Oxford University Press.
Broadcasting Research Unit (1985) *The Public Service Ideal in British Broadcasting – Main Principles*, London: Broadcasting Research Unit.
Brooks, R. (1996) 'The ex files', *Guardian*, 26 August, p.8.
Brown, A.D. (1998) *Organisational Culture*, London: Financial Times Publishing.
Brown, D.H. (1991) 'Citizens or consumers: U.S. reactions to the European Community's directive on television', *Critical Studies in Mass Communication*, 8: 1–12.
Bryman, A. (1988) *Quantity and Quality in Social Research*, London: Routledge.
Burns, T. (1977) *The BBC: Public Institution and Private World*, London: Macmillan.
Campbell, A., Devine, M. and Young, D. (1990) *A Sense of Mission*, London: Century Business/Economist Books.
Chandler, A.D. (1962) *Strategy and Structure*, Massachusetts: MIT Press.
Clemens, J. (1996) 'The forces shaping the future', *EBU Diffusion*, summer 1996: 41.
Cloot, P. (1994) *BBC Producer Choice: A Case Study*, Briefing Paper Number 16, Major Projects Association, Oxford.
CNN (1994) Untitled Information Pack, Atlanta.
CNNI (1994) Untitled Information Pack, Atlanta.
Collingwood, R.G. (1974) *Essay on Metaphysics*, Chicago: Gateway.
Collins, R. (1998) *From Satellite to Single Market: New Communication Technology and European Public Service Television*, London and New York: Routledge.
Commission of the European Communities (1989) *Council Directive of 3 October 1989 on the Coordination of Certain Provisions Laid down by Law, Regulation or Administrative Action in Member States Concerning the Pursuit of Television Broadcasting Activities* (OJ No. L298, 17.10.1989, pp.23–30), Brussels.
Congdon, T. *et al.* (1992) *Paying for Broadcasting*, London: Routledge.
Cramer, C., speech at Financial Times New Media & Broadcasting Conference, London, 23/24 February 1998.
Cronkite, W. (1996) *A Reporter's Life*, New York: Knopf.
Culture, Media and Sport Committee of the House of Commons (1998) 'The Multi-media Revolution' *Report and Proceedings*, Session 1997–8, 1, London: The Stationery Office.
Curran, J. and Seaton, J. (1997) *Power without Responsibility: The Press and Broadcasting in Britain* (5th edn), London and New York: Routledge.
Deal, T.E. and Kennedy, A. (1982) *Corporate Cultures*, Reading, Mass.: Addison Wesley.
Deming, W.E. (1986) *Out of the Crisis*, Cambridge: Cambridge University Press.
Dennis, E. (1994) *Mapping and Understanding the Information Superhighway*, speech to The Global Networking Society, University of Madrid, May 1994.
Denzin, N.K. (1970) *The Research Act*, Chicago: Aldine.
Downes, L. and Miu, C. (1998) *Unleashing the Killer App: Digital Strategies for Market Dominance*, Boston, Mass.: Harvard Business School Press.
Drucker, P.F. (1998) *Peter Drucker on the Profession of Management*, Boston, Mass.: Harvard Business School Press.
Euromedia Research Group (1992) *The Media in Western Europe: The Euromedia Handbook*, London, California, New York: Sage.
Fombrun, C., Tichy, N. and Devanna, M.A. (1984) *Strategic Human Resource Management*, New York: Wiley.
Forman, D. (1987) 'Will TV survive the politicians and the media mercenaries?', *The Listener*, 16 July, London.
Frank, R.H. and Cook, P.J. (1995) *The Winner-Takes-All Society*, New York: Free Press.
Froschauer, U. and Lüger, M. (1992) *Das Qualitative Interview zur Analyse sozialer Systeme*, Wien: Universitätsverlag.
Frost, P.J. (ed.) (1991) *Reframing Organizational Culture*, Newbury Park: Sage.

Gates, B. (1995) *The Road Ahead*, New York: Viking.
Georgiou, M. (1998) 'Television use in the digital age: a personal perspective on change', *Reuter Foundation Paper* 63.
Gergen, K.J. (1989) 'Organization theory in the postmodern era', paper presented at the *Rethinking Organization* Conference, University of Lancaster, September 1989.
Giddens, A. (1979) *Central Problems in Social Theory: Action, Structure and Contradictions in Social Analysis*, London: Macmillan.
Glaser, B.G. and Strauss, A.L. (1965) 'The discovery of substantive theory: a basic strategy underlying qualitative research', *American Behavioral Scientist*, 8(6): 5–12.
Goldman Sachs (1995) *UK Cable Market*, UK Research.
Gomez, P. (1993) 'Organising for autonomy', in R. Espejo and M. Schwaninger (eds) *Organisational Fitness: Corporate Effectiveness Through Management Cybernetics*, New York: Campus.
Gomez, P. and Probst, G. (1991) *Vernetztes Denken: Ganzheitliches Führen in der Praxis* (2nd edn), Wiesbaden: Gabler.
——(1995) *Die Praxis des ganzheitlichen Problemlösens: Vernetzt denken, Unternehmerisch handeln, Persönlich überzeugen*, Bern: Paul Haupt.
Goold, M., Campbell, A. and Alexander, M. (1994) *Corporate Level Strategy: Creating Value in the Multibusiness Company*, New York: Wiley.
Granovetter, M. (1991) 'Economic action and social structure: the problem of embeddedness', *American Journal of Sociology*, 3: 481–510.
Guba, E.G. and Lincoln, Y.S. (1988) 'Do inquiry paradigms imply inquiry methodologies?' in D. Fetterman (ed.), *Qualitative Approaches to Evaluation in Education: The Silent Scientific Revolution*, New York: Praeger.
Hamel, G. and Prahalad, C.K. (1994) *Competing for the Future*, Boston, Mass.: Harvard Business School Press.
Hampden-Turner, C.M. (1990) *Charting the Corporate Mind: From Dilemma to Strategy*, Oxford: Blackwell.
——(1994) *Corporate Culture: From Vicious to Virtuous Circles*, London: Piatkus.
——and Trompenaars, F. (1993) *The Seven Cultures of Capitalism: Value Systems for Creating Wealth in the United States, Britain, Japan, Germany, France, Sweden and the Netherlands*, London: Piatkus.
Handy, C. (1985) *Understanding Organizations*, Harmondsworth: Penguin.
——(1989) *The Age of Unreason*, London: Business Books.
——(1994) *The Empty Raincoat*, London: Hutchinson.
Hargreaves, J. (1996) 'Interview: John Birt', *New Statesman*, 21 June, pp. 16–17.
Hassard, J. and Parker, M. (1993) (eds) *Postmodernism and Organizations*, Newbury Park: Sage.
Hassard, J. and Pym, D. (1990) (eds) *The Theory and Philosophy of Organizations*, London: Routledge.
Heller, R. (1996) 'Bravo for the bean counter', *Management Today*, November: 12–15.
Henzler, H. (1998) *Communications and Media in the Digital Age*, speech to mcm Forum, St. Gallen.
Hofstede, G. (1991) *Cultures and Organizations: Software of the Mind*, Maidenhead: McGraw Hill.
Holland, P. (1997) *The Television Handbook*, London: Routledge.
Horrie, C. and Clarke, S. (1994) *Fuzzy Monsters: Fear and Loathing at the BBC*, London: Mandarin.
House of Commons (Session 1997–98), *The Multi-media Revolution*, Report and Proceedings of the Culture, Media and Sport Committee, 4th Report, London: The Stationery Office.
Information Strategy in association with INSEAD and Novell (1998) *Global Internet 100 Survey 1998*, Special Report, London.
Jeffres, L. and Atkin, D. (1996) 'Predicting use of technologies for communication and consumer needs', *Journal of Broadcasting and Electronic Media* 40: 318–30.
Johnson, G. and Scholes, K. (1993) *Exploring Corporate Strategy*, Hemel Hempstead: Prentice Hall.
Kao, J.J. (1989) *Entrepreneurship, Creativity and Organizations*, Englewood Cliffs: Prentice Hall.
Kay, J. (1993) *Foundations of Corporate Success: How Business Strategies Add Value*, Oxford: Oxford University Press.
Kilmann, R.H., Saxton, M.J. and Serpa, R. (1986) *Gaining Control of the Corporate Culture*, San Francisco: Jossey-Bass.
Köcher, R. (1985) *Spürhund und Missionar: Eine vergleichende Untersuchung über Berufsethik und Aufgabenverständnis britischer und deutscher Journalisten*, unpublished thesis, Universität München.
Kotter, J.P. (1995) 'Leading change: why transformation efforts fail', *Harvard Business Review*, March/April 1995: 59–67.
Kotter, J.P. and Heskett, J.L. (1992) *Corporate Culture and Performance*, New York: Free Press.
Krathwohl, D.R. (1985) *Social and Behavioural Science Research: A New Framework for Conceptualizing, Implementing, and Evaluating Research Studies*, San Francisco: Jossey-Bass.
Kuhn, T.S. (1970) *The Structure of Scientific Revolutions*, Chicago: University of Chicago Press.
Lansley, S. (1994) *After the Gold Rush: The Trouble with Affluence: 'Consumer Capitalism' and the Way Forward*, London: Century.
Laurent, A. (1983) 'The cultural diversity of western management conception', *International Studies of Management and Organisations*, 8: 75–96.
Lawrence, P. (1995) *Management in the USA*, Newbury Park: Sage.

Lawrence, P.R. and Lorsch, J.W. (1967) *Organization and Environment*, Boston, Mass.: Harvard Graduate School of Business Administration.

LeCompte, M.D. and Preissle, J. (1993) *Ethnography and Qualitative Design in Educational Research* (2nd edn), San Diego: Academic Press.

Levitt, T. (1983) 'The globalisation of markets', *Harvard Business Review*, May/June: 92–102.

Lewin, K. (1951) *Field Theory in Social Sciences*, New York: Harper & Row.

Linstead, S. and Grafton-Small, R. (1992) 'On reading organizational culture', *Organization Studies*, 13/3: 331–55.

Lorsch, J.W. (1985) 'Strategic myopia: culture as an invisible barrier to change', in R.H. Kilmann, M.J. Saxton and R. Serpa (eds), *Gaining Control of the Corporate Culture*, San Francisco: Jossey-Bass.

Macdonald, S. (1994) 'Selling British culture in Europe', in A. Sögren and L. Janson (eds) *Culture and Management in a Changing Europe*, Stockholm: Institute of International Business.

McCracken, G. (1988) *The Long Interview: Qualitative Research Methods*, 13, Newbury Park: Sage.

McGregor, D. (1960) *The Human Side of the Enterprise*, New York: McGraw Hill.

McIntyre, I. (1994) *The Expense of Glory: A Life of John Reith*, London: Harper Collins.

McKibben, B. (1992) *The Age of Missing Information*, New York: Random House.

McNair, B. (1996) *News and Journalism in the UK* (2nd edn), London and New York: Routledge.

McQuail, D. (1987) *Mass Communication Theory: An Introduction*, Newbury Park: Sage.

——(1992) *Media Performance: Mass Communication and the Public Interest*, Newbury Park: Sage.

——and the Euromedia Research Group (1990) 'Caging the beast: constructing a framework for the analysis of media change in Western Europe', *European Journal of Communication*, 5: 313–31.

Mintzberg, H. (1983) *Structure in Fives: Designing Effective Organisations*, Englewood Cliffs: Prentice Hall.

——(1987) 'Crafting strategy', *Harvard Business Review*, July/August: 65–75.

——(1989) *Mintzberg on Management*, New York: Free Press.

——(1994) *The Rise and Fall of Strategic Planning*, Hemel Hempstead: Prentice Hall.

Morgan, G. (1986) *Images of Organization*, Newbury Park: Sage.

Moss Kanter, R. (1984) *The Change Masters: Corporate Entrepreneurs at Work*, London: Allen & Unwin.

Murdoch, R. (1989) *Freedom in Broadcasting*, MacTaggart Lecture at the Edinburgh International Television Festival, 25 August.

Negroponte, N. (1995) *Being Digital*, London: Hodder & Stoughton.

Noam, E. (1991) *Television in Europe*, New York: Oxford University Press.

Nonaka, I. and Takeuchi, H. (1995) *The Knowledge Creating Company: How Japanese Companies Create the Dynamics of Innovation*, New York: Oxford University Press.

Nossiter, T.J. (1986) 'British television: a mixed economy', in *Research on the Range and Quality of Broadcasting Service*, A Report for the Committee on Financing the BBC/West Yorkshire Media in Politics Group, London: HMSO, pp. 1–71.

OECD (1992) *Telecommunications and Broadcasting: Convergence or Collision?*, Paris: OECD.

——(1995) *Governance in Transition in OECD Countries. Conclusion of the Public Management Committee*, Brussels: OECD.

Ouchi, W. (1980) *Theory Z: Meeting the Japanese Challenge*, Reading, Mass.: Addison Wesley.

Parker, M. (1992) 'Postmodern organizations or postmodern organization theory?', *Organization Studies*, 13/1: 1–17.

Pascale, R.T. and Athos, A.G. (1981)*The Art of Japanese Management*, New York: Simon & Schuster.

Patton, M.Q. (1990) *Qualitative Evaluation and Research Methods*, Newbury Park: Sage.

Peacock, A. (Chairman) (1986) *Report on the Committee on Financing the BBC*, London: HMSO.

Peled, A. (1998) 'Digital Broadcasting will Revolutionise the Way we are Entertained and Informed', speech to *E-Screen '98 Conference*, Monte Carlo, 19/20 February.

Peters, T. (1992) *Liberation Management: Necessary Disorganization for the Nanosecond Nineties*, New York: Knopf.

—— and Waterman, R.H. (1982) *In Search of Excellence: Lessons from America's Best-Run Companies*, New York: Harper & Row.

Pettigrew, A.M. (1973) *The Politics of Organizational Decision-Making*, London: Tavistock.

——(1985) *The Awakening Giant: Continuity and Change at ICI*, Oxford: Blackwell.

Phyllis, B. (1995a) *The BBC in the International Multi-Media Marketplace*, speech at Financial Times Cable, Satellite & New Media Conference, London.

——(1995b) *The BBC in the Marketplace*, speech to the Royal Television Society Cambridge Convention, London.

——(1996) *Broadcasting in Europe – Serving the Citizen, Satisfying the Consumer*, speech to the Viewer and Listener Forum, London.

Platt, R. (1989) 'Reflexivity, recursion and social life: elements for a postmodern sociology', *Sociological Review*, 37(4): 636–67.

Pollitt, C. (1990) 'Performance indicators, root and branch', in M. Cave, M. Kogan and R. Smith (eds) *Output and Performance Measurement in Government: The State of the Art*, London: Jessica Kingsley.

Porter, M.E. (1980) *Competitive Strategy*, New York: Free Press.

Potter, D. (1994) *Seeing the Blossom*, London: Faber & Faber.

Power, M. (1992) 'The audit society: monitoring as a technology of government', paper presented at *History of the Present Workshop*, London, November 1992.

Puttnam, D. (1996) *Dilys Powell Memorial Lecture*, Hay on Wye.

Quinn, J.B. (1992) *The Intelligent Enterprise*, New York: Free Press.

Robins, M. (1995) 'Juiced-up CNN is ready to try again', *Variety*, 19–25 June, p. 21.

Ronen, S. and Shenkar, O. (1985) 'Clustering countries on attitudinal dimensions', *Academy of Management Review*, 10(3), July: 435–54.

Rosenstiel, T. (1994) 'The myth of CNN: why Ted Turner's revolution is bad news', *The New Republic*, 22&29 August, pp. 27–33.

Rumelt, R.P., Schendel, D.E. and Teece, D.J. (1994) *Fundamental Issues in Strategy: A Research Agenda*, Boston, Mass.: Harvard Business School Press.

Sackmann, S.A. (1991) *Cultural Knowledge in Organizations: Exploring the Collective Mind*, Newbury Park: Sage.

Samuelson, P.A. (1954) 'The pure theory of public expenditure', in *Review of Economics and Statistics*, 36: 387–9.

Saxer, U. (1989) (ed.) *Unternehmenskultur und Marketing von Rundfunk-Unternehmen*, Stuttgart: Kohlhammer.

Scannell, P. and Cardiff, D. (1991) *Social History of Broadcasting 1922–1939: Serving the Nation*, Oxford: Blackwell.

Schein, E.H. (1983) 'The role of the founder in the creation of organizational culture', *Organizational Dynamics*, summer: 3–18.

——(1987a) *The Clinical Perspective in Fieldwork*, Newbury Park: Sage.

——(1987b) *Process Consultation*, 2, Reading, Mass.: Addison Wesley.

——(1992) *Organizational Culture and Leadership* (2nd edn), San Francisco: Jossey-Bass.

——(1993a) 'On dialogue, culture, and organizational learning', *Organizational Dynamics* special edition: 40–51.

——(1993b) 'How can organizations learn faster? The challenge of entering the green room', *Sloan Management Review*, 34: 85–92.

——(1995) 'The role of leadership in the management of organization transformation and learning', *OD Practitioner*, 27(1): 17–24.

——(1996) 'The three cultures of management: implications for organizational learning', *Sloan Management Review*, 38(1).

——(1997) 'Organizational learning: What is new?', in M.F. Rahim, R.T. Golembiewski and L.E. Pate (eds), *Current Topics in Management*, 2, Greenwich, Conn.: JAI Press.

Schneider, S.C. (1989) 'Strategy formulation: the impact of national culture', *Organization Studies*, 10/2: 149–68.

Selznick, P. (1957) *Leadership and Administration*, New York: Harper & Row.

Senge, P.M. (1990) *The Fifth Discipline: The Art and Practice of a Learning Organisation*, London: Random Century.

Setstrup, P. (1989) 'Transnationalization of television in Western Europe', in C.W. Thomsen (ed.), *Cultural Transfer or Economic Imperialism?*, Heidelberg: Carl Winter Universitätsverlag.

Siune, K. and Truetzschler, W. (1992) *Dynamics of Media Politics*, Newbury Park: Sage.

SRG (Schweizerische Radio- und Fernsehgesellschaft) (1994) *Geschäftsbericht*.

Stalk, G., Evans, P. and Shulman, L. (1992) 'Competing on capabilities: the new rules of corporate strategy', *Harvard Business Review*, March/April: 62–9.

Stevenson, N. (1995) *Understanding Media Cultures: Social Theory and Mass Communication*, London: Sage.

Stewart, C. and Laird, J. (1994) *The European Media Industry: Fragmentation and Convergence in Broadcasting and Publishing*, London: Financial Times Business Information.

Tayeb, M. (1994) 'Organizations and national culture: methodology considered', *Organization Studies*, 15/3: 429–46.

Tichy, N. and Charan, R. (1989) 'Speed, simplicity and confidence: an interview with Jack Welch', *Harvard Business Review*, September/October: 37–52.

Tichy, N. and Sherman, S. (1993) *Control your Destiny or Someone Else Will: How Jack Welch is Making General Electric the World's most Competitive Corporation*, New York: Doubleday Currency.

Time Warner Inc. (1997), Annual Report, New York.

Tiven, K.D. (1993) 'Global television news in the new age of video', SID speech, May 1993.

——(1994) Untitled speech, December 1994.

Trompenaars, F. (1993) *Riding the Waves of Culture: Understanding Cultural Diversity in Business*, London: Economist Books.

Tunstall, C. (1993) *Television Producers*, London and New York: Routledge.

Turner Broadcasting Systems, Inc.(TBS) (1995) *1994 Annual Report*, Atlanta.

US Department of Commerce, Secretariat on Electronic Commerce (1998) *The Emerging Digital Economy*, Washington.

Venturelli, S.S. (1993) *The Imagined Transnational Public Sphere in the European Community's Broadcast Philosophy: Implications for Democracy*, unpublished paper.

Vogel, H.L. (1994) *Entertainment Industry Economics: A Guide for Financial Analysts* (3rd edn), Cambridge: Cambridge University Press.

Wallace, D. and Marer, M. (1991) 'Renegades 91', *Success Magazine*, 38(1), 5 February: 22–30.

Warner Burke, W. (1994) *Organization Development* (2nd edn), Reading, Mass.: Addison Wesley.

Wassenberg, A. (1997) 'The powerlessness of organization theory', in S. Clegg and D. Dunkerley (eds), *Critical Issues in Organizations*, London: Routledge.

Watzlawick, P. (1978) 'Wie wirklich ist die Wirklichkeit', in *Aulavorträge*, St. Gallen: Hochschule St. Gallen.

Wegg Prosser, V. (1996) *Producer Choice and the Management of Organisational Change*, unpublished notes from PhD dissertation, London.

Weick, K. (1996) 'Interview with John Geirland', *Wired*, April: 137.

Weischenberg, S. (1994) *Legitimation als Gegenschäft: Warum CNN zum Symbol journalistischer Dummheit geworden ist*, speech presented to Media Symposium, Luzern, 26 November 1994.

Wernerfelt, B. (1984) 'A resource-based view of the firm', *Strategic Management Journal*, 5: 171–80.

——(1989) 'From critical resources to corporate strategy', *Journal of General Management*, 14(3), 4–12.

Whittemore, H. (1990) *CNN: The Inside Story*, Boston: Little, Brown.

Whittington, R. (1993) *What is Strategy and Does it Matter?*, London: Routledge.

Wilke, J. (ed.) (1987) *Zwischenbilanz in der Journalistenausbildung*, München: Ölschläger.

Willis, E.E. and Aldridge, H.B. (1992) *Television, Cable and Radio: A Communications Approach*, Englewood Cliffs: Prentice Hall.

Wood, D. (1996) 'A new set of tools for television', *EBU Diffusion*, Autumn: 46–8.

Wyver, J. (1996) 'Audience participation', *Wired*, October 1996: 33–5.

Young, E. (1989) 'On the naming of the rose: interests and multiple meanings as elements of organizational culture', *Organization Studies*, 10/2: 187–206.

Index